Our Brother's Keeper

Our Brother's Keeper

My Family's Journey through Vietnam to Hell and Back

Jedwin Smith

WILEY

John Wiley & Sons, Inc.

Library of Congress Cataloging-in-Publication Data

Smith, Jedwin.
    Our brother's keeper : my family's journey through Vietnam to hell and back / Jedwin Smith.
        p.   cm.
    ISBN 0-471-46759-6 (alk. paper)
    1. Vietnamese Conflict, 1961–1975—Psychological aspects. 2. Vietnamese Conflict, 1961–1975—United States. 3. Smith, Jedwin. 4. Smith, Jedwin—Family. 5. Brothers—Death—Psychological aspects. I. Title.
    DS559.8.P7S65   2005
    959.704'3'092—dc22

                                                    2004025687

Printed in the United States of America
10 9 8 7 6 5 4 3 2 1

This book is dedicated first and foremost to my brother,
PFC Jeffrey Earl Smith, 2359214, U.S. Marine Corps.

It is also dedicated to his comrades in arms, whose only commonality at first was a desire to do something important for their country. That goal became fused in the heat of combat with an unyielding commitment to do whatever it took to protect the man fighting beside them. Some had nicknames—Giant, Rat, Coffee, Frenchy, and Smitty—but all were "Magnificent Bastards" of Foxtrot Company, 2nd Battalion, 4th Marines. Most especially to me and to my family, each and every one in some way was my brother's keeper. I am proud to call them friends.

However, it would be dishonorable to speak of the living—Jim Arnold, Gunny Brandon, Ron Dean, Chuck Elliott, Ken Fickel, Michael Gavlick, John Kachmar, Steve Klink, Dave Leverone, Lonnie Morgan, Richie Tyrell, and Jim Wainwright—and their sacrifices of youth, sound bodies, and peaceful sleep, without having roll call for those who forever march through their memories. In addition to Jeff, what follows is a list, compiled by their comrades, of some who gave all: Victor Patrick Andreozzi, Joseph William Baker, William Jay Balfour, Jedh Colby Barker, Richard Lee Bartlow, Kenneth Carl Baxter, William Aaron Berry, James William Bettis, David Richard Bingham, Lawrence Anthony Branigan, James Robert Burke, Conal Joseph Byrne Jr., Daniel Peter Cappello, Walter K. Cleveland, Louis George Cohen, Lenard Coleman, Stephen Rae Cunningham, Jimmy Douglas Curry, Alan Jay Dick, Francis Stanley Devine Jr., Ronald Lee Favourite, Robert Bruce Findlay, Thomas Ryan Fleming, Jerry Wayne Frazee, Dennis Jerome Fries, David Frank Garrett, Richard Alan Hamblin, Gary Paul Hill, William L. Holland Jr., Brent Arthur Holte, Louis Howard Huff II, Theodore Johnson, Albert Arthur Kedroski Jr., Chris John Larsen II, Willie B. Lee, William Allen Machacek, Adolph Alfred Martinez, Randall Lee McElreath, Jeffery Evans Mead, Daniel Victor Michel, Kenneth Michael Montone, Michael B. O'Connor, Michael Dee Oliver, Norman Ira Phipps, Kenneth Leo Plumadore, Edward Francis Rogers, Rickey Dovie Smith, Gregory Joe Staples, Richard John Stewart, Matthew Earl Sutton Jr., Michael Autrey Teague, James Edward Trushaw, Ismael José Valdez Jr., Ralph Levon Washington, Kenneth Maurice Watkins, Robert Lee Weeden, Thomas Mitchell White, and Franklin Wilson.

Admittedly and regrettably, this list is incomplete. Because it is my desire to honor all who served in Fox 2/4, but especially those who died during my brother's tour of duty, I invite any reader to send me the name, with rank and serial number, of any who should be listed with these honored dead in any future printings or editions of this book. My e-mail address is: Jedwin@mindspring.com.

The greatest thing in this world is not so much where we are, but in what direction we are moving.

— *Oliver Wendell Holmes*

Contents

Acknowledgments

This journey would never have been completed without a handful of very special gifts from God. First and foremost is my wife, June; if ever anyone deserves the title "saint," it is she. She has always blessed me with her love, not to mention four beautiful daughters.

My brother Joe, a great soldier and leader, pointed the way. One could not ask more of a friend or a brother.

Dave Andersen helped rescue me from hell and myself, teaching me to live one day at a time. Lanny Franklin continually prodded me to forgo my hatred; he also encouraged me to be accurate, moderate, forceful, and concise. I cannot think of anyone I would rather have walking point.

J. Stanford Fisher has always been my second set of eyes, voice, and conscience. Scary that he should know my heart as well as I; even scarier that he saw my vengeance in its most vile degree, yet still chooses to cover my flank. During the darkest and most dangerous moments of this trek, it was he who held aloft the light.

I wish to recognize two special friends: George Scott, who was the first bookseller to promote me; and Jeff Dennis, the first bookman to praise me.

I also would like to thank my agent, Marilyn Allen, who continues to fight the good fight. Much like my wife, she, too, is a saint. There are not enough words to adequately praise the kind folks at Wiley, especially my editor, Tom Miller, who continually pushed me to dig deeper and deeper for the emotions I had long suppressed.

1

KIA

I deeply regret to confirm that your son PFC Jeffrey E. Smith died 7th of March 1968 in the vicinity of Quang Tri, Republic of Vietnam. He sustained shrapnel wounds to the body from hostile mortar fire while on an operation. Please accept on behalf of the United States Marine Corps our sincere sympathy in your bereavement.

—Gen. Leonard F. Chapman Jr., March 9, 1968

Saturday, March 9, 1968. I was up late last night drinking with my father. The hangover this morning was why I was running late to help wash the windows and clean the blinds. Mom didn't really need my help with the cleaning; it was what would come next that she could not handle. For when the cleaning was over, we would pop a few beers on top of those we would have already consumed and then pack another goodie box for my younger brother Jeff in Vietnam.

My presence would serve to lighten the moment. Crack a few jokes, play the role of Jerry Lewis or Bob Hope to Ma's Dean Martin or Bing Crosby. She would sing, then invariably lapse into tears. My job was to make her laugh and I was good at it. I would say something that would elicit her memories of lighter moments when the household tension wasn't quite as unbearable. I was Ma's

1

sounding board, not only the elicitor of mirth but also the deflector of her wrath and sorrow. It was a role I had dutifully served since childhood.

I was twenty-two, the oldest of Ma's six children and the first to leave home. I had married my wife, June, fifteen months earlier. Jeff called my wedding "The Great Escape," referring to the popular war movie of the day about Allied soldiers tunneling out of a Nazi prison camp. Serving as my best man at the wedding, Jeff joked about my pulling a Steve McQueen on him, hopping on my motorcycle and riding off into the sunset with my young bride, leaving Jeff to deal with the turmoil at home.

And then less than three months later, Jeff engineered his own getaway from the dysfunctional household, cutting his shoulder-length hair and setting aside his guitar, not to mention his crusade against war and all things confrontational. He enlisted in the Marine Corps. Our family's own dominoes tumbled forthwith: Ma and Dad separated within days of Jeff's departure for boot camp, then Ma filed for divorce as soon as Jeff was sent to Vietnam. The rest of our brood—teenagers Joe and Jude and my youngest siblings Jim and Jane—were left more confused than when they had entered this world.

As for myself, I struggled with my loose grasp on maturity, providing for my wife while juggling my spare time between my parents. The consumption of more than my fair share of beer seemed to help. But the lubrication was a blessing and a curse. Especially now that Jeff was halfway across the world, slugging it out along the DMZ with Fox Company of the 2nd Battalion, 4th Marines.

My wife was not overjoyed about how I was spending the day. Helping Ma was okay—no harm in that. But June knew we would be drinking as much as we worked. Her irritation was óbvious when she kissed me good-bye before driving up the road to Rockford, where she worked as a hair stylist.

I checked the clock. It was almost 10 AM. *Dammit,* I had told Ma I would be there bright and early.

"That sonofabitch has brainwashed all of you kids. I don't know what you see in that sonofabitch." I knew those would be the first words out of Ma's mouth as soon as I arrived. She blamed

Dad for Jeff's having enlisted in the Marines. She blamed Dad for driving a wedge between her and me, my father being able to share beers with me at the Elks Club while Ma worked the overnight shift as a switchboard operator at the telephone company, making sure the twelve thousand residents of Belvidere, Illinois, were properly connected to each other and to the outside world.

I shuffled out of the second-story apartment's back door and down the steps. It was a cool day. No sun, just a white glaze from the blanket of gauze hanging overhead. I kick-started my Honda 450cc and released a sigh, leaning back as the engine cleared its throat with a steady rumble, its throbbing in sync with the pounding inside my head.

I thought of Jeff's words and laughter. "The great escape—yep, that's what you've pulled off, bro." Remembering his joy and light-heartedness made it possible for me to endure what would surely come next. But just to make sure, I stepped back into the apartment, popped the top of a can of Pabst Blue Ribbon, and chugged it in three swallows.

"Here's to your health and good cheer, bro," I said aloud, toasting Jeff with a belch and a tear before dropping the empty can into the wastebasket. And then I returned to my motorcycle, revved its engine, raised the kickstand, and toed it into first gear. With a spray of loose gravel I gunned the bike from out of the alley and onto State Street, heading north to my mother's house.

The headache would not go away. It hammered away without letup despite the cool wind ripping through my hair as I zipped along on my usual route, timing the traffic lights perfectly, as I usually did. About the only thing different on this ride was the jerk driving the ugly green car that seemed to be tailgating me. To return the favor, I drove erratically, easing off on the throttle and downshifting to third gear from time to time. I hung a left onto Oak Street and zipped past the old brown clapboard house our family had lived in when we first moved to Belvidere five years earlier, and then cut over one block, downshifting again and laying the bike almost horizontal to the pavement. Showing off, I shot the throttle coming out of the turn and did a wheelie—nailing it perfectly in both gears, making my black-and-silver bike dance—

before downshifting again as I cut sharply into the driveway on the right side of Ma's two-story white house.

Overjoyed that I'd won some sort of nonsensical race, if only in my mind, I killed the cycle's engine and was preparing to drop its kickstand when I heard a car pull up in front of the house—the same damn ugly green car that had been riding my ass.

Because I had not been wearing goggles or sunglasses—or even a helmet, for that matter—I wiped chilled tears from my eyes, blinking to adjust them to the sky's haze. And then the moment focused in perfect clarity.

Invisible hands seized my throat. No breath, no air, no sound other than a rumbling deep within my gut. My knees went limp. The motorcycle dropped onto its side. I didn't hear the metallic crash of the bike's gas tank crumpling against cracked concrete, didn't hear the sharp footsteps of the well-dressed men as they solemnly made their way up the driveway. Both wore Marine Corps dress blues.

The taller of the two was a lieutenant colonel; the shorter, a staff sergeant, obviously diminished by war wounds, shuffling slightly as he dragged a stiff right leg. There were no handwaves of recognition, no smiles. Their eyes were awash with cold determination, which only enhanced my numbness.

The colonel asked, "Is this the residence of Mr. and Mrs. John E. Smith, the parents of Private First Class Jeffrey Smith?"

I nodded, my eyes riveted on the Western Union telegram in the colonel's left hand. When I asked what had happened to my brother, the colonel said he needed to speak with Jeffrey's parents.

"I'm his goddamn brother!" I yelled. "What happened to Jeff? Is he okay? He's only wounded, right?"

The colonel lifted his chin slightly and sucked in a breath. Then he bowed his head and hesitantly glanced at the sergeant. Neither spoke; their silence was thunderous, telling me that my brother was dead.

I can't tell you what my thoughts were. I'll always remember the noise, though, that of a big jet's afterburners cranking up, full blast, making me shake and shudder, at the same time numbing my mind. And I'll always remember the pain, like someone smacking me with a thick board—first slamming it flat across the back of my neck, then nailing me again, this time driving the sharp edge into my flesh, short-circuiting all circulation, slicing through every nerve. My mind was racing, telling me to grab a weapon and kill these bastards.

But I couldn't. My arms hung limply at my sides.

My breathing quivered as I led them through the back door into Ma's house. Through the kitchen and into the living room, where my mother smiled broadly when she saw me, then collapsed and started sobbing when she caught sight of the uniforms; screaming how she'd always hated the Marine Corps, damning Christ and flailing her arms, damning my father and hysterically pounding her fists on the floor. I was on my knees, at my mother's side, trying as best I could to soothe her. I hugged her, holding on for dear life until she screamed herself hoarse. But even then her sobbing continued, now in harsh, gruff gasps spewed between hiccups.

The colonel tentatively approached Mom, bent down to offer his apologies, but she slapped at his hands and arms. All the colonel could do was say, "I'm so sorry, Mrs. Smith," which he repeated over and over.

Odd, but I don't remember the colonel ever saying my brother was dead. My mother would tell me years later that she had no recollection of it either.

What remains is a blur of bits and pieces. I made a lot of telephone calls, pleading for assistance, and friends and neighbors gathered to help sustain my mother through the horrible hours and days ahead. I phoned our parish priest and Mom's best friend, Betty Brenner; they both arrived shortly thereafter. Once Ma was in stable hands, I got into the backseat of the official green car and pointed out the directions to the interstate, where my father worked weekends at the Standard Oil service station. The Marines were cordial, sharing what little information they knew, but it was difficult to understand them because the roaring inside my head wouldn't go away. And then we arrived at the gas station.

"You'd best wait here," I told the Marines, which didn't sit well with the colonel. He wasn't used to being ordered about by a mere civilian, but he wasn't aware of my father's hair-trigger temper.

In younger days I would have smirked and not issued a warning, content to see my father's fists at work, enthralled by the madness. Like when I was eight years old, and a neighbor—a man much bigger and younger than my father—wouldn't give back the football that Jeff and I had accidentally bounced into his flowerbed. I ran into the house and told Dad, who stormed out the door. The neighbor, unafraid, said, "Your little bastards—" That's when my father destroyed the man's face, hitting him with four punches that sprayed blood everywhere. Dad handed me the football and told me to be more careful kicking the ball from here on out. And then he smiled and said, "I don't want to have to do that shit again, you hear me?"

I usually heeded my father's advice. I also tried to stay on his good side because he terrified me.

Now, the colonel was just the messenger. So as he got out of the car and attempted to follow me across the asphalt, I said, "Why don't you just wait here, sir. I'll take care of it. Dad won't hit me."

The colonel, obviously confused by my casual warning, halted.

My father had stuck his head out the door of the station when he had seen the car pull up and block the entrance to the gas pumps. His pissed-off expression evaporated when he recognized me. "Hey, son!" he shouted as he approached, smiling and waving. But then he froze when he noticed the Marines standing behind me, knew immediately what their presence meant, and then screamed "No!"

Thirty-six years later, I can still see my father's face. He is the toughest man I've ever known, and I had never seen him show weakness, had never seen him back down from anything or anyone. But at that instant his body seemed to collapse—mouth agape, arms limp at his sides, eyes welled with tears. Sobbing. And then, as if someone flipped a switch, he attacked—lunging, his hands aimed at the colonel's throat. Dad would have killed the officer had I not thrown my arms around him and pulled him away. Much to the colonel's credit, he did not attempt to protect himself. Neither did the sergeant step in to stop my father.

I don't remember the drive back to my mother's house. What transpired once we returned remains a fractured jumble of bits and pieces—Dad rushing to Ma's side and her screaming for him to go away, that Jeff's death was his fault; Ma's close friends looking at my father with contempt; the parish priest mumbling inane shit about my brother's death being "God's will"; my dad taking a step toward the priest and me jumping between them; the house filling to capacity with sorrowful friends and neighbors; the Marines who had delivered the news of Jeff's death standing off by themselves, speaking to no one because no one desired their company.

I have no recollection of seeing my younger brothers and sisters.

Later, over beers with Dad and me at the local VFW post, the two Marines spoke about having the shittiest job in the Corps. For the past five weeks, ever since the North Vietnamese had launched the Tet Offensive, it was the duty of these two warriors to visit quaint little homes throughout northern Illinois and deliver the worst news any parent can ever receive. Not that I really gave a shit about their troubles—they were alive; my brother was dead. The hell with compassion. I wanted answers. Yet they had nothing to add other than what the official Marine Corps telegram offered.

"Vietnam is a weird place," the sergeant offered, then abruptly cut short his evaluation when the colonel caught his eye. Something unspoken passed between them, so we lapsed into silence, which had a strange comfort to it.

My father had been a killing machine in his youth, a Marine's Marine with a chest full of combat decorations earned at hellholes called Guadalcanal, Tarawa, Saipan, and Tinian. But now, as we shared beers with the Corps' messengers, my father looked old and defeated.

Later that evening, sitting in a dark room at my wife's cousin's house in Chicago, I was alone with my misery, a beer in my right hand, the fateful telegram in my left. I kept reading the damn thing over and over. Willing the message to miraculously change, willing myself to snap out of the nightmare. But no matter how hard I cried, how fervently I prayed, how blasphemously I condemned a heartless God, the message never altered.

What was eating away at me was the guilt. I had always been there to keep Jeff out of harm's way. His fights were my fights. No one screwed with my brother. But when he had needed me most, in the heart of a real combat zone, I wasn't there to help him. In the biggest test of Jeff's life, I was convinced I had failed him.

I was sick to my stomach. And then I lay back and cried until there were no more tears. Only memories.

I drank myself into oblivion once the Marines had informed us of my brother's death, sitting alone in darkened rooms clutching the damn government telegram in my fist.

Still drunk ten days later at the Witbeck-Wheeler-Sabien Funeral Home, I entered an enormous sanctuary paneled with walnut, empty except for the open casket pushed up against the far wall. Dad, my brother Joe, and June stood back as I approached Jeff's body. It was as if I floated to the casket, my feet not striking the ground; a loud roaring filled my ears. I have no idea how long I knelt beside my brother's coffin, speaking with him as if he were still alive—telling him everything I had felt too foolish to tell him so long ago. I apologized for past hurts and petty jealousies. I told him for the first time that he truly was the better brother, the better pole vaulter, the better football player and basketball player.

I told Jeff that I wished it were me in that coffin and not him— I told him how much I loved him, how I wished I had told him that before. Then I stood and bent over the coffin. I brushed my hands across his Marine dress blues, thinking that at least the Corps had cleaned him up, sending him beyond in style.

Jeff's face was chalky, serene, so at peace. I kissed him on the forehead, then on the cheek. But I wasn't ready to say good-bye. Dad and my brother Joe had to drag me away.

My memory of the funeral, held on Tuesday, March 19, is a blur. I sat in the front row of St. James Catholic Church, shaking uncontrollably, hearing nothing that Father C. K. McCarren said. I sat beside my father in the front seat of the hearse on the ride to the cemetery, my body racked by spasms.

I was still shaking at the graveside service, then roughly shaken by the sharp cracks of gunfire from the Marine Corps honor guard. I cried in silence as the buglers played "Taps."

Jeff's body was lowered into the ground.

I'm told it was a cold, rainy day. I don't remember.

A close friend of mine, a member of that honor guard, pressed two spent cartridges into my hand. When he did this exactly, I don't know. But once I returned home, I drilled a hole through each one and linked the shells with a piece of rawhide, then draped the necklace around my neck.

Less than two weeks after Jeff's funeral, I stopped by the house in hopes of cheering up Ma, plus making sure my sisters and brothers were doing okay. Of course, I knew my mother and I would share a few beers. Not that I was desperate for a drink. Hell, drinking was as natural as breathing now—I had been doing nothing but since the day the Marines had arrived at Ma's back door with the telegram. In this instance, though, I had worked my way through at least three Pabsts when the knock came at the door. When I opened it, a young Navy seaman stood on the porch, a clipboard in his right hand, his left resting atop a seabag. Numb once again, I signed the receipt for my brother's belongings that had been shipped from Vietnam, then carried the seabag into the living room.

Mom was still in the kitchen when I opened the bag. The first item I pulled out was a bloodied, torn fatigue jacket, which I immediately carried outside and burned on the front lawn. By the time I returned to the living room, Ma was crying as she lifted out Jeff's personal belongings. Blinded by rage that some twisted, sick asshole in Nam had piled a bloodstained combat jacket atop Jeff's belongings, I had no idea what items Ma had already retrieved from the seabag. Nor did I ask. She told me that there was neither a wallet nor pictures.

My arm felt ice cold as I reached into the bag and extracted the few remaining items: a utility cap, starched utility shirt and trousers, and a watchband, which added to my confusion. The Viet Cong would strip the dead, taking weapons, uniforms, and watches. They used the watches as timing devices for their booby traps. But the Marines said Jeff's body had been immediately recovered, so how could the enemy have taken the watch? Had the Marines lied to us? Why would they do something like that? Did Jeff really die as we had been told? I knew he had used drugs before joining the Corps. Was my brother doped up when he was killed?

After Jeff died, my dysfunctionality took on extra dimensions. Not only did I thoroughly embrace alcohol, but I also became kind of psychotic. Although happily married, I would leave the house without warning, slide behind the wheel of our car, and disappear into the darkest corner of my soul—to drink, to bury my grief, to escape; it was all one and the same.

I suspect that June knew what I was up to all along, but much to her credit she never complained, never protested.

The visitations were always made long after the obligatory last call at Lynie's or the B&A Tap, my favorite taverns. With a six-pack of Pabst in hand, I would drive up State Street and hang a left onto Appleton Road. My destination was about a mile away, directly across from the VFW post. Visiting Jeff was simply a matter of stepping over the rusted fence of St. James Catholic Cemetery and making my way deep into the shadows.

My brother's grave was easy to spot, despite its not yet having a headstone. The Veterans Administration was working on that problem, but admittedly it had its hands full. The war in Vietnam had slipped into the shitter, and the enemy's Tet Offensive had caused the agency overwhelming bureaucratic grief. American servicemen were dying in large numbers; thus the backlog in headstone distribution. Not that it mattered, for the mound of black dirt drew me like a beacon.

I had been coming here almost every night since Jeff's funeral and burial four weeks ago. We shared beers. Mine were gulped; Jeff's were dropped sparingly on his grave. But this night was far more difficult to endure.

It was April 17, 1968—Jeff's birthday.

Normally, this was a time of reverent festivity in our Irish Catholic household—Holy Week, Christ's Resurrection. But all that seemed meaningless now, which is why I had avoided our church's Easter celebration three days earlier.

Today, Jeff would have turned twenty. Instead, he remained forever nineteen.

As I kneeled in the mud at the foot of his grave, I heard Jeff's words ringing in my ears: "Time to go huntin' some gooks. Yes, sir, am I gonna look good in them dress blues or what, bro?"

The memories came flooding back—Jeff and me sneaking into our father's closet and carefully pulling out his dress uniform, each of us taking turns slipping into his blues; running our fingers gently over the bronze ball-and-bird emblems fastened to each of the collars; our fingers tracing the path Dad had chosen, tiny fingers touching the row of campaign ribbons fastened to the uniform's left breast that testified to his participation in the Marines' historic Pacific island-hopping and other ribbons signifying his Bronze Star, Purple Hearts, and the Presidential Unit Citations.

"How many of these are you gonna win, bro?" Jeff asked.

Without hesitation, I said, "More; more than Dad."

Jeff laughed. "Yeah, me, too."

I repositioned myself in the mud at the foot of Jeff's grave. I listened to the rain splatter onto the mud, heard a dog barking in the distance. For a moment, I thought I heard my brother's laughter. I shuddered, then opened another beer, sharing it with Jeff.

That goddamn dog barking was driving me nuts. I pounded my fists into the mud. "Dammit, Jeff, I'm sorry . . . I'm so sorry. You've gotta believe me. You know I always was there, fighting your fights, never allowing you to get hurt. Then when you needed me most I . . ."

My brother's silence was deafening. There was no absolution. I had failed in the biggest test of my brother's life. Now he was dead. What I had sought on the anniversary of my brother's birth was a sign from God, something spiritual—anything other than the bitter cold and soaking rain that seemed not so much to fall on me as to define me.

Somewhere into the last beer I passed out, relinquishing one nightmare for another, waiting to hear a voice that never came.

And when that voice didn't come in the nights that followed, I hated God even more as I fantasized about killing the son of a bitch who had killed my brother.

2

Brotherhood of Pain

Bro: Right now I'm in my second week of recruit training. I'm beginning to get used to getting up early, sneaking smokes, etc. It's just like you said, bro. Hasn't changed a bit. The DIs are bad, but you get used to that too. . . . Drink a few beers for me and keep it cool. JES

—July 2, 1967

I was born on January 2, 1946; Jeff was born on April 17, 1948. According to the baby book my mother kept, my first complete sentence was: "Shut that damn door." My first spanking was received shortly after Jeff was born. Seems that I wanted him to play catch with me, so I tossed a baseball into the crib, the ball smacking him in the head.

Memories are fragile commodities. Pictures help jog what time has long buried. There are no pictures of my father's parents, Clarence and Elinor, or of their farm that I remember with such fondness. There are no pictures of my mother's father, George, who died when she was only a few months old. There are a few photos of Grandma Genevieve, my mother's mother, and a few photos of Ma's brother George; his wife, Barb; and their son Butch. But thank God there are lots of pictures of Jeff and me as we struggled through childhood to adolescence.

I look at the photos in Ma's dog-eared albums and I see Jeff looking up to me—always a head shorter, always grinning. Jeff's wide eyes, which always seem to be filled with equal parts amazement and glee, and his smile dominate his face. The governing feature of my childhood face is a shit-eating grin. I look into my eyes and I can almost see the wheels in my young mind spinning, calculating how to get the upper hand. And behind the old Kodak camera, focusing in on Jeff and me is our mother. I don't have to close my eyes or force my mind to wander in reverse to recall what she is saying. From the moment I started recording memories I can still hear Ma's words, speaking of Jeff: "Oh, you're such a sweet one. You'll be a poet, Jeffrey. Or a priest. Wouldn't that be wonderful. So innocent, so compassionate. There's no anger in you. Yes, you're *my* son."

And then Ma would look at me, her hands on her hips, a contagious smile spreading across her beautiful face. "And you," she would say, her words spoken without a trace of anger, "you're definitely your father's son. Now wipe that damn smirk off your face. We don't want you to break this camera."

Jeff and I feared both Mom and Dad, but for different reasons. Our father's anger was deep-rooted; it took quite a bit to piss him off. But once he gave it vent, it wasn't easily checked. Our mother's fury was always close to the surface, only an eyelash away from eruption. She wasn't as quick to grab the belt and whale away. Her specialty was her tongue—she could render Jeff and me motionless with a simple warning: "I'll tell Smitty." She would say this even when we were perfect gentlemen. She loved to see us tremble. She was a master manipulator.

My siblings and I were raised in a household of electric tension, brief moments of screaming followed by prolonged silence. We walked on eggshells—afraid to speak, afraid to question, afraid even to disturb our father. You didn't dare place a hand upon him while he slept. I did it once as a child, and paid the price, getting knocked senseless across the room. When I came to, my mother was cradling me in her arms and screaming at Dad, "You and your goddamned Marine Corps."

But Jeff and I loved Ma dearly, without prodding, even when she punched our buttons to make us quick to seek her approval, to do her bidding.

Loving Dad was always a work in progress.

I can still see Jeff's eyes. Brown eyes filled with equal parts wonder and puzzlement; eyes locked onto mine as we huddled in the backseat of the police cruiser, eyes anticipating from me some sort of worldly wisdom in response to the confusion in which we found ourselves.

But I had no answers. I was every bit as mystified as my little brother.

It was the dead of night. Pitch black, no moon. And as we nervously stood on the backseat, moving our heads from side to side to get a better view through the windshield, we saw our father move once again into the glare of the car's headlights as he stumbled down the gravel road, a beer bottle clutched in one hand, his other waving back and forth, as if fighting off someone's groping hands. Dad was yelling at someone or something unseen.

"Japs," Jeff whispered, his eyes now filled with tears. "Them Japs are coming for Dad again."

Our mother, sitting in the front seat with Uncle Don Carper, an Illinois state trooper, turned her head toward us and glared. Her face, contorted in pain and anger, was enough to render us into silence. Ma turned to our uncle and said, "It's that stupid Marine Corps. They made him crazy; he doesn't give a shit about my boys and me. All he cares about is going off and being a hero. Thinks it's funny killing people."

Jeff grabbed hold of my hand, tears running down his freckled cheeks. To reassure him, all I could think of to say was what I had heard Dad and his buddies say, the gospel according to warriors: "It's okay to kill Japs and Commies; Nazis, too."

Uncle Don turned his head toward me. He was neither angry nor smiling. At that moment he seemed just as confused as Jeff and me. "See what I mean?" my mother shouted. "He's brainwashed my boys. Filled their head with all that shit . . ."

Uncle Don winked at us. Except for that momentary lapse, he was all business; didn't seem too concerned about what was happening, didn't seem in a hurry either as he idled his cruiser from time to time, slowly keeping pace with Dad. In a soft voice he said to Ma, "Just let him cool off, June. Give him some room; he's not going anywhere now. They don't need him. It's not easy for a man to find out he's not needed."

"Not needed? What about us? Who gives a damn if the Marines don't want—"

Uncle Don finally had heard enough. "Just shut up, June. I'll handle this." Ma started crying. Jeff and I remained silent, listening to the stones pop beneath the car's tires, listening to our father's unfathomable screams as they cut through the darkness of a summer night.

I was almost five years old, Jeff three. The Korean War had started, and Dad had returned home from Camp Pendleton, California, that morning. The Marines had called him back to active duty, but then released him from his obligation. Since he was a recent graduate from Northern Illinois State Teachers College, not to mention being married with two children, Dad wasn't going off to kill Communists, though I'm sure he wanted to do it because he didn't seem too overjoyed upon his return. He and Ma had a few beers, which eventually led to another argument. Somewhere during the course of that day-long feud, Dad had stormed off. And then Jeff and I awoke in the backseat of Uncle Don's police cruiser, its headlights following my father as he traipsed down the narrow dirt road.

Finally, my father stopped walking. He pitched the beer bottle into the cornfield, then collapsed to his knees as Uncle Don and my mother exited the car. "For Christ's sake, Don, she just doesn't understand," I heard my father say. When Ma tried to interrupt, Uncle Don turned to her and said, "Leave us alone, June. Just shut the hell up and leave us alone. I can handle this." My mother reluctantly got back in the car and slammed its door shut.

Dad and Uncle Don talked for the longest time, my father crying and saying time and again, "We're at war, for Christ's sake. Doesn't she understand that?"

My mother did. But for all Jeff and I knew, it was a war of her own making.

When Jeff and I awoke the next morning, we were at our grand-parents' farm in Wyanet. We ate breakfast in silence, then accompanied Granddad Clarence into the barnyard, being careful to place our feet on the stones leading down from the house, past the well pump and the garden, past the dilapidated wooden outhouse. There was no grass in Grandma's yard, only mud and stepping-stones. We helped Granddad feed the chickens and the pigs. The chickens had no character, simply scurrying around and mindlessly pecking away at the grain. The pigs, however, were thick and power-ful, snorting their gratitude as we tossed corncobs to them, nuzzling up to me as I held the cobs in my outstretched hand. Granddad said, "Got yourself some friends there, boy."

Not that I needed any more friends. I had Jeff.

When I asked Granddad if my brother and I could live here forever, he grunted and then dipped some snuff. "Got no place for you here, boy. Besides, you'll be seeing your mama pretty soon." When I asked about my father, Granddad scowled and said, "Don't know nothin' about *that* sonofabitch. Never did, never will."

I had no idea what Granddad was talking about; wouldn't know until decades later. So I simply let the words slide past me, which was easy to do because Jeff and I were enjoying ourselves. There were no arguments, plenty of food, and lots of hugs from Grandma Elinor.

A few weeks later we were reunited with our parents in Nepon-set, Illinois, where Dad had landed his first teaching job. There was no mention of what had happened on that dark, lonely coun-try road with Uncle Don. No mention of why we had spent time with our grandparents. Jeff and I were afraid to ask, content that Mom and Dad were together once again.

We fought, we argued, we teased each other endlessly. Following our parents' lead, Jeff's and my relationship was inexplicably linked by time and place. We wore matching shirts and shorts, handmade by our mother. When she wasn't cooking, cleaning, or working at the telephone company, Ma could be found hunched over her Singer sewing machine, stitching drapes or tablecloths, but mostly making shirts and britches for us boys. She was proud of us. Even prouder that when we weren't bickering, we were constantly looking out for each other.

"These are *my* boys," she would tell new acquaintances, never distinguishing between the older or younger son. And once the stranger was out of earshot, Ma would kneel, wrap her arms around us, and then say, "Wouldn't it be great if you were twins." Mom tried her best to make it happen. She dressed Jeff and me alike. We wore identical shoes. Even our haircuts, close-cropped GI style, were the same. But despite Ma's best efforts, the match was only superficial.

The greatest irony of all is that Jeff and I became best friends.

As far back as I can remember the most often asked question in our presence was: "Are you two *really* brothers?" In response, Jeff would chuckle knowingly and whimsically shrug his shoulders. I would laugh, too, but coldly.

Jeff and I were as opposite as the poles—different hair and eye color, different builds, completely different views of the world. While I was constantly wary, always wondering when someone was figuratively going to make me eat another shit sandwich, Jeff was constantly grinning, allowing the world's troubles to roll off his back. And if a shit sandwich was given to him, he accepted it with sincerity.

My right was Jeff's wrong, my temper was his compassion, my selfishness was his generosity, my continual struggles with grades and athletics was his intuitive excellence. It was often maddening and frustrating as hell to be in his company, yet I had sense enough to be his constant companion. Most of the time he was my conscience, coaching me through one difficult or dangerous situation after another. While I fully understood the difference between right and wrong, black and white, I was all too willing to walk the fine line between the two. And when I did, Jeff was there to caution me: "But what if?"

*   *   *

I received a chemistry set for Christmas 1957, which led to a fasci-
nation with making gunpowder. We were living in Wethersfield,
Illinois, the fifth town in seven years, and I kept playing around
with the chemicals until at last I stumbled upon an explosive mix-
ture. When I announced that I wanted to blow up one of the
bridge supports at nearby Windmont Park, Jeff talked me out of it.
One slip or one inadvertent spark, he cautioned, and I would lose
a hand or my life. So I chose to blow up a fire hydrant instead. The
explosion was powerful, but not enough to destroy the hydrant. We
shared a laugh, then I abandoned my explosive experiments and
moved on to other pursuits.

That same year Jeff discovered my diary, read the passage about
my smoking my first cigarette with Mergy Greenhagen, then showed
it to Ma, who showed it to Dad, who in turn showed me the belt.
"Sorry, bro," Jeff said, failing to hide his grin. "Honest to God, I
didn't think Dad would make a big deal out of it." Yeah, right. And
then we ran over to Windmont Park, where I shared a cigarette
with Jeff, his first.

The next summer we mastered the art of lock picking, entering neighborhood homes when the owners were away on vacation.
It was loose-change and piggy-bank thievery, not that big a deal.
Then Jeff's conscience kicked in and he reminded me that if we
got caught—both of us knew our luck couldn't last forever—he was
too young for reform school and would only get a whipping from
Dad. Because everyone knew I was "an ornery little sonofabitch,"
though, Jeff joked, the cops wouldn't hesitate sending me away.
We had a good laugh over that, knowing neither of us was quite
old enough for reform school. But then Jeff, with a touch of clarity
well beyond his years, pointed out how our getting pinched would
reflect disastrously on Dad's and Mom's reputations. A sobering
realization, indeed.

As for the pocketful of change each of us was lugging around,
Jeff thought it best that we unburden ourselves of the guilt. Always
the good Catholic, my brother said that our quarters, dimes, and
nickels were no different from the silver that Judas received for
betraying Christ. There was no way we could return it to those

whose homes we had pilfered, so he suggested we ditch the coins in the cornfield at the end of our subdivision. Jeff pitched his deep into the cornrows first; I followed suit, yet hoarded a handful of quarters on the sly. More to the point, Jeff thought that rules were put there for our own good and should be obeyed without question.

Jeff was my conscience and friendly antagonist. Arguing in 1959, Jeff threw a few punches that I halfheartedly blocked. Thoroughly pissed at his inability to hit me, he ran into the kitchen, grabbed a paring knife, and heaved it at me, the knife barely missing my head as it stuck in the front door with a sharp *thunk*. "Goddamn, bro. You've gotta learn to control your temper," I said. Then both of us laughed our asses off and harmonized the theme song from the TV show *Jim Bowie*.

Good things just seemed to fall into Jeff's lap, while I had to fight and claw for everything I wanted. Or thought I wanted. From my earliest recollections, I had to be the center of attention—not just a good basketball or football player, but the high-scoring shooting guard and the team's star quarterback. I was more than willing to do whatever it took to attain these goals, even if it meant practicing around the clock. I was never content with being second best. It was all or nothing. In essence, reaching for the stars, which, in most instances, is setting oneself up for failure. For much of my life, that's precisely what I became expert at. Jeff, on the other hand, thought small, or what my concept of "small" was. He was satisfied with whatever came his way—the smallest piece of cake, hand-me-down clothes, or the worn-thin comic books. He was as thrilled with a Jerry Coleman or Moe Drabowsky baseball card as I was upset because I didn't have an Ernie Banks or Mickey Mantle. And invariably, because he seemed satisfied with whatever came his way, in most instances it turned out to be good fortune.

Jeff laughed at life's absurdities, seeing vast areas of gray and accepting the incongruities without concern. I viewed life as a life-or-death struggle.

Jeff enjoyed games; I never knew the meaning of the term.

Whereas I was quick with my fists, Jeff was quick on his feet. When confronted with a difficult situation, I would blindly dive in headfirst, without hesitation, and slug my way through it. Jeff would hesitate, study the issue at length, then tell himself he could reach his goal with a deft flanking movement.

Because our father was a highly regarded schoolteacher who steadily progressed in his profession, moving up the pay scale from one school to another, Jeff and I were always leaving our friends behind. Do that often enough and you develop a self-defense mechanism of intentionally never getting close to people. At least that's how I approached our family's frequent shuffling from town to town; Jeff and I attended four junior highs and two high schools. The only constant we had was each other's companionship. We were inseparable. Unlikely allies united by a common bond—the dysfunction we found ourselves ensnared in.

Ours was a brotherhood of shared pain, and Jeff and I took turns covering for each other.

We borrowed a neighbor's hatchet one day and played mumblety-peg, seeing how close we could throw the ax to each other's foot. When my toss embedded the ax in the toe of Jeff's shoe, he convinced Ma that it was an accident; he had somehow dropped the ax on his own foot, thus saving me from my father's wrath. But it wasn't being saved from a whipping that I remember most. Instead, it was Jeff's apology to Mom—saying how sorry he was for ruining his shoe.

I returned the gesture months later, shortly after Ma had treated us to a Tarzan movie. Trying to emulate the African tribesmen on the big screen, Jeff and I fashioned our own spears, then went in pursuit of each other in a make-believe war game. Jeff was on the roof of a neighbor's shed and managed to "kill" me by thrusting the sharpened end of a spear into the top of my head. En route to the hospital for stitches with Jeff holding my hand all the way, I blamed my injury on another kid on the block, Bernie Salzer. I can still see Jeff's puppy-dog eyes looking up at me; his smile was as warm as I can ever remember it, proclaiming to the world: Big brother just saved me from an ass whipping.

Deflecting blame was hereditary. According to Ma, Dad's violent outbursts were the Marine Corps' fault. According to my father, Mom's drinking was the offshoot of too much stress from holding down a full-time job while trying to raise an ever-growing family. No one was at fault; everyone was at fault. I learned at an early age the art of self-delusion. I also learned the perverse concept of manhood—that real men absorbed pain without complaint; save your tears for later, take your punishment like a man; stand up for what you believe is right. Don't question the reasons why, just do it, dammit. A real man is willing to sacrifice himself for others.

My sacrifices for Jeff had nothing to do with heroism.

I remember his getting whipped only once. Although he accepted his punishment with the usual amount of crying, he did so with aplomb—he did not attempt to twist away from Dad's grasp as the belt was laid to his butt, nor did he scream. Instead, his eyes were locked on Dad's. Puppy-dog eyes. And after a few whacks, I remember my Dad shaking his head. Failing to smother a smile, he said, "Jesus," then laid aside the belt. In return, Jeff smiled and hugged our father. Then it was my turn with the belt. Try as hard as I could, it was impossible for me not to fight against my father's grasp, impossible for me not to turn my butt away from the crack of his leather belt, thus taking the brunt of the beating on my thighs; impossible for me to look him in the eyes with anything other than hatred. All of which induced more whacks on the ass and legs.

Indeed, Jeff and I were made of different stuff. So when it came to accepting blame for one household transgression or another, I pushed my brother aside and willingly stepped forward—taking the punishment like a man, taking solace in the fact that I was the best brother because no amount of pain was too much for me, knowing I'd gag if ever again I was forced to see Jeff's puppy-dog eyes at work.

I learned early not only how to carry excess baggage but also how to laugh in the face of disaster, which, according to my mother, is a thoroughly Irish trait.

The same can be said for stubbornness. While Jeff learned the value of a smile and a hug, both of which easily won over Dad's attention, I was too hardheaded to grasp the gentler side of life. Instead, I went out of my way to antagonize my father. Because he didn't have a great sense of humor, didn't like getting squirted by a toy squirt gun, I would *accidentally* squirt him. "Jesus Christ!" he would yell, then run me down and jerk the toy gun from my grasp. In one swift motion he would step on the gun and smash it, then slip off his belt. The whipping was worth it, simply to have seen the startled look on my father's face when I had shot him.

Dad didn't like cats, either. So Jeff and I would wait until he was asleep on the couch, napping between jobs, then argue over which one of us would toss our cat (mine was named Pepper, Jeff's Salt) on Dad's bare chest. Because my cat was the ornerier, I would sneak up behind the couch and drop Pepper over the edge. My cat did his thing, digging his claws into Dad's chest. It was impossible for Jeff and me to keep from laughing, rolling on the floor over our father's reaction—his startled scream of pain from Pepper's claws; Pepper screeching in protest as Dad flung him across the room, then Dad bolting to his feet and running me down. The whipping was worth it.

I've always had a problem with overkill, though. The next time I dropped Pepper on Dad's chest was the last time. I should have known better, because Dad was moaning in his sleep. I dropped my cat on Dad's bare chest anyway. But there was no cry of pain this time. Instead, Dad's right hand shot out and snatched Pepper by the throat. The cat was dead before he hit the ground. Then my father lay down and went back to sleep.

Too stunned to say anything, I looked at my brother, my eyes wide with terror and disbelief.

Jeff shook his head, released a deep sigh, and said, "Them Japs came after Dad again."

3

The Never-Ending War

Dear Dad: I know I told you that there wasn't much going on up here at C4, but we went out 5 days ago and got a little bit of action with no casualties. Yesterday 2 squads went out and got hit by the gooks. We took 4 wounded and 1 dead. We ran into a reinforced platoon of gooks. You're the only one I write to about what happens here. I have to tell someone, and I know you understand. Just had enough time to fill you in. I'll write later. Have a Merry Christmas. Love—Jeff

—December 11, 1967

We saw the unframed print every time we walked past the open door of our parents' second-floor bedroom. Attached to the wall by a thumbtack above Dad's dresser was the white fist holding aloft the big yellow flame with the numeral 2 inside it, surrounded by five white stars in a field of red. There were no words on the print, nothing stipulating what it stood for.

According to my mother, the print signified stupidity. But she never said so in my father's presence. To him, the emblem of the 2nd Marine Corps Division stood for things just and precious, all things worth fighting for. "A lot of good men wore it during the war," Dad told us. "Lot of good men died attempting to keep evil from ruling the world."

Downstairs in a hall closet was Dad's mottled camouflage jacket with the Marine Corps emblem, the globe and anchor, stenciled in black over the left breast. The jacket was well worn, threadbare in spots, with brown stains on the left collar and left sleeve. From time to time I would sneak inside the closet and slip on the jacket, my arms barely making it halfway through the long sleeves, the bottom of the jacket dragging at my feet. All I ever wanted was to someday be big enough and man enough to wear such a jacket, to walk in my father's courageous footsteps. The first time Dad found me wearing the jacket, I figured he would lay the belt to me. Instead, he ran a rough hand through my hair and rolled up the jacket's sleeves to give me a better fit.

But his smile disappeared when I asked about the brown stains. "That's blood, son," he said, rubbing the cloth between his thumb and forefinger, as if trying to eliminate the stains. "Damn Japs tried to kill me. Came close, but I was tougher than those bastards. All of us were."

I don't recall exactly what year it was that Jeff and I discovered the pictures of Dad's trek through the South Pacific, pictures tucked away beneath some correspondence in the center drawer of his desk. Graphic pictures of Guadalcanal, Tarawa, Saipan, Tinian, and Okinawa; dead Marines floating up against the beach, hundreds of wounded Marines strewn in haphazard fashion on the beach, dead Japanese in their bunkers or scattered about riverbanks; thick jungle and emaciated faces of young men seemingly struggling to catch a breath; palm trees blown apart, burned tanks with shattered turrets, and lots of white crosses stretched out across the sand. Each island campaign was assigned to a specific envelope, and Jeff and I were careful to return each picture to its proper place.

Every time Ma caught us leafing through the photos she threatened to tell our father. I don't ever remember his reprimanding us, though. Not even when Jeff and I asked him about the pictures, wondering if he would tell us some stories about the war. In response, Dad looked away, then walked out of the room.

His war would remain a mystery, one we tried without success to solve throughout our childhood.

As close as we came to learning the totality of our father's war exploits came at the old musty-smelling tavern in his hometown of Wyanet, Illinois. Jeff and I spent a lot of time there, tagging along with Dad whenever he visited his parents. The tavern was always his first stop, probably because that was where my father's childhood friends could always be found—those friends of his who survived World War II.

I remember best the trip we made during the summer of 1955, before I started fourth grade. Jeff and I were sitting in the tavern's wooden booth against the wall, seeing only Dad's back and the backs of his buddies as they hunched over the bar, talking about old girlfriends and high school teachers who had given them a hard time, talking about their jobs and their ever-growing families, talking about what it would be like to own a new car or maybe even a new house—talk that bored the hell out of my brother and me, even though Dad and his buddies kept us well supplied with Cokes and potato chips.

When I slid out of the booth and asked Dad if we could go see Grandma and Grandpa, Bud Olds, Dad's best friend, said it was too damn early to cut short the party. He bought another round of beers, then handed me two dollars and told Jeff and me that we ought to check out the store next door. "They got all kinds of plastic models over there, boy. Go get yourself one," Olds said.

So Jeff and I walked out one door and through another, coming face to face with a whole shelf of model airplanes. I don't know how long it took me to pick out the neatest plane, but as soon as we returned to the tavern and showed off the purchase, Dad yelled, "Jesus Christ! Get that goddamn thing out of my sight!"

The plane I had chosen was a Japanese Zero.

Bud Olds hustled me out of the tavern and back into the store, where he exchanged the model for a German Stuka. "Now, this is one scary goddamn plane, boy," Olds said. "Was a Stuka that hit my tank, got me wounded; liked to tore my leg off. Germans aren't that bad a people, so no one's gonna make a big fuss about you putting together one of their planes. But them Japs—shit, them bastards were worse than animals. Don't you ever forget that, hear?"

I heard him loud and clear. For the next hour or so, to be exact. Once Olds was again hunched over at the bar, and Jeff and I had settled back into the booth taking turns examining the pieces of the model Stuka, Dad and his buddies went on a tirade about the Japanese. That's when I first heard him talk about a tropical hellhole called Guadalcanal, how Dad had fought almost four months behind enemy lines scouting enemy positions, subsisting on roots and pigs' feet, and feasting on an unquenchable rage for all things Japanese.

"Your father lived with savages," Olds said, referring to Guadalcanal's Melanesian natives, who helped the Marines eliminate the Japanese from their island. And then he told a story about Dad, whom Olds said scoured the jungle looking for Japanese camps. And when our father came across one he would kill the sentries, and then the natives would cut off the sentries' heads, propping them up like they were sleeping—repositioning their heads, of course.

"Next morning," Olds said, "the Jap officers were pissed because the sentries were asleep. They'd shake the little bastards and the heads fell off. That's when your Dad and them natives opened up and killed 'em all. Japs didn't have a chance."

My father, seemingly embarrassed, sipped his beer and tried to change the subject. When that didn't work, he said, "Yeah, I hated those little sonsabitches. Even that shitty rice wine of theirs tasted like warmed-over piss."

Everyone laughed at that comment, including Jeff and me, and then the bar lapsed into silence.

Later, on the drive home to Kewanee, Dad turned melancholy and apologized for jumping my ass about my wanting to build a model of a Zero. "I saw more of those damn planes than I ever want to see again," he said. "I'll be seeing 'em in my sleep tonight."

Jeff and I knew what that meant, so we didn't say anything. Several miles down the road, Jeff finally broke the silence. "What about Grandma and Grandpa? How come we didn't go see them?"

Dad didn't respond for the longest time. Finally he said, "We'll be seeing your grandma next week."

As was always the case, Dad never made a reference to his father.

* * *

My father was the youngest of ten children reared by Elinor Marier and Clarence Augustus Smith during the Depression in the rural northwestern Illinois community of Wyanet. It is a small town, its population less than three thousand.

As a child in the 1950s, I remember Wyanet as a drab, dark place filled with even darker secrets, a community in which poverty seemed to touch everyone. Although my aunts never spoke of the conditions under which they were raised, my Uncle Floyd told me about the bank repossessing the family farm when Dad was eight, how he and my father worked the fields from dawn to dusk to help feed their sisters, working for as little as a nickel a day.

What Granddad did, other than drink, no one ever said.

My earliest recollection of my Grandfather Clarence is of his running a rough hand through my hair and calling me "Little Johnny Bullshit." Granddad was a gruff, humorless man who smelled of snuff and the barnyard in which he toiled. I don't remember ever seeing him smile or laugh. My most lasting memory of him was his constant reference to my father as "that son of a bitch." Until I called my mother the same thing in my father's presence at Jeff's sixth birthday party, I was under the impression it was a compliment. I never used the phrase again after the ensuing whipping.

My most lasting memory of Grandma Ellie is her silence in Granddad's presence, which I would learn, decades later, had been beaten into her. Clarence was a domineering man who doted on his eight daughters and oldest son, Floyd. But for reasons my father has never fully explained, Clarence refused to have anything to do with Dad.

"He always told me that I wasn't *his* son, that I was a pain in the ass who was always underfoot," said my father. "Even as a small child, I'd go out to the barn or the fields to help him do chores, but he'd always tell me to get the hell out of his way, that he didn't want me around. Other than that, my father never ever spoke to me."

Granddad Clarence never praised my father, never took him fishing, and never saw him compete in high school athletics. When my father enlisted in the Marine Corps in December 1941 at the outbreak of World War II and was away from home for almost three years, Clarence never bothered to write him a letter. And when Dad finally returned home in October 1944—after almost twenty-nine months of constant combat, twice wounded, and a decorated war hero—almost everyone in town was there to greet him at the train station, including his mother, his brother Floyd, and sisters Hazel, Lola, Dorothy, Margie, Belva, Betty, Mildred, and Margaret.

Not his father. Dad told us that even when he got home, he stuck out his hand, but Granddad wouldn't even acknowledge it.

My father loves his mother to this very day, even though she has been dead since 1961. When he speaks of her, his eyes fill with tears. To him Ellie will always be the kindest, gentlest person he has ever known. Why Clarence refused to believe that Dad was his son, Ellie would never say. Whenever my father asked, she always dismissed his pleas by saying that *someday* she would explain. But she never did. It was a secret she took with her to the grave.

What has never been buried is my father's hatred for his father. Dad grew up with Grandpa Clarence's drinking and his physical abuse directed at Grandma Ellie. This ended only upon Dad's return home from the war. "I told my father that if he *ever* laid another hand on my mother I'd kill him." Grandpa Clarence never slapped Grandma again.

What my father is left with are memories of love and rejection and memories of crushing poverty. When not working as a field hand, Dad was always looking for anything he might steal to help his family—swiping sacks of potatoes, peaches, watermelons, and grapes from the back of delivery trucks whose drivers stopped in Wyanet for a bite to eat; hopping onto moving freight trains during the winter, stealing handfuls of coal or firewood to help heat the home; he and his buddy, Bud Olds, stealing chickens, doing whatever they could to help feed their families. Stealing not to get rich, stealing because they were hungry.

And then, through a bizarre twist of fate, being able to step away from the poverty by going off to war—for the first time in his life being properly clothed and fed, actually having an *extra* pair of new boots, being handed a new rifle and all the ammunition he could possibly use. In return, all that was asked of my father was that he kill those who had driven the free world to the edge of the abyss.

Dad did it well. So well that the memories always remained close to the surface. Living in the stench, mud, and often impenetrable jungle that was Guadalcanal in 1942; outnumbered and outgunned, killing every Japanese soldier he came across. Never taking prisoners. Just killing until there was nothing left to kill. Killing in record numbers on Saipan, where at Kaberra Pass on July 9, 1944, he was awarded the Bronze Star for killing more than three hundred Japanese during one day-long battle. Being written about in glorious text in *Leatherneck,* the Marine Corps magazine, his picture appearing in the *Saturday Evening Post.*

Without a doubt, my father was a genuine, bona fide hero. Yet he was a hero who to this day considers himself a failure.

Grandpa Clarence died of heart failure in the spring of 1964. A few days before he died, my father and I went to visit him at the hospital in Princeton, Illinois. Dad's sisters were there, gathered around Clarence's bedside, crying. When my father stepped forward and stuck out his hand, Granddad stared coldly at him and asked, "Who are you?"

"I'm your son, Edwin," my father replied.

"I don't have a son named Edwin," said my granddad.

I remember my father's tears when he returned to the car that day. He did not explain his sorrow; he said nothing as we made the long drive home. Decades later, his eyes again filled with tears and his face contorted in rage as he said, "I felt so empty at that moment. I wanted to punch him in the mouth, but I didn't because my sisters were there and I didn't want to make a scene. They loved him so much; he was always very kind to them."

So instead of exploding at his father, Dad turned his back on him and walked away.

My father did one last thing before leaving the hospital. He had some blood work done, then had a doctor compare his blood with Granddad's. The result was irrefutable: the blood work matched.

Granddad Clarence was indeed my father's father—in name only.

4

War Games

Dear Bro: The monsoons have set in and it's cold and wet. We'll be pulling back about the 15th of December. We should be on ship by the 1st of January. Boy I hope we spend some time on ship. For all I care, three to six months would be great. There's not much going on now. We patrol by day and set ambushes at night. Sorry I can't be there for your first anniversary, but I'll be home to celebrate the next one. Love: Your little brother Jeff

—December 3, 1967

Before Jeff and I became make-believe Marines, we were cowboys. Not just any cowboys, though—we were mirror images of Hopalong "Hoppy" Cassidy. We first listened to his exploits on the radio, spellbound as he tried to keep his small town of Long Valley free from thieves and other desperadoes. Then we gravitated to the movie theater, every bit as enthralled as was Ma, watching Hoppy work his Bar 20 Ranch with sidekicks California, Lucky, and Windy. When evil presented itself, Hoppy and his boys knocked it aside with a few well-directed punches to the jaw. Or if the action was stepped up a notch and guns were drawn, the good guys dealt with it by drawing their own six-shooters and winging the bad guys in the shoulder. Justice was swift but never deadly.

Jeff and I couldn't get enough of Hoppy. Even Ma got into the act, helping drill "Hoppy's Creed" into our heads. As every good cowboy knows, you can't ride the range without a creed. Hopalong Cassidy's creed appeared in the newspapers each week, accompanying his syndicated column. We would help Ma with the dishes, standing side by side on a chair at the kitchen sink, and she would say, "Okay, number four." I would shrug my shoulders, my eyes glazed. Then Ma would respond, "Only through hard work and study can you succeed."

Ma would then ask Jeff, "Number two?" And Jeff, who was always asked to repeat Hoppy's second point of the creed, never number four, responded, "Your parents are the best friends you have. Always obey them." Jeff would then stick his tongue out at me.

Jeff and I drank our milk from Hopalong Cassidy mugs and ate lunch and dinner off our Hopalong plates—always eager to eat everything because that way we got a clear look at Hoppy's image, him dressed in black and sitting erect on his white stallion. We wore Hopalong Cassidy hats and vests, even fired away at imaginary bad guys with our trusty Hopalong six-shooters, none of which bothered our mother. It was she who managed to save enough money to buy us these goodies.

But then Jeff and I discovered true warriors, the first of whom was Pa Edwards. As close as I can recall, this happened during the summer when I was seven, Jeff five. We lived in Geneseo, Illinois, and Pa Edwards, the grandfather of a friend of ours who lived at the end of the block, had fought in World War I. Jeff and I had no idea of what that meant, other than that this old man surely was heroic. This is exactly what we told him one day as we sat at his kitchen table and listened to his tales of fighting the Huns, about poison gas and endless artillery bombardments, how someone in authority would blow a whistle and then everyone would climb out of their holes in the ground and charge the enemy.

Other than it sounding like grand fun, I screwed up my courage and finally confessed to being greatly confused. I asked, "What's a Hun? What's gas? What's artillery?" Jeff, every bit as wide-eyed as I, nodded his head in agreement. We needed to know the answers to these questions; knowing might make it easier for us to be just like Dad, who we knew had been a hero in the other war, against the Japanese.

I remember Pa Edwards giving me a strange look, and I immediately cringed. At my house, an innocent question often had
dire consequences. Jeff and I were on the edge of our seats, ready
to duck if necessary, ready to soak up the old man's information if
he wanted to talk. He smiled, then led us outside to his backyard.
He disappeared inside his barn and returned moments later with
a shovel and pickax in hand. "In order to understand what it was
like," he said, "you've gotta live it."

With that, he started slamming the pickax into the ground,
digging up huge clods of dark soil. Within half an hour he had
made great progress, producing a fairly big hole, which grew even
deeper and longer as soon as the rest of the neighborhood kids
showed up and discovered what Pa Edwards's intention was. All of
us took turns wearing the old man's World War I doughboy helmet and the gas mask, which resembled a pig's snout. In no time
at all, with the help of extra shovels pilfered from various tool
sheds, the trench was complete—a thing of beauty. I can still smell
the moist dirt, how I moved about the trench from one end to the
other; I remember trying to peer over the trench's edge and failing, watching in wonder as Pa Edwards deftly dug out a ledge for
me to stand on, and then I stepped up and carefully peered over
the edge, my eyes scanning past the distant flowerbed in search of
the enemy, my imagination running wild.

The rest of the day was spent in the trench, listening to Pa
Edwards's interpretation of what his war on the Western Front was
like. For the longest time he was every bit as childish as his audience. I do remember his wife angrily berating him for filling our
heads with nonsense. I don't recall what Pa Edwards said to her,
but he obviously won the argument because we continued to play
in the trench. But as the day wore on, as all of us kids asked questions we didn't realize were embarrassing—"Who were your buddies?" "How many of those Huns did you kill?"—a haunting veil
seemed to drop over Pa's face and he seemed to grow older and
older. That's when Jeff, obviously embarrassed by the old man's
tears, tired of the ordeal and went home, leaving me alone to con-
template one of life's mysteries.

From that day forward Jeff and I traded in our Hopalong Cassidy six-shooters for homemade weapons resembling those used by our father—M-1s and Tommy guns—and our neighborhood became an imaginary battlefield, the names of which we wouldn't fully appreciate until many years later: Kasserine Pass, Anzio, the Bulge, Tarawa, and Guadalcanal. We would take turns fighting the Nips and the Krauts—moving across our neighbor's apple orchard, sweeping past the dilapidated sheds in another neighbor's backyard, and making grand flanking movements in the open fields behind Pa Edwards's place—and we would do it in grand style, complete with GI helmets, ammo pouches, and Eisenhower jackets, whatever relics we could lay our hands on. Every kid in the block would invade the closet in his father's bedroom and help himself to any assortment of war souvenirs. My father had brought home enough goodies to outfit Jeff and me—a Jap helmet he had picked up on Saipan, and the Jap pistol holster and camera he had picked up at Guadalcanal. Armed with these goodies, we set about playing at being Marines.

Ma was furious, yelling, "For Christ sake, Smitty, stop them from playing that shit." My father never objected, except on the one occasion when I tried to walk out of the house with his Japanese battle flag, a tattered and bloody souvenir he lifted from the shell-pocked helmet of a Jap he killed on Tarawa. Dad gave me a couple of whacks on the butt with his hand, then informed me that under no circumstances would I *ever* again touch that flag, which he referred to as "one of my proudest possessions."

In 1955 I was paralyzed from the waist down. We had moved once again, this time across town into the Wethersfield School District, and I was doing jumping jacks in gym class when my legs suddenly went numb and gave out on me. The teacher yelled at me, thinking I was up to my usual antics, playing the role of class clown. When he checked out my legs, though, and saw the welts, he immediately drove me to the hospital. It was there that I heard Mom's explanation, given to a neighbor who had stopped by to wish me well: "Smitty and his goddamned Marine Corps," Ma told her. "It's his temper. He's always beating my boy."

I never gave her opinion much thought, figuring I must have been doing something wrong to get whacked. Besides, I was too busy enjoying the peace and quiet of the hospital. Not to mention the wide-open spaces.

Our household was bursting at the seams. Brother Joe had joined us in August 1951. Then Mom had finally hit the jackpot when Jude was born on January 3, 1953. Of course, that made our living arrangements even more compact, meaning that Joe now shared a bedroom with Jeff and me. All of this equated to nonstop noise typical of all large families.

Life at the hospital was pretty cool, though. And even though my first roommate, an old gray-haired gentleman hooked up to a bunch of plastic tubes, died in his sleep one evening, my second roommate was much younger and a lot of fun. He was a member of the National Guard and had accidentally shot himself in the thigh while hunting rabbits. What I remember most about him is that he taught me how to play poker, which certainly didn't endear him to my mother. Other than that, life was grand—there were meals in bed, a television, no shouting and screaming, no one reaching for a belt. I figured I was destined to stay there a long time, maybe for the rest of my life. After all, the doctor said as much, saying I had some form of leukemia, a rare blood disorder, and would never walk again, that I was paralyzed for life.

But then the doctor screwed up, repeating his prognosis in front of my father, who responded by grabbing hold of the doctor's throat, slamming him into the wall, and saying, "You'd best fix my boy's legs. If he doesn't walk again, neither will you."

I don't remember the doc's response, but Dad's reaction was enough to spur me on to recovery. I worked hard for months at physical therapy, graduating to a wheelchair and then crutches. And then on the day I finally walked out of the hospital under my own power, Dad took me to the junior high gymnasium for a game of shoot-around. At that point in my life, basketball was everything. It was a sport I could master on my own terms, without benefit of dominant stature. Until my hospitalization, I had shared stardom with my good buddy Johnny Perkins on Wethersfield Junior High's lightweight team, which was comprised of fourth-, fifth-, and sixth-graders. Because I had been in the hospital for three months, I had missed almost the entire basketball season.

"I don't know if you'll ever catch up, son," my father said as we drove to the school's gymnasium. Dad's words were worse than the numbness I had once experienced in my legs. He was the coach of the heavyweight team comprised of the school's *real* basketball stars. Making that team, playing for my father, was my real goal. I was more than willing to do whatever it took to make Dad's team, so I shot baskets in a half circle that day, moving from one spot to another *only* after making a basket. The way Dad and I played the game was that you had to start all over if you missed a shot, winning the game by moving around the half circle by being perfect. A wooden paddle in the hands of my father, and a crack on the ass, provided incentive every time I missed a shot.

I made it home that night without too much pain. And although to this day I can still shoot the eyes out of a basket, I never did catch up with my buddy Johnny Perkins, for he and his family moved out of town the next summer.

Nor did I ever catch up with my father. He jumped schools the next year, switching allegiances to the larger, more prestigious Kewanee school system, teaching and coaching at Central Junior High while Jeff and I remained at Wethersfield. We merely shrugged it off, taking it for granted that Dad would always be out of our reach.

Some of the Wethersfield students weren't as forgiving, however. One kid in particular, an eighth-grader named Danny Ramsey, cornered me after school. I was on my bicycle, its basket filled with newspapers I was intent on delivering, when Ramsey punched me in the face and called me a traitor, called Dad a backstabbing bastard for teaching at Central Junior High. Ramsey punched me in the face a few more times, then walked away.

I had never given much thought to how intense the rivalry between Wethersfield and Kewanee was; never given much thought to why Dad was such a highly regarded teacher. Seems he was always assigned the kids from broken homes, the students who spent more time on the streets smoking cigarettes or messing around with gangs. Dad's job was to straighten them out, get them properly educated, so the school system would be rid of them.

More often than not, Dad talked the repentant thug into joining the Marines. My father was good at this, a natural-born recruiter. After all, he would say, if the Marines could straighten out his life, carrying him out of the clutches of poverty and into the white-collar world of respectability, that of a schoolteacher, then they could straighten out anyone's life. So on the first day of class he would do a little show-and-tell, showing off to the class that Jap flag and his combat decorations, then tell a few war stories. The tough kids quickly learned that they weren't as tough as they thought. Dad became their mentor, allowing them to hang out with him nights at his second job, at the Sinclair service station. I would join them sometimes, listening to the town toughs trying to outdo each other with tough-guy stories.

When I finished delivering my newspapers that evening, I bicycled to the Sinclair station. When Dad asked what the hell had happened to me, I told him how Ramsey had beaten me up. Dad said nothing. Neither did the three Wethersfield toughs, all sixteen-year-old career eighth-graders. I figured no one gave a shit, figured I had better learn how to defend myself, or people would be beating on me the rest of my life. When I asked the toughest of the thugs if he could help me, he took me into the service bay with its hydraulic lifts and showed me some techniques—proper stance, throwing a punch, and rolling with a punch. Then he gave me some advice I have never forgotten: "Fight's never over until you say it's over. If you can take the pain, take a punch, then no one's gonna kick your ass. Only way you're gonna beat me is by killin' me. Everyone knows it; they don't dick with me 'cause they know I'm crazy that way."

We messed around for half an hour or so, the thug allowing me to shoot punches at his head, which he deftly avoided; then we worked on my footwork. After a while he called a halt to the lesson. "One thing you gotta remember," he said. "You don't ever want to start a fight because then they'll dump your ass in reform school. But once you take that first punch, it's fair game. Don't stop beating on that other sumbitch until he's out cold. As for Ramsey, don't pay him no mind. He won't be botherin' you anymore."

Danny Ramsey did not return to school for three days. When he did, the bruises were still quite visible on his face. He never bothered me again. Nor did anyone ever again question my father's loyalty in my presence.

Because the doctors feared that my growth had been stunted by the long hospitalization, they said my recovery would be greatly aided by being outdoors as much as possible. That's when Mom and Dad decided to be caretakers of Pike Lake Resort, a fishing camp on the Minnesota-Canadian border, that summer.

Pike Lake was every little kid's dream come true—endless miles of trackless forest; a twelve-mile-long lake dotted with long-abandoned cabins; peace and quiet interrupted only by an occasional bear or moose traipsing through camp. Jeff and I ran wild, scouting the woods until we knew much of it as well as we knew the backs of our hands. We fished from dawn to dusk; sometimes even later, rowing a wooden boat to our favorite fishing holes, dropping anchor, then catching walleyes until the mosquitoes had eaten us alive, forcing our retreat to shore.

We were kids; yet, for the most part, we were allowed to call our own shots. The only rule was letting Ma and Dad know where we were headed—across the lake to scout out an abandoned cabin or to follow a trail we had stumbled upon, playing in the abandoned icehouse or down at the end of the lake in the boathouse, or taking the raft Dad had built for us and navigating down the shoreline. Jeff and I were both good swimmers. Besides, we weren't stupid; we didn't take inordinate chances on the lake. Because of the lay of the land and the location of the cabins our parents took care of, Ma and Dad always had a good idea where we were playing, if not being able to keep a distant eye on us. And even though we occasionally stumbled upon a moose or a bear, we gave them a wide berth. Especially bears, this coming after the great awakening I had one day when I lit after one while trying to emulate Davy

Crockett, star of my current favorite TV show. Knowing Davy killed him a bear when he was only three, I figured I could do the same thing, being all of eleven years old. Besides, all Davy had was a knife. I had my trusty .22-caliber rifle. So I lit out after the bear, gaining on him as Jeff screamed at me, warning me about being stupid. But what did Jeff know, him being only nine? So I'm running down this bear, who's not appearing to be all that fearsome. And then the critter tires of the game, stops and turns toward me, then stands up and gives me a mighty growl.

"Man, you should have seen your face," Jeff said, laughing himself silly later, once we made it back to our cabin, having run for our lives. "That old bear starts roaring and you turn ghostly white. Swear to God you surely shit your drawers, bro."

Jeff was more observant than I ever gave him credit for. He also had more patience than I did. When we weren't playing Marines, making beach landings down at the boathouse, we were emulating the Vikings, sacking imaginary lands far across the lake. It was Jeff's idea to invite little brother Joe along. I figured our little brother, at six years old, wouldn't know one end of our homemade rifles from the other. But he fooled me—manning the oars of our boat as if he had been doing it for years, and swimming ashore without missing a stroke when Jap mortars hit our landing craft. And when it came to charging those machine-gun nests, he lobbed grenades with the best of us.

Joe was irritating, though, because no matter how much I bossed him around, he took it with a smile. He was a mirror image of Jeff—identical pudgy cheeks, same infuriating grin, and the same quick wit. I would tell him that Jeff and I were going across the lake to fish and that he would have to return to the cabin with the girls, meaning Ma and Jude, and Joe would say, "Okay. But I bet I'll catch more fish than you guys, just fishin' off the dock." And damned if he didn't do just that.

Or I would elbow him aside down by the boathouse, kneeling at the stream to get an ice-cold drink of water, and Joe wouldn't bat an eye. He would wait until I had drunk my fill, then say, "I just got done pissin' upstream. How's it taste?"

Joe didn't laugh; he simply smiled, which made it impossible for me to smack him.

But the most irritating thing about Joe was that he became the center of Dad's attention. Dad's temper had been greatly improved by the summer of '56, which is why Jeff and I desired nothing else than being at his side. It was like waking up one day and discovering that the person you feared had suddenly turned into a pussycat, rendered harmless by a wonder drug normally used to subdue wild beasts. But as hard as Jeff and I tried, we never found Dad approachable—at least not in the affectionate sense that he displayed with Joe, hugging him, then holding his hand as they walked about the fishing camp. This is why Jeff and I mocked our little brother by calling him "Little José from Pike Lake." And every time we did so, Joe would grab hold of Dad's hand and lead him away, pausing only long enough to turn and flash us a knowing grin.

While Joe was a pain in the ass, our little sister Jude was a soft-spoken angel. She was afraid of fish and afraid of the wild animals that roamed the encroaching woods, but she made up for those flaws by entertaining the rest of us kids in the evening with her singing and dancing. During the day Jude was Ma's shadow, helping her with the laundry and cleaning cabins, even helping with the meals, which, because of our still-tight financial affairs, amounted to us living on freshly caught fish twice a day. And when Jeff and I entered the kitchen, Jude would break out into a smile and song, pirouetting around the room. And then she would ask us to join her, which I refused to do because I thought it was silly. But not Jeff, who gently took Jude's hands in his, doing their own rendition of Fred Astaire and Ginger Rogers.

The only downside to Pike Lake Resort was the occasional family feud. We kids never knew what it was that Ma and Dad argued about, for we were always caught up in our own imaginary worlds. But as soon as we entered the main cabin, the atmospheric ice chilled us instantly. Mom would shout something derogatory at Dad, who simply said, "Jesus Christ, June, lower your damn voice." Other than that, he ignored her. And before we knew it, Ma's shouts would escalate to screams, and we kids would scramble to the bedroom. There were no other diversions—no television, no radio, nothing to read. All we had was each other, so we huddled together, trying to make sense of the latest storm.

The worst of these swept down on us near the end of the summer, shortly before we had to pack up the station wagon and head south, toward Illinois. We had gone to sleep to Ma's screams, then awoke to her rough hand shaking us in our bunk beds. "I'm leaving the sonofabitch," Ma said. "If you want to go with me, fine. If not . . ." Just like that, we had to make a decision. Jeff, Joe, and Jude said they were going to stay with Mom. I opted to live with Dad. No way could I leave him alone. He needed me.

But then, just as quickly as it had erupted, the storm passed. There was no outward peace agreement, no shaking of hands in front of us kids. Instead, our mother told Jeff, Joe, and me that Dad needed our help transporting minnows, so we all ran out to the pickup truck and jumped in. Sitting in the back of the truck, Jeff gave me a confused look, then asked, "What made you decide to stay with Dad?" Try as hard as I might, I was unable to put my thoughts into words. I hemmed and hawed, then grudgingly admitted that I was every bit as mystified as was Jeff. In response, he shook his head and laughed.

5

Our Own Broadway Star

Dear Mom: I have been selected for an interview for Sea Marines, but I'm not sure I'll become one. It may keep me away from the war, but I'm not sure I'd want that. I feel obligated, but so does every Marine. . . . I miss home and your cooking, Mom, and being around the best brothers and sisters anyone ever had. You're going to be surprised when I casually pop in some day. I'll surprise the hell out of you. Everyone take care. Don't work too hard, Mom, and stay happy. Love: PVT JES

—August 1, 1967

My mother is forever beautiful and free-spirited, a red-headed hellion with wit, wisdom, and a tongue that could cut you to the quick in a heartbeat. That she was Irish is a given. She was the epitome of women's rights, an uneasy mix of Gloria Steinem and Barbra Streisand—an angel singing the melodic scathing of men, particularly my father. She was a religious mulatto—part atheist, part evangelist—condemning the church to the very pits of hell in one breath, praising it to heaven's highest edifice the next.

In my mind's eye, my mother never ages.

Saying Ma was a contradiction is being kind. She hated war with every living breath, yet unaccountably married into it. She despised

41

poverty, yet found it impossible to rise far above it. She hated fighting of all sorts, yet gloried in it, holding her own in the worst of circumstances. She prayed every day and night and grudgingly adhered to the Ten Commandments. With minor exceptions. God help you if you crossed my mother, for she neither forgave nor forgot. Wrong her, and you were an enemy for life. But if she considered you to be pure of heart and deed, she quickly became the truest, most trustworthy friend anyone could ever be blessed with.

I never looked at Ma as simply my mother. She was my friend, a confidante, someone I could truly trust. As quick as she was to threaten me, she was even quicker in jumping to my defense—bragging to her friends what a gifted athlete I was, what a gifted student I would someday become. And despite my aversion to singing and dancing, my reluctance to play a musical instrument, and my antipathy for Catholicism, we got along quite well. "You're going to be just like your father," she would say, shaking her head in disgust. Her words never hurt, however, because I could detect the deep sense of pride with which she made the statement.

When the Sunday school nuns reprimanded me for fighting with another youngster, Ma stood by my side because I had punched a kid who was teasing Jeff. When those same nuns kicked me out of class for asking "dangerous" questions about what Adam and Eve truly looked like—I told the nuns about the pictures I had seen in Dad's encyclopedia, pictures depicting early men as hairy apes, which led me to wonder aloud in class if Adam and Eve were *really* monkeys—Ma listened patiently as the nuns went ballistic, then asked, "Well, how do you explain the archaeological evidence?" Later, at home, Ma cracked me on the butt for mocking the church, first telling me that faith and belief went hand in hand, then telling Jeff that he shouldn't listen to my nonsense.

Having to have the last word, I asked Ma if she knew what Satan looked like. She gave a stern look, then smiled, almost as if she knew what I was going to say. "I bet Satan looks just like Sister Mary Catherine," I said, referring to the nun who was always reprimanding me.

Ma's response was, "She's a mighty ugly one, isn't she?" And then we spent the rest of the day doing our duty—Ma washing the dishes and me drying, Ma doing the laundry and me doing the folding. Between the chores, Ma would dance with Jeff.

The dancing and chores aside, Ma always remained a mystery. She would tell us a few stories of her past, yet left so much unsaid. And whenever Jeff and I pressed her for more details, she dismissed our inquiries with the same response: "I'm going to write a book someday. Lot of sonsabitches are going to squirm, that's for sure."

That was my cue to get Mom a beer, and then Jeff and I would sit by her side, listening once again to stories that by now we knew by heart.

My mother, a Smith before she married a Smith, was raised with the doctrine that there were only three things of importance in life: family, self-reliance, and the Catholic Church. "As long as we've got God and each other, we've got everything," she said time and again.

Ma's mother, Genevieve, was the daughter of Mary Ellen Cain and John V. Kearns, who was an Irish mercenary who provided militant protection for the Mormon prophet Joseph Smith. No one ever spoke of Great-Granddad John's exploits. Grandma Genevieve, the youngest of five children, was born in 1888 in Sheffield and lived to be eighty-six; she had nineteen grandchildren and twenty-seven great-grandchildren. She was a strong woman who walked to St. Patrick's Catholic Church every day without fail. Attendance was not negotiable. After all, God was watching over her.

"And you can thank Jesus Christ himself that Grandma never misses church," Mom would say. "She's praying for you, for each and every one of you. Praying that your sins are forgiven, God help us. And praying for my father, too."

Ma had no memories of her father, George Smith, who died in 1923, seven months and four days after my mother was born. No one in her family ever spoke of Granddad, other than saying that he died young, the result of a terrible accident. My father, without a hint of condemnation, told me that Granddad George was drunk when he died, hand-cranking his Model-T car when it somehow slipped into gear and crushed him against a tree.

In the years that followed, Grandma Genevieve supported her children—Mary, Katherine, Gladys, George Jr., and Mom—by doing other people's washing and ironing, refusing to be a burden on society by accepting the government's offer of financial relief. Everyone pitched in to make ends meet: teamwork and determination were the backbone of the family. Overlook the present situation, work diligently, and don't buckle under to the system; study hard, smile, and the world will smile with you—those were the qualities my mother came to grasp.

Whenever I close my eyes and dream of my mother, I see Maureen O'Hara playing opposite John Wayne in the movie *The Quiet Man*. Mom was every bit as beautiful as Miss O'Hara; as equally mismatched with my father as the redheaded star was with the Duke; as headstrong, feisty, and combative in real life as O'Hara was on the big screen. In the movie, not in my mother's life, love was the victor.

I have my own film clip of Ma, an old black-and-white version choreographed in the 1950s—a decade before the births of our youngest brother and sister, Jim and Jane. I see a short, red-haired Irish lady with an ever-present cigarette in one hand and an equally ever-present bottle of beer in the other. Of course, Mom was working. No matter the hour or the day, she was always working—full-time as a telephone switchboard operator, full-time at home, too: cooking or cleaning, hunched over a sewing machine or standing before an ironing board, making sure her and Dad's ever-growing brood of children were properly cared for.

"We might not be as well off as other people," she would say, a mischievous smile playing across her face, "but, by God, we're not poor. At least there's a roof over our head, food on the table, clothes on your back, and we're clean. Squeaky clean, right?"

She said this with her chin jutting out in defiance, which actually made us proud of our somewhat threadbare economic state.

And then, as the night grew longer, the music would fill the house. It always began with the zaniness of Spike Jones, then gravitated to sad laments from Patsy Cline and Connie Francis. Ma would play their songs on the record player, singing the mournful tunes so often that I came to know the lyrics as well as my multiplication tables. And when Ma tired of song, the dancing would begin—from the kitchen to the living room and back again, her children trailing close behind. It was like celebrating Christmas in the middle of the summer, a refreshing bit of gaiety and lightheartedness in an otherwise tension-filled home.

In those moments, we actually had fun. No worries, no fears, laughing at the silliest things. We were taking a break from reality, the washing and ironing and folding of clothes. Doing, I would imagine, what normal folks did all the time.

Of course, Jeff and I used the moment to clown around, for there were no reprimands at that late hour. Dad was away, either toiling at a second job or attending a faraway college, bolstering his teaching career by working on his master's degree in mathematics. So, for the time being, seriousness was forgotten. We were in an almost make-believe realm of uncontrolled silliness. Roughhousing around on the floor with little José from Pike Lake, making faces at one another, maybe poking fun at Ma's zany antics. Kids being kids, except for our little sister Jude, who actually took Ma seriously. Jude was every bit as theatrical as Mom, tagging along step for step, twirling in sync, her every move completed as flawlessly as Ma's—waltzing along, oblivious to the faraway cast of Mom's eyes.

Even though we had seen it all before, time and again through the years, my brothers and I didn't have the heart to tell Jude what was really going on, that Mom was dancing with her long-dead love, her fiancé Jack, an Army Air Corps pilot who had crashed his plane into a nameless peak somewhere in the China-Burma-India Theater in late 1943.

Shortly after Jude was born in January 1953, Ma blurted it out for the first time. I don't remember why. I don't even recall if she had been drinking. Nonetheless, I remember her words—harsh, possessing the biting sting of a hand across the face: "If it hadn't been for that goddamn war, if Jack hadn't crashed his plane into that goddamned mountain . . ." And then Ma collapsed onto her knees and started crying.

Jude still has the picture of Mom taken in 1943, the one that Ma always kept on her nightstand. It shows a serious young lady, as beautiful as ever, wearing a white blouse and jacket upon which is pinned, just above her left breast, Jack's Army Air Corps wings.

We never knew Jack's last name, nor did Ma tell us how she met him or where they became engaged. She spared us that.

What we were left with was Ma's anger, unexplained anguish, and the everlasting oath "If Jack hadn't died, dammit to hell, I would have never married that son of a bitch."

Ma was referring to my father, whom she met on the Wyanet High School football field in October 1938 during her sophomore year. Ma attended Sheffield High, a few miles up the road. Sheffield was a more affluent town, and, for the most part, the towns-people looked down their noses at anyone from Wyanet—the same sort of animosity separating Wethersfield from Kewanee.

"Smitty's one of them damned, worthless fighting Kentuck-ians," my mother told me when I was a youngster. I took her words verbatim, figuring Dad had been born and raised in Kentucky. Decades later I would learn the truth, how during the Depression men from the neighboring state of Kentucky flocked to Wyanet, underselling their labor to the local farmers. Kids in neighboring communities made a joke of this, calling anyone from Wyanet a Kentuckian.

Sheffield versus Wyanet, the annual football grudge match. Mom's brother George, playing offensive end, cut across the mid-dle and caught a pass. My father, playing defensive back that day, introduced himself via a leg-breaking tackle. So upset was my father at what he had done that he drove to Sheffield and apologized to my mother's mother.

Mom loved the movies, and Shirley Temple was her favorite actress. She could always identify with whatever circumstances little Shirley was depicted in, more often than not those of an orphan. Of course, the best parts of those movies were the singing and dancing. Ma would watch Shirley tap-dancing up and down the mansion's staircase with Bill "Bojangles" Robinson in *The Little*

Colonel or performing with Jimmy Durante in *Little Miss Broadway,* all the while dreaming of someday being just as famous.

Ma was destined for the stage, Hollywood or Broadway. A natural-born entertainer, she had a gift for mimicking. She picked up her tap-dancing prowess by watching film clips of the Radio City Rockettes. She also could quote Scripture and poetry at the drop of a hat.

"My ambition," Mom told me time and again, "was to dance for the Rockettes. I would have made it if it weren't for that goddamned war, if it weren't for that accident."

In 1940, then a telephone operator in Champaign, Illinois, Mom was sitting in the front passenger seat of an automobile driven by a friend, the name of whom we were never told. The driver was drunk and took a corner too wide, smashing into the back end of a parked flatbed truck. The driver and a backseat passenger were killed instantly. Mom's rib cage was crushed, and she suffered a double-lung puncture. Pronounced dead at the scene, it was en route to the morgue that an attendant noticed that Mom was barely breathing.

"That Negro boy saved my life," my mother said, "so there'll be no prejudice in this family. Not one bit, you hear me? God placed that Negro boy and me at that very spot for a reason. God's plan, that's what it was. Jesus Christ himself was looking over me that night. Am I making myself clear?"

All of us children nodded, wide-eyed at the tale.

Like the contradictions of her dictums about how to live our lives, Mom was a physical contradiction—great physical talent in a body left frail after her accident, functioning with only one reinflated lung, and missing several ribs. So massive were her injuries that the doctors told her that not only would she be incapable of conceiving children but she also would not live to see her twenty-second birthday.

It seemed only fitting that my mother would prove everyone wrong, living thirty-nine more years and bringing six children into the world, thus having the last laugh in a life filled with broken dreams and shared misery.

*   *   *

When we moved to Kewanee, Illinois, Jeff and I spent every free moment playing baseball. From dusk to dawn, pickup games or Little League. It never occurred to us to ask Ma to join us. After all, she was a woman, and the world was quite different in 1955.

If Jeff and I weren't playing ball, we were watching it being played. Windmont Park, two blocks up the road, was our second home. The ball diamond was always busy, and the highlight of our week was watching the Kewanee Blackhawks, a women's fast-pitch softball team, beat the dickens out of whomever they faced. I don't recall seeing the Blackhawks ever lose a game. Better yet, most of the young ladies were gorgeous—especially their pitcher, who had long red hair, tied back in a ponytail. The team's best hitter was a thick-necked third baseman—a somewhat odd lady, according to Dad.

"For Christ's sake," he said, "she's nothing but a bull dyke; her and all the rest of them . . . ah, players."

In the summer of 1956 the team was looking for new blood, having lost the world championship for the first time in three years.

"Now don't tell your father," Mom told Jeff and me one morning, "but I've been asked to try out for the team."

Good grief. Jeff and I looked at each other and laughed. Mom certainly was as pretty as that ponytailed pitcher and a whole lot shapelier than the thick-necked third baseman and several of the other gals. But no way did Ma possess anything close to the Blackhawks' athletic abilities. I mean, Ma was Ma.

Mom glared at us. Then that leprechaun smirk spread across her face, and she grabbed my baseball glove, tossed it to me, and then said, "Okay, let's go outside and toss the ball around."

Outside, in the yard, Jeff, always the peacemaker, handed his baseball glove to Mom and was in the midst of showing her how to properly insert her fingers into the respective grooves when Ma expertly inserted her hand in the glove, then snatched the baseball from Jeff's grasp and unloaded a head-high fastball in my direction. *Crack!* The stinging in my glove hand was almost unbearable. Just to show her up, I fired the ball back to her and she deftly snatched it out of the air and fired it back to me. *Crack!* It was obvious that I wasn't going to win this game of burnout, so I told her to pick up a bat and see if she could hit my fastball.

One pitch was all it took to make Jeff and me believers.

Ma timed the pitch perfectly, and the ball exploded off the bat and arced high and deep—sailing across the field, across the street, and through our neighbor's window. Jeff and I could do nothing more than stand there in shock. We had never seen that thick-necked third baseman hit a ball that far. Nor any of the other Blackhawks, for that matter.

Once we had regained our senses, Jeff and I rushed to Mom's side, congratulating her, telling her she was fantastic, that she would be the greatest Blackhawk of them all. She wasn't listening to us, though. All she could think of was the damage she had done, breaking that window. "My God," she said, "please don't tell your father I did that."

No sweat. I took the blame for busting the window, which resulted in a couple of whacks on the butt from Dad. I figured it was worth the pain, though. Not only was I credited with the greatest home run in the neighborhood, but in the process I also acquired a partner in petty crime.

Mom never attended that Blackhawks' tryout, nor did she ever tell us why she didn't.

Long before balladeer Kris Kristofferson popularized the song "Don't Let the Bastards Get You Down," all of us children knew and loved Mom as a walking, talking contradiction, a resolute person who first and foremost preached to us to stand our ground and not to ever let life's bastards get the upper hand. Of course, in her eyes, bastards came in varying shapes and sizes: the clergy, the wealthy, those better educated, or more athletically endowed. Survival, if not the key to success, was to never ever give the "bastards" the satisfaction by seeing you quit on yourself.

Mom had a comical way of always seeing the bright side of whatever calamity her family might be facing. By God, we might be lacking in funds and food, but it was only temporary. Jesus Christ himself would rectify the situation, providing we attended cate-chism classes and church without exception, including those days commemorating various saints. Providing we were faithful in our prayers, the recitation of our Hail Marys and Our Fathers. Provid-ing we stood up for each other and never gave ground, no matter what sort of confrontations might arise.

In our family, mixed messages were the norm. Fight but don't fight. Honor your mother and father—"And where is that son of a bitch going now?" Never use the Lord's name in vain—"I'm going upstairs right now and get down on my goddamn knees and pray that Jesus kills that bastard tonight." Patriotism, love of our God and our country was of the utmost—"But if it hadn't been for that goddamned war and that goddamned plane crashing . . ." Always tell the truth, never tell a lie . . . well, a little lie didn't really count; after all, we were Irish—"God will protect us. If not God, then it's up to you boys."

Work hard, be loyal to yourself, and all's well that ends well. "St. Patrick himself has blessed us," Mom would say, toasting the blessed saint with another bottle of Pabst Blue Ribbon. And then she would place her rough, worn hands in mine and we would dance across the living room floor. Her laughter was musical, almost as enchanting as the songs she was singing. We swirled about the room until I became lightheaded. Of course, I was laughing with Ma, making up the words to the songs I had not yet memorized.

And although it had taken a great deal of practice, I also pre-tended not to notice her tears, having by then convinced myself that they were tears of joy.

More than anything else, we children learned to make do with the circumstances, expecting and accepting with a resolute shrug the worst possible of life's scenarios, knowing that it was easier to laugh than to cry.

6

The Home Front

Dear Mom & Family: I finally made it over to Vietnam. Today is Friday the 24th of November. In Belvidere it's Thanksgiving. Right now I'm in Quang Tri. I'm in Fox Company, 2nd Battalion, 4th Marines. The company moves all around. The guys tell me it's a good outfit. We are up towards the DMZ, patrolling the area. I've been separated from all my close friends and really feel lost. But I know I'll meet more good buddies pretty soon. Don't worry; I'll be okay. Pray for me. Love: Jeff

—November 24, 1967

Jeff and I survived childhood through sports. Baseball, football, basketball, or track, it didn't matter. Just as long as you could hit it, throw it, run with it, or dribble it, the game kept us occupied. When the weather was too bad—by our standards, meaning more than two feet of snow or a blinding rainstorm—we played football and basketball indoors. A rolled-up sock became our ball for a game played on our knees in the hallway leading to the back bedrooms. We even allowed Joe to play, mostly using him as a tackling dummy. Joe never seemed to mind; he was just glad to be included. And while Joe was getting run over by Jeff and me, Jude was standing in the doorway, cheering us on.

Even when I tried out for my first organized school sport, the Wethersfield lightweight football squad during the sixth grade, my brothers and sister got into the act. I managed to memorize the entire offense with Jeff's help, but only after several days of pop quizzes. I would wake up to Jeff's questions: "Pitch right, who's taking out the defensive end? Who's blocking the outside linebacker?" En route to school, Jeff would run through the plays and blocking assignments. On the way home after practice, Jeff would set up various game situations, then grill me over which play I should run: "Third and three at your own forty-five: pass or run? And remember, bro, the right-side linebacker has been stopping you all day, and your arm ain't that strong."

Day after day I rattled off the blocking assignments until I knew every player's assignment on any given play. Damn, I was proud of myself, actually believing I was an offensive whiz, a pint-sized version of Johnny Unitas. Only years later did it dawn on me that Jeff had grasped the entire offense at a glance.

And once I had mastered the playbook, Jeff gathered Joe and Jude into the backyard and worked on my technique. We ran the plays with me at quarterback, Jeff switching between running back and fullback, and Joe lining up opposite us as the enemy linebacker. Jude also got into the act, cheering us on from the sidelines. Before I knew it, my quarterbacking skills were flawless. For the longest time I actually believed I would become a star because I was a natural athlete.

When we weren't immersed in sports, we kids entertained ourselves by putting on neighborhood circuses. This was the most fun of all because everyone took a turn at being the center of attention. Jeff and Jude ran the show, brainstorming the various acts and entertainment. Jude, of course, would be a dancer, enthralling the neighborhood kids, and even their parents, with her feet. She would even sing a song or two, sidling up to Jeff for a duet. Joe was the strongman, slipping into a set of my long johns and stuffing socks up his arms, thus doubling his biceps. My role was always the same, slipping on the boxing gloves and whipping the bejabbers out of anyone foolish enough to step into the ring with me. Ma would sell Kool-Aid and homemade chocolate chip cookies; then Jude and Joe would slip into the clown outfits that Ma had originally made years earlier for Jeff and me. The entire day would be spent laughing our way through our very own three-ring big top.

And then, as darkness descended, we would put everything away and return to the basketball court, playing a game of two on one—Jeff and Joe against me.

Because Mom was Mom, we never lacked an outlet to be as zany as we sought to be. And because Dad was a coach—always drilling us to improve, to be the very best—everything about our lives was competitive. We never lacked for self-motivation or intensity of spirit. Or for sporting equipment, for that matter. We kept busy, coaxing our muscles through games of strength and agility, perfecting the outside set shot, the long pass to an end cutting across the middle of the defense, knowing exactly how much speed we had to generate running down the beaten path before slamming the end of our bamboo pole-vaulting pole into the slot and pulling ourselves up and over the crossbar. Becoming bigger and stronger, becoming fairly gifted athletes; competing always, arguing over who was the fastest, the strongest, the best athlete in our father's eyes.

Jeff and I pretty much raised ourselves, locking in our ideals and morals by what we observed on the home front. Dad was up and out the door by seven o'clock to teach school. Between coaching and working second jobs, his return was long after we kids had gone asleep. He worked for the police department or on the railroad during the summer. Dad swore Jeff and me to silence about the railroad. "If any of those guys I work with found out I was educated, they'd stick a knife in my ribs," our father said. Mom worked various shifts, which required that Jeff and I spend our evenings baby-sitting our younger brothers and sisters. Asking why we had to do this never entered our minds; we were family, and it was our job to help each other. There were times when we ate nothing but oatmeal or ham and beans for weeks on end. Peanut butter was a luxury; we'd snack on crackers crushed in a glass of milk.

Jeff eventually tired of the games and fell in love with music, discovering that he had a knack for playing a guitar and could carry a tune. Ricky Nelson was his first teen idol, then Bob Dylan. My brother's infatuation with music was one thing, but his choice in television programs was another. While I couldn't get enough of *Gunsmoke, Have Gun Will Travel,* and *Wanted Dead or Alive,* Jeff was glued to the TV set whenever *The Adventures of Ozzie and Harriet* was on, spellbound by Ricky Nelson. In retaliation, I teased the hell out of him, first pointing out how stupid the show was—Ozzie never used a leather belt on Ricky or his older brother, David; Ozzie and Harriet never engaged in knock-down, drag-out shouting matches; and you never saw either of them slugging down a beer. Hell, everything in the Nelson household was always peaches and cream—total harmony, which both of us knew to be bullshit. Jeff didn't give an inch, though. He simply smiled at my rebuttals and started singing "I'm Walking." I didn't get it, so to keep pace and to keep the heat turned up on our friendly rivalry, I chose Edd "Kookie" Byrnes, the slick-haired sidekick in *77 Sunset Strip.* It didn't matter that Byrnes couldn't sing a lick. He was cool. Besides, in the show's premiere he was cast as a sociopathic teenager. Something clicked; I made a connection, right or wrong.

During the summer of 1960, shortly after we moved from Wethersfield to Kewanee, Jeff placed an election poster of John F. Kennedy in our bedroom. I told him he was nuts, that Kennedy was a squid—a derogative word used by Marines to describe Navy personnel. I had heard Dad use it often. Besides, Dad liked Ike. And if Ike liked Richard Nixon, then the choice was a no-brainer. Jeff said I was stupid, that I should learn to think for myself. Again, I had no idea what he was talking about. To my way of thinking, my brother was strange. *Must be the damned music,* I thought, mimicking my father's comments.

We gained another brother shortly after JFK's inauguration and almost lost Mom in the process. She was under doctor's orders not to have any more children. Being an Irish Catholic, though, she had her own thoughts on the matter. Never mind that she lost a lot of blood during the birth, so much so that a priest had to administer last rites. Never mind that a doctor, concerned about the critical condition of my mother, said it would be best if she aborted the child. Mom screamed, "Just deliver my goddamned baby! Forget about me!" This the doctor did, without further comment. That's how Jim came into the world on July 12, 1961, screaming and hollering, yet cradled in the loving arms of a mother who was willing to sacrifice her life for that of her unborn child.

Of course, our household became more crowded than ever: Jude still pirouetting around the house in her tutu, singing and dancing up a storm; Joe carrying on by emulating his hero-of-the-moment, GI Joe, gunning down make-believe villains; Jeff shuffling from room to room, amplifying his singing with a handheld microphone, numbing us all with his Ricky Nelson tunes; and baby Jim seemingly crying endlessly. Dad was away more than usual, working two extra jobs—still pumping gas at the Sinclair station during the week, bartending on weekends, and attending college in Michigan during the summer to finally obtain his master's degree.

Between caring for all her kids and still holding down a full-time job at the telephone company, Ma somehow made ends meet. Lots of oatmeal, spaghetti and sauce made from tomato soup, peanut butter and jelly sandwiches, and ham and beans. No one went hungry or was improperly clothed. Everyone helped around the house, whether it was baby-sitting or padding the grocery fund. Jeff shoveled snow or mowed neighborhood lawns, and I peddled ice cream during the summer for Street Treats, earning two cents for every ten-cent bar I sold. On good days I earned eight dollars. It was with a deep sense of pride that Jeff and I handed over our earnings to Mom, who said she used it to help purchase groceries. Even if she didn't, it was no big deal.

By this time our parents had mellowed. Dad no longer laid a hand on me; better yet was the cessation of hostilities between our parents. They still argued, but not with the intensity and frequency of the past.

High school was the great eye-opener. I had always viewed academics as a form of punishment, equating education with my father, unconsciously believing that if I studied hard and got good grades I would be double-crossing Ma and lending truth to her frequent accusation that I would turn out to be "just like your goddamn father." By my freshman year, though, I ceased giving a shit. I actually took school seriously and studied, and surprised my classmates and myself by becoming an honor student. I escaped through books *and* sports. I would either become the best of athletes, someday winning a scholarship to Notre Dame or, failing that, I could distance myself immediately by plunging into such exotic literature as *The Catcher in the Rye* and *Strong Men Armed*.

In the summer of 1963 we uprooted once again, moving farther north, to Belvidere, Illinois. The summer before my senior
year, Jeff caught wind of a group of long-haired Englishmen and
actually wrote to their manager requesting more information.
Next thing we knew, three large cardboard boxes crammed with
posters, flyers, and a handful of record albums were delivered to
our house. My brother had a leg up on Beatles mania. It was obvious to all that his future was etched in stone; he would someday
make it big on the rock 'n' roll circuit.

As to what escape plans my other brothers and sister might be
aspiring to, I had no idea. It never seemed important enough for me
to ask, because I was looking for my own way out. The Marine Corps
seemed to be the perfect answer. Having by now sustained almost a
dozen concussions, plus twice dislocating my left shoulder, I had
long abandoned my dream of leading Notre Dame's Fighting Irish
to the national championship. So on the early evening of March 31,
1964, two Marine sergeants decked out in dress blues showed up at
our home to officially swear me in. Because Dad had been such a
kick-ass warrior, the Corps wanted to make this a family function.

Mom would have none of it. She stayed in the bedroom during the entire swearing-in ceremony, making an appearance only
out of necessity.

"Okay, Smitty, it's time," she said, walking to the door with suitcase in hand.

"Guys, this is my wife, June," Dad said proudly. "Help yourself
to the beer. I'll be back in a few hours."

The jaws of the Marine recruiters were comical, hanging as
low as they did on this occasion. I hadn't thought to tell them my
mother was pregnant with her sixth child. I hadn't thought anything odd about it, in fact.

So the recruiters stood there dumbfounded as Dad rushed
Mom to the hospital, where she suffered through another excruciating, near-fatal birth—having the last rites again pronounced over
her as she chose to give life even at the expense of her own. That's
how sister Jane joined the clan, born shortly before I was inducted
into the Marine Corps.

Dad made it back in time to hoist a few more beers for the
glory of the Corps, sharing war stories with the two sergeants, who

turned their backs briefly when Dad handed me a beer, clinked his bottle against mine, and said, "Son, you're about to become a man."

Mom would later joke that she lost one child that day, yet gained another. "God's will," she said, then drank another beer and added, "But please, Lord, please damn the goddamned Marine Corps." She lapsed into silence, then said, "And I would have said exactly those words right to those goddamned recruiters' faces if I hadn't been giving birth to your sister."

My brother Jeff watched my swearing-in ceremony, though. He was proud of me, he told me later. But the seriousness of my rite of passage did not stop him from punctuating the event with his special brand of humor. He gave me the finger just as I was repeating the oath about defending the life and liberty of these United States, and then he grinned and silently mouthed, "You're an asshole."

My stint in the Corps was short-lived. Another dislocation of my left shoulder, this one occurring during a fistfight with another boot, necessitated my rehabilitation at the Navy's Balboa Hospital, and then I was honorably discharged in November 1964. Feeling as if I were snakebit, Jeff consoled me at Chicago's O'Hare International Airport. The twelve-pack of Pabst that he had brought with him also helped ease my humiliation. "Hell, bro," he said, "the good Lord has better things in store for you. Where's your faith?"

In truth, it was beginning to waver as I stumbled through a maze of confusion, jumping from one menial job to another before finally settling in at the local Chrysler assembly plant. Jeff's prophecy came to light on January 7, 1967, when June Rush agreed to become June Smith, joining me at the end of the altar at Belvidere's First Baptist Church. To no one's surprise, Jeff was my best man. And he carried out his duties with typical flair, using a Magic Marker to write "Help" on the sole of my left shoe and "Me!" on the sole of my right, knowing that the instant I kneeled at the altar, the crowd would burst out laughing. Which it did. And when I looked at my brother, his innocent, wide-eyed puppy dog expression made me laugh, too.

Three months later, Jeff shocked everyone by walking away from his peacenik lifestyle and enlisting in the Marines. He never did explain his actions.

7

The Long Good-bye

Dear Mom & Family: Don't know what to say exactly. We've been out on an operation, which we still are, and there's nothing to talk about. We've been seeing monkeys around here. That might interest the kids. If you get a chance to send some goodies, do it. Food is precious in the field. If you do send something, send mostly canned goods—fruit, ravioli, and stuff like that. I'll be sending another check home when they pay us. I'm with a great bunch of guys, so you don't have to worry about me. God bless you all: Jeff

—February 5, 1968

We toasted Jeff's departure in typical Smith fashion—with friends, family, and an endless supply of beer. It was far from being a joyous occasion, though. The intensity of the Vietnam War had been turned up a notch in the summer of 1967, and it was impossible to ignore the horrific television reports about besieged Marines at an otherwise innocuous place called Con Thien. For the most part, no one spoke of war and death.

Instead, my brother sat on the living room couch with a know-ing smile as Dad and I regaled everyone with semiserious stories of boot camp—getting slapped around by our drill instructors, get-ting our asses run off day in and day out, how other boots got their asses chewed out for not qualifying as expert on the rifle range. When someone asked Dad what islands he had fought on during World War II, my father dismissed the inquiry with a curt "too damned many of 'em," which prompted our laughter. When someone else asked Jeff if he was afraid of being sent to Vietnam, there was at first an uncomfortable silence. Then my brother made light of the subject.

"Vi-*et*-nam? You've gotta be shittin' me, bro?" he said. "Hey, if the Corps is dumb enough to send me over there, I'll just pacify the damn place with some of my flower power." Even Ma thought that was funny, slugging down beers with the rest of us. She did not slip into depression until Jeff boarded the military bus that transported him to O'Hare.

Before he departed, Jeff pulled June and me aside and hugged us both. "Don't worry, bro, all them medals you wanted to win, I'll win 'em for you," he said. We talked about the war games we played in our youth—hiding out in the snow in the cornfields, awaiting the Nazi tanks; the beach landings we made at Pike Lake, some-how always avoiding the Jap machine guns; we even reminisced about Pa Edwards digging that trench so long, long ago. And then Jeff turned serious. "You know, bro, you getting discharged was the best thing that's happened to you—that and marrying June. Hell, you got the best of the bargain." And then he smiled, punched me in the arm, and added, "Of course, I'll always be the best man."

My wife broke into tears, holding onto Jeff for the longest time, and then she assured him that both of us would be praying for him constantly.

Jeff had the last word. "While you're at it, June, don't forget to pray for my stupid brother here. He surely needs it more than me." Moments later he boarded the bus to become a member of the 2nd Battalion, Platoon 2004, the battalion's honor platoon. He graduated from boot camp on August 19, 1967, then underwent advanced infantry training at Camp Pendleton. Upon receiving orders for Vietnam in early November he was given a far-too-brief reprieve at home, just time enough to say his good-byes and drink a lot of beer.

My wife and I threw a farewell party for Jeff, inviting all of his friends. The record player blared all evening, a loud and constant medley of Monkees tunes as we drank ourselves semiconscious, once again reliving our yesterdays and bullshitting about our tomorrows. Somewhere during the course of the evening I told Jeff that he would survive this little war with no sweat, that he would come home carrying his shield, not being borne on it. What I didn't share was the numbness that was slowly encasing my heart, my fear that he was marching to his death. Try as I might to muster the courage to relay my fears to my brother, I just couldn't. Macho bullshit, I guess; afraid to show weakness, afraid to show that I truly cared, that I actually *loved* my brother. And Jeff, acting equally as stupid as I—probably wishing not to spoil anyone's fun—played the John Wayne game perfectly and said he would try his damnedest to take it easy on the gooks.

Each of us drank two more beers from a fresh six-pack of Pabst, and then I made a big ceremony of placing the last two beers in the back of the refrigerator, saying we would drink them upon his return. We hugged each other, and then Jeff turned and walked away.

There was no shaking my fear. Never before had I felt so distant, so cold—not during any of the brutal fistfights I had had in the past, not even when I was scared out of my mind as a child, watching Dad unbuckle his belt, muscle memory telling me how bad the whipping would be. I wanted to cry but couldn't. My hands shook, my heart seemed to shudder, to vibrate out of sync with everything else I was feeling. When I tried to wash away the creeping terror with another beer, I gagged.

It wasn't until early the next morning that I finally shared my feelings with my wife. Cradled in her loving arms, I told her that I didn't think we would see Jeff again, not here among the living. Only then did I cry, but only briefly—a few tears that quickly dried up when June said my fears were unfounded. After all, she would be praying for my brother every day, she said. God would protect Jeff.

But then she, too, broke into tears, sobbing deeply as she repeated Jeff's parting words to her: "Promise me that if anything happens to me, you won't let my brother go back in the Corps. Revenge solves nothing."

* * *

With my brother gone, I got stuck with being the family's peace negotiator. My first and last attempt failed. I could not keep Mom and Dad from divorcing. They had not been sharing the same bed for almost a year—my mother sleeping in their upstairs bedroom while my father slept on a cot in the dirt-floored basement next to the furnace.

As soon as Jeff departed for Vietnam, Mom filed for divorce. I found out about it in typical fashion, walking into the middle of an argument shortly after Thanksgiving.

"That son of a bitch is out of my life for good!" my mother screamed at no one in particular as I entered the house. I had heard her talk like this many times before, ranting and raving after too many beers. The storm usually burned itself out within a few hours. But never before had I seen Ma this upset, this distraught. Still not believing she would go through with it, I simply shrugged and approached her with a dumb smile, my arms outstretched to embrace her. But she slapped my hands away, turned her back, and then went into the kitchen for another beer, her words trailing behind her, "That son of a bitch isn't living here anymore—not under *my* roof."

I heard Dad upstairs, slamming drawers. Panicked now, I bounded up the stairs and entered Mom's bedroom. Dad was crying as he packed an old suitcase. He wiped away his tears and gave me an embarrassed look, then opened the closet and pulled out his three suits. I tried to form words, but my heart was lodged in my throat. Finally I said, "Dad, you can't leave us. You've got to talk to Ma, work it out."

Dad's hands were shaking, his eyes wild, his voice as trembling as mine as he said, "For Christ's sake, she calls me an atheist. How the hell does she think I survived that goddamn war? No way in hell I'd have lived if I hadn't—Jesus, that woman is crazy."

And then he reached into the drawer in which he kept his socks and pulled out a small prayer book that a chaplain had given him at Guadalcanal. "I read this damn thing till I was blue in the face; read it every night when the Japs hit us, read it every damn day when the Jap destroyers were shelling us. I prayed and I prayed. She's never understood any of it; never understood me, none of it."

Dad paused to finish packing, then turned to me and said, "I'm sorry, son, but your mother wants me out; I've got to go." He started to say something else, but couldn't because of his tears. Finally he said, "This place is a goddamn nuthouse," and then he brushed past me and stormed down the stairs.

I don't know how long I stood in the bedroom, my mind racing back and forth—from all those moments in my youth when I wished my father were dead, this the result of a whipping; to the good moments, and there were plenty of those, when Dad found the time to build me my very own Soapbox Derby racer, when he built the raft for Jeff and me at Pike Lake. Damn it, I hated him and I loved him. Just like Ma had, I guess. And now he was gone.

For the first time in my life, I felt alone. Abandoned. Dad was gone, and for some damn reason I was convinced that it was my fault.

When I finally shuffled down the stairs and into the kitchen, Ma would not look me in the eye. She was standing at the sink, her back to me. I opened the refrigerator and grabbed a beer, then set it aside without opening it. "What about the kids?" was all I could think of to ask. When Ma turned around, I embraced her. Our tears fell on each other's shoulders.

"We'll be okay," she said. "Your father will still take care of us, so don't worry. We just can't live together. Me and the kids will be fine." She paused to open my beer, handed it to me, and then said, "Whatever you do, don't tell Jeff. Promise me?"

I agreed, then gave Ma another hug. We spent the rest of the afternoon reminiscing about the good times; every one of Ma's stories seemingly started the same way: "Remember when Jeff . . ."

For the most part, I listened—trying to soothe Ma's tears, desperately trying to fill the void that now seemed to have taken over my heart, thinking there was no way in hell I could ever feel any worse.

Jeff died less than four months later.

8

Running toward
the Abyss

Dear Bro: Got your letter of Feb. 4 the other day. The mail was
fouled up for a while, but now it should be straightened out. I
enjoyed your poems. Send me some more if you will. I showed
your poems to a buddy and he liked them. Hope to be playing
some basketball with you next year. I won't be much for running
and shooting, but when the roughhousing starts under the basket and I start throwing grenades—well, you know! My prayers
go out to you and June. Love you, Bro Jeff

—February 28, 1968

O ur mother conducted an eleven-year wake for Jeff.
Her first act was to turn her dining room wall into a
memorial to him. Pictures of Jeff were hung from floor
to ceiling—Jeff holding an armload of fish from our childhood days
at Pike Lake, Jeff driving the 1965 Homecoming Queen's Court in
a convertible during the annual parade, Jeff shooting a free throw
for the Belvidere Bucs, Jeff flying high over the cross-bar in '66
to set the local high school pole vaulting record, Jeff being awakened drunk from the going-away party before leaving for Vietnam,
Jeff glassy-eyed in a Philippine bar with an unidentified Marine.

The pictures ran on and on, including the Purple Heart citation issued by the Defense Department.

Whenever Jeff's closest buddies stopped by, and at times it seemed as if they spent as much time commiserating with Ma as they spent with their own parents, the Wall was always the first stop.

"Who's the guy with Jeff?" someone would invariably ask, pointing to the Philippine bar shot. Ma would simply shrug and say, "Jeff never told us," then slip into the kitchen to grab a couple of beers.

Upon seeing that picture for the first time, my question to Ma was: "Where did this come from?" She gave me a sheepish grin and said, "Your brother's belongings. There was a roll of film."

"Were there any other pictures from Nam? Anything else in that seabag of his?" I asked, biting my tongue, trying not to get pissed at Ma for having lied to me.

Another sheepish grin. "Nope, just that one picture; nothing else. You want a beer?" Indeed, I did. Several, in fact.

And then I would join Jeff's buddies as they gazed upon the Wall, scanning the pictures, most of them the source of memories of time they had spent with Jeff, memories that grew in such proportion that an outsider would have thought Jeff to be a saint.

I knew better. He was vindictive at times, manipulative like everyone else in our family, and enjoyed scaring the hell out of me. A couple years before June and I were married, I took her to see the movie *Strait-Jacket* starring Joan Crawford, who played the role of a modern-day Lizzie Borden, the alleged ax murderer. The scary part was when the innocent-victim-of-the-moment was about to get axed; it was always preceded by the sound of metal bracelets tinkling somewhere in the shadows. Spooky stuff. Later that night I returned home and got into bed. Just as I started to drift off, I heard bracelets tinkling. And then Jeff leaped out of the closet and onto my bed.

No one knew better than I that Jeff was far from being a saint. But he sure as hell was a great friend.

Ma's second act at immortalizing Jeff was to use his government death benefit to purchase a cabin on Lake Ripley, just outside of Cambridge, Wisconsin. According to Ma, Jeff had stipulated that if something terrible should happen to him in Vietnam, she should use the money to "do something nice for the entire family." Ma took possession of the five-room, slate-board dwelling during the summer of '69, and subsequently spent almost three weekends a month relaxing there—doing a little fishing, a lot of sleeping, and a great deal of drinking. The cabin, "Jeff's cabin, and don't any of you ever forget it," became a family watering hole, literally and figuratively. The beer flowed as much as the swamp that inched closer and closer to the cabin as the years went on, eventually consuming the dwelling in the fall of 1978.

But long before that happened, Ma gathered all of us together on weekends at the cabin and talked endlessly about better days down the road. And when Jim and Jane were out of earshot, we would talk about Jeff.

I would be lying if I said I recalled every conversation, every moment that my wife and I spent there. I'm sure our young daughters, Julie and Jill, who were born in 1969 and 1972, enjoyed some grand moments there, because we have pictures of their joyous faces. And I know I must have enjoyed most of my moments at the cabin because I have vague memories of playing tackle football with my high school buddy Mike Plumley and brothers Joe and Jim in the partially flooded grassland separating two long rows of similar cabins. And I remember bits and pieces of other great days water-skiing with my wife and my friend Johnny Lowry. But most of all, I used Jeff's cabin as an excuse to stay drunk. If I laughed, it was empty laughter.

For the most part, I sat with Ma on the screened front porch and listened to her talk, never getting upset that every story inevitably led to Jeff. I would listen and drink, then glance at the painted-on-burlap rendition of Joan Baez. "Jeff could sing almost as good as she could. She hates that goddamn war as much as I do," Ma would say, lapsing into tears.

I would listen and drink, then shift my eyes to the poster of Che Guevara. "Jeff also had a revolutionary streak in him. He protested that damn war, you know," Ma would say, then grin triumphantly. Her grin reminded me of a death's-head. When she flashed it, it seemed so damned exultant. She was getting revenge the only way she knew how, striking out at all those she perceived to be responsible for my brother's death.

*   *   *

My wife, June, truly believing I was a gifted writer, encouraged me to quit my job on the Chrysler plant assembly line and enroll in college. June's faith in my writing talents lay solely on a few score poems I had written to her during my senior year in high school and my brief stint in the Marines. With nothing more than that, in September 1968, nineteen months after our marriage, I enrolled at Northern Illinois University, my father's alma mater—majoring in journalism and drinking, with minors in history, literature, and bar fights. I did fairly well educationwise; piss poor mentally. No matter where I turned it seemed as if I bumped up against the Vietnam War. My best friends were veterans, my worst enemies the campus hippies who protested against the war.

In the spring of 1969 I was walking through the student union and found myself staring at a Marine Corps enlistment poster. Beside the poster, his hands flat upon the table, was a Marine captain decked out in dress blues. We shook hands and exchanged a few pleasantries, and then he inquired about my background. I laid it all out for him—my prior service, my brother's death, my being married. In less than two hours, without consulting my wife, I signed the document that made me the newest member of the Corps' Platoon Leaders Class.

"I've been expecting it for some time," June told me that evening, fighting back her tears. "I know it's something you *have* to do. Remember two things: Jesus and I love you, and I will always be praying for you. No matter what."

My wife has always known me better than I've known myself. She knew the guilt that was eating away at me. More important, she knew the source—in her eyes, the Darker Power. My mother's reaction was a tight smile, which I interpreted as her blessing for me to exact revenge—seeking out and killing the man who killed Jeff.

Lost amid the bravado of my signing up for the PLC program was that June was pregnant with our first child, the birth expected sometime in December. It didn't matter. I had to serve; duty and honor were eating me alive. Never mind that almost everyone in the country, including those who were fighting the war, wanted us out of Vietnam. Never mind that I was drinking to excess and was probably borderline psychotic. What the hell, I still wanted to be a grunt—a member of the elite lean, mean fighting machine. So, without further ado, I soon found myself at Quantico, Virginia, running from dawn to dusk, firing an M-16, learning leadership tactics and setting ambushes, air-assaulting from Hueys, escape and evasion. Cool stuff. Playing war games, just as Jeff and I had done as kids.

Granted, there were a few minor obstacles I had to overcome before climbing into a bunk in an outdated Quonset hut at Camp Geiger. Although my chronic dislocated left shoulder had been surgically repaired in 1966, a Navy doctor put me through a battery of tests, smiling as he did so, saying, "I just want to make sure you can hoist the flag on Mount Suribachi." Later, another Navy doctor sat me down and asked a battery of questions, all of which dealt with *why* I wanted to reenlist. I was twenty-three, married with a pregnant wife, had prior service, and was doing well in college, which gave me an automatic exemption from the draft.

"Enlighten me," the doctor ordered. I didn't hesitate. I looked him square in the eye and said, "I just want to kill the sonofabitch who killed my brother."

The doc smiled and approved my enlistment. Next stop, Quantico—six weeks of simulated hell meant to prepare the survivors for Officers Candidate School the next year. I breezed through the PLC course without too much difficulty, despite being drunk half the time. When not undergoing training, I spoke with as many Nam vets as I could find, looking for anyone who had been in Vietnam with Fox Company, 2nd Battalion, 4th Marines, 3rd Marine Division. In return I received nothing but condolences and unsought advice: "Man, get out of the Crotch as quick as you can. That fuckin' country over there ain't worth dying for." Indeed, but the bastard who had killed Jeff was probably still lurking out there, so I pressed on, making it through graduation.

But just when I was ready to take the next step toward dying for my country, President Nixon decided to let the South Vietnamese fight and die for their own lost cause; my brother's division furled its flag and returned to the States. My wife likes to say that the hand of Providence was involved. Years after the fact, I referred to it as *luck*—I was lucky to be spared, and the Corps was lucky that I didn't get sent over to Nam and do something tragically stupid, thus soiling its reputation.

No matter. In February 1970 I was handed another honorable discharge and told to have a nice life. The upside was being able to see my newborn daughter, Julie Lynne, the most beautiful baby any father could ever spoil and adore. The downside, finishing college or not, was that I had to join the real world and find a job. Quite naturally, the last place I wanted to work was my hometown. Too many bad memories. Chances are I would have landed a newspaper job far from Belvidere had I not stopped for a beer at Dodge Lanes; one beer led to another, and being the smart-ass that I am, I started joking with a dude seated across the bar. He was wearing an Army uniform, which meant he was fair game. Turned out that Bill Hetland had just returned from Vietnam.

Talk about the hand of Providence. Before volunteering for the army, Hetland was editor of Northern Illinois University's student newspaper, the *Northern Star*. While in Nam he wrote a weekly column for our hometown newspaper, the *Belvidere Daily Republican*. What I didn't know at the time was that Hetland had just been named editor of the *BDR*. He was looking for a sports editor and had learned from an NIU journalism professor that I was a pretty good sportswriter. That evening, Hetland offered me a job. I accepted. Over the course of the next three years, Hetland became as true a friend as anyone could ever ask for. He worked my rear off, polished my writing, encouraged my propensity to dig and dig even deeper to get the story. In return, I taught him every move I had mastered on the basketball court, then tried my best to teach him the finer points of boxing.

About the only thing my friend and I disagreed on was how to handle rage. An avowed pacifist, Hetland had volunteered for Vietnam out of his sense of duty. Once there, his education and editing skills landed him in an awards and decorations detachment, where he did nothing but compose heroic verse for posthumous acts of heroism.

"Did nothing but handle Medal of Honor and Distinguished Service Cross documents. Now, if that doesn't drive you crazy, nothing will," Hetland told me one evening over drinks. "Yet even though I drank myself silly in the evenings, I didn't allow it to take me over the edge. But you—Jesus, you've got to stop allowing everything to piss you off, stop throwing punches."

I was pissed at my father, who had remarried in 1969. Dad's wife, Darlene, brought seven children to the marriage; my father was now spending more time with my stepbrothers and stepsisters than he was with his *own* children.

I was pissed at President Johnson and Robert McNamara for not allowing us to win in Vietnam. I was pissed at President Nixon for abandoning the war. Hell, I was even pissed at Hetland and the *BDR* brass because every Memorial Day and Veterans Day the newspaper ran a picture of my mother placing a wreath at the foot of the VFW monument at the city park.

About the only person I wasn't pissed at was my wife, who, for reasons that were and remain far beyond my grasp or understanding, tolerated my instability. Her strength of character made up for my lack of it; her love overrode my self-loathing; her compassion filled the emptiness dominating my heart. And amid our inexplicable bond, June gave birth to our second daughter, Jill Elizabeth, in July 1972.

Despite the love that embraced me within the sanctuary of my own home, living and working in Belvidere was like working within a tomb. No matter where I turned, I embraced my brother's death at every turn; it was a community that never tired of honoring the memory of the county's only Vietnam fatality. The high school coaches I interviewed for various sports stories had been Jeff's coaches. Belvidere High even named its track room in my brother's honor and also awarded an annual scholarship in his name to its best track athlete. The teachers I drank with were some of Jeff's teachers. Those with whom I played industrial league basketball were Jeff's friends. Jeff's grave was just down the road from where my wife, our two daughters, and I lived; the cemetery was like a second home.

There also was family strife, juggling my time between Dad and Ma. As hard as I tried to hate my stepbrothers and stepsisters, I came to like them a lot. Liking my stepmother, Darlene, would take another decade. No one could replace my mother. While hating Darlene, I found myself loving my mother more and more, trying even harder than I had in the past to keep her smiling.

It was a full-time job, though. She would call me in the middle of the night and tell me about a dream she kept having, how Jeff had walked into the bedroom and told her that he "wasn't in pain anymore." Or the police would call and ask me to come down to the station and pick up Ma; she had been pulled over, drunk. When I arrived at the jail, Ma was shouting about police brutality, how this sonofabitchin' cop had laughed at her, which she interpreted as them laughing because Jeff had been killed. No charges were ever filed. The police, like everyone else in town, had nothing but sympathy for my mother.

"Just take her home and sober her up, Smitty," the arresting officer would say. I would do a half-assed job of it—taking Ma home, where we would sit up half the night drinking and talking about Jeff. My mother would cry; I would sit and listen, my rage building.

In the winter of 1973, I was drinking at the VFW with Dad. Ma was checking coats, doing her part for the annual Gold Star Mothers' dance. I could feel my ears burning, knowing Ma was in the other room, fuming that I was having a good time with my father. To give her equal time, I stepped into the other room and got in line at the coat check, working my way to the front just to say hello. Ma's eyes sparkled when she saw me. The older gentleman in front of me saw my mother's smile, then turned to his wife and said, "That's Smitty's ex, isn't it? What's that bitch grinning about?" I leveled him with two punches. When I was pulled off him, Ma was still smiling.

I was married with two young daughters, making $185 a week, paying $135 a month rent in a home owned by the newspaper, and surrounded by friends and family. After that one-sided fight at the VFW, I knew I had to get out of town before I killed someone or someone killed me. So I accepted a job as a sportswriter for *Cocoa Today* in Cocoa Beach, Florida. Without bothering to check out either the newspaper or the community in which my family and I would live, I moved as far away from the past as I could. It didn't matter that I took a $50 a week pay cut to work at a larger newspaper. Didn't matter. Happiness was Belvidere in my rearview mirror. Another plus was that I would work with Ron Martz, a fellow Marine and a gifted reporter. Martz taught me to write with passion. We also became best friends.

I covered sports of all kinds, from high school gymnastics to the Miami Dolphins. I lived the job day and night, racking up a wall full of writing awards. I was a workaholic and an alcoholic. But I did stay sober long enough to continue my search for anyone who might have known Jeff in Vietnam. I interviewed Sergeant Greg Hargis, the Marine embassy guard in Saigon, officially the last Marine out of Vietnam when the country fell to the Communists in 1975. I wrote scores of feature stories on Nam vets, quizzing them about what their experiences had been like—listening but never fully comprehending their horrors.

And because I never came to grips with what was eating away at me, I continued to run away. From Cocoa Beach to St. Petersburg, spending less than a year covering the NFL's newest entry, the Tampa Bay Buccaneers, for the *Evening Independent.* Then moving my family out of the sun and into Wisconsin's winter chill to become sports editor of the *Racine Journal-Times.* It was there that Paul Bodi and Ted Findlay took me under their wings, refining my journalistic skills and making me an even better reporter, a more passionate writer.

In May 1977, the *Chicago Tribune* hired me to design sports pages. The move had two benefits. After an absence of five years, the guilt I felt about having abandoned my mother was overwhelming; having at the same time abandoned my brothers and sisters never entered the equation. Also, I would no longer have to write. Problem was, my drinking had become so intense that I would stumble home from an interview, have a few more beers, then forget all about having conducted an interview. My notes were of no help; I was unable to decipher my own handwriting.

At the *Tribune,* all I had to do now was design pages, make them look pretty and appealing, something I could do in my sleep. Even drunk or hung over.

And through it all, praying day and night for God to relieve me of the demons bedeviling me, was my wife. June attended church and Bible study classes without fail. She gathered with other tortured souls in various Christian charismatic groups, becoming a member of Women's Aglow. June refused to give up on me. Although a loving and caring husband and father, my heart was buried. I had a cold, mean streak and a hair-trigger temper, which I directed at almost everyone except my family. I was thoroughly agnostic.

For the most part, I did a superb job of hiding my pain while I went through the motions of living, moving from one state to another, from one newspaper to another, forever trying to place more distance between myself and the specter of my brother's grave. And always failing, for it was impossible not to close my eyes and drift away, opening the door for the nightmare.

Jeff is moving through the clearing, through the gunfire and explosions, and then he falls face-forward, clutching his stomach. I run to help him, pushing aside the Marines standing over him, screaming at them to call a corpsman, to radio for an evacuation helicopter. But the damn grunts seem ambivalent, staring at me with glazed expressions, immobile and indifferent.

I see Jeff's blood seep into the sandy soil. I watch him die. And then I turn to speak to the men in his rifle squad but now they have no faces. They're young men with names I'll never know. Mortar rounds come whistling in but no one seems in a great hurry to scurry to safety. Cigarettes are lit, then one by one Jeff's buddies crouch at his side, their hands brushing his forehead. They're saying something to my brother; their mouths are moving, but I hear no words.

And then I wake up, shaking, drenched in a cold sweat. Unable to sleep, I go to the refrigerator and open a beer. Sitting alone in the dark with tears welling in my eyes, but unable to cry. Waiting to heal, yet watching the wound fester even more. Saying to hell with it and grabbing another beer. Then waiting for the sun to come up, waiting to go to work.

9

King Cobra

Dear Mom: Don't have much time to write now, but I wanted to
let you know that I picked up a radio and at night when we're
on ship I can pick up the Armed Forces radio network. From
7–10 they play popular music. It's really great. Unfortunately, I
can't take the radio with me into the field. Keep praying. I strive
to be a better Catholic. God bless all of you. Love, your son—Jeff

—*January 27, 1968*

What goes up eventually comes down. Everyone has a
bottom. Luckily for me, when I finally came crashing
down, I bounced instead of splattering.

My descent began in Chicago, which was, indeed, my kind of
town. Not only had I reached the ultimate in the field of journalism, but also the city never closed its doors. I had the best of both
worlds, watching my beloved Bears and Cubs whenever I wanted,
plus being the center of my family's attention—in my muddled
mind, at least. Ma and Dad never ceased bragging about me. And
if there was a lull in the conversation, I was the first to drop
a hint about being a hotshot journalist, the design editor of the
Tribune's flashiest product, *SportsWeek*.

I had it all—my dream job, making more money than ever
before, even more than my father made; for the first time in our
marriage, June and I were able to pay most of our bills on time.

We also purchased our first home, in Schaumburg; and our daughters, Julie, eight, and Jill, six, were attending a first-class school and making good grades.

The best part, however, was that my wife was reunited with childhood friends and family. She had grown up in Chicago; most of her relatives lived there. And Belvidere, still home to her three brothers and sister, was only a forty-minute drive to the northwest on the interstate.

Indeed, life was grand. Irish bars seemed to adorn every corner, and Guinness was the beer of choice. I was working with some of the finest people I had ever known: Bill Parker, Skip Myslenski, Art Dunn, Bob Verdi, Mike Kiley, Randy Youngman, Gordon Edds, Kevin Costner, and a Nam vet I knew only as "Mouse." Although I certainly wasn't the greatest page designer in the land, I made up for my deficiencies by working harder than the next guy. And when I wasn't working, I was partying fast and furious, sometimes until dawn.

The trouble started in September 1978, shortly after the Bears' home opener, when my mother was diagnosed with inoperable lung cancer. While that news caught me totally unprepared, the realization that there was no one at home to take care of her really blew me away. Other than Ma and my brother Joe, I had completely lost track of my family. My own troubles were more than enough to handle, so all I knew with any degree of certainty was that Ma had been given only a few months to live, and that Joe was in the California Army National Guard, living in Oceanside with his wife, Mary, and their three children—daughters Jenny and Rhiannon, and newborn son Jeff. I would learn that Jude and her daughter Morgan—*how the hell could I have forgotten about Morgan?*— had left home years earlier and were living somewhere in California, and that my brother Jim, now seventeen, had dropped out of high school and moved to neighboring Rockford; Jane was fourteen.

Always the most levelheaded of my siblings, Joe immediately packed up his family's belongings and drove cross-country, moving in with Ma. He and his wife became Ma's caretakers. To lighten Joe's burden, I officially became Jane's guardian, moving her into our Schaumburg home. Between monitoring my mother's chemo-therapy treatments and trying to keep a handle on Jane's ongoing problems—she had diabetes and was immersed in the day's drug culture—I was experiencing blackouts, although I certainly didn't recognize them as such. I would spend the weekend in Belvidere, visiting Ma at the hospital as she tried to recover from a chemo-therapy treatment, then down beers with Joe on Saturday night and Sunday afternoon. I would drive to work in downtown Chicago on Monday morning, then lose all track of time, stumbling out of a fog on a Thursday or Friday. This went on for a few months; then I started losing entire weeks. What I did remember scared the hell out of me.

There were seemingly endless arguments with Jane. She wanted her bedroom painted black; my wife and I held our ground, in-stead painting the room pink. We demanded and succeeded in dressing Jane like a proper young lady—none of that hippie shit, no beads or peace emblems. Jane also attended school without fail; with Ma, Jane was constantly skipping classes for days on end. In retaliation, Jane threatened my daughters. It happened only once, and ended with me backhanding her, breaking her glasses. The most difficult part of monitoring my sister was making sure she ate properly, keeping her away from sugar-laden sweets and sodas. That we succeeded in keeping Jane from killing herself was largely the result of my wife's vigilance and determination.

Other than flying off the handle and pushing my sister up against a wall, I was of little help. There were early-morning visits to Chicago's rough South Side bars, oblivious to the patrons' stares, sitting contentedly and minding my own business while hoping someone would start a fight—no one did; I guess I was a happy drunk. But screwed up as hell. Crawling on my hands and knees on piss-soaked sidewalks, unable to stand, trying to figure out where the hell my car was. Then finally finding it and driving erratically out of the city, somehow finding Schaumburg and pulling into my driveway, then sleeping for a few hours before driving back into the city to work.

And then, picking up the phone receiver at work on the first day of October 1979 and hearing my brother Joe's voice on the other end: "Mom just died. I need your help, bro." *Jesus Christ!*

I stood there for the longest time, immobile, my mind a blank. Then the realization hit me hard in the stomach: my mother is dead. I reacted by punching out the closest thing to me, a filing cabinet, punching it until my hands bled; punching and screaming, then being smothered by the soothing arms of my boss's secretary, Lois Gerber.

What would strike me as odd about my behavior that day—although the realization did not occur until almost three years later—was that the news of my mother's death did not bring any tears. My heart hurt, deeply, but there was no visible show of grief, only rage. Not when I sat with my brother Joe in Ma's kitchen that night, drinking and reminiscing about our mother's zaniness; not at Ma's wake a few days later, when her closest friends extended their condolences. My face was a stone-cold mask, for by now I was living in an emotionless vacuum. I truly didn't care about anything.

Most frightening of all, though, is that I have no recollection of my mother's funeral. I know she was buried in St. James Cemetery, next to my brother. I can't even tell you what shape Jeff's grave was in, whether anyone had been taking care of it over the years. I had not been to visit his grave since leaving Belvidere six years earlier.

Everything was blurred and out of sync. Days disappeared, then weeks and months. I smiled and clowned around to keep up appearances; I sure as hell didn't want anyone to think I was losing my mind, going insane. Being thought of as a little crazy was okay. But God help me if friends, family, and coworkers viewed me as a certifiable nutcase.

Our third daughter, June Alice, was born on March 6, 1980. I celebrated her birth, thinking privately that *maybe* there was a God after all— He gave my wife and me another beautiful child on the anniversary of Jeff's death. Of course, I had the dates wrong— Jeff was killed on March 7—which shows how far I had plummeted.

The bottom was two years away, even though I remember it as a mere handful of days. It began with a September 1980 telephone call from Ted Findlay, my mentor from the *Racine Journal-Times* who was now living in Kansas. He said the *Kansas City Times* was looking for a sports editor with big-city experience. I applied for the job and was promptly hired. What appealed to me was the fact that, unlike in Illinois, Coors beer was sold in Missouri. The downside was leaving my wife and children behind. The plan was for June to sell the house, then join me in short order. In the back of my mind I knew my sister Jane wouldn't want to leave Illinois. I was right. Within a week of my leaving to assume my new job, Jane left to live with her sister Jude, who had moved back to Belvidere shortly after our mother's death.

I lasted 198 days in Kansas City, the job a poor fit for both parties. I left in mid-April 1981 with a three-month severance package, four cases of Coors, and what would prove to be three lifelong friendships—Brent Frazee, Joe Coleman, and Tom Whitfield. My next stop, this time with the entire family in tow, was Atlanta, Georgia. Van McKenzie, whom I had known in 1976 during my brief stint in St. Petersburg, Florida, was now the executive sports editor for the *Atlanta Journal.* June's prayers were obviously working because I left Kansas City on a Thursday and was hired as McKenzie's Sunday sports editor nine days later. Not only that, but also our house in Schaumburg, which had been on the market for seven months without anyone showing interest, was sold two weeks after I accepted the Atlanta job.

According to my personnel file at Cox Enterprises, the multimedia conglomerate that owns the *Atlanta Journal* and the *Atlanta Constitution,* I began work on June 8, 1981. Considering the physical and mental shape I was in at the time I joined McKenzie and deputy sports editor Gary Caruso and their staff, I have only a vague recollection of the eighteen months after my hire. I lived the job, working virtually around the clock. The same can be said about my drinking with some of my *Journal* cohorts, although most of the times and places remain a mystery. That I helped construct award-winning sports sections is verified by the plaques and certificates squirreled away in an old file cabinet; I actually remember designing some of the pages, but not all. The sporting events these pages were designed around are, for the most part, lost in a void of booze.

I do remember the Braves, under new manager Joe Torre, winning thirteen straight games to open the 1982 season, then clinching the Western Division pennant only because the Los Angeles Dodgers lost their season's final game. June through August remain a blank. I remember the University of Georgia Bulldogs, on the strength of running back Herschel Walker, running off eight consecutive victories and looking like a lock to win another national championship. While all of my Mondays through Fridays of that season are blank, I do recall working from noon Saturdays until two o'clock Sunday mornings, designing four editions of award-winning sports sections, then drinking until sunup with friends— right up to October 30, the day the Dawgs crushed Memphis State.

My best guess is that it was June 1982. It was early morning and, as had been the case for the past few days, I was unable to sleep. So, with all of the lights turned off, I reclined in my easy chair in the den of our Duluth, Georgia, rental home, my feet propped up, my head laid back as I stared mindlessly at the ceiling. I chain-smoked cigarettes and drank beer, hoping the chaos racing through my mind would eventually wind down.

But it didn't. So I snubbed out my cigarette and flipped on the overhead light, with the intention of grabbing one of the three-score books I had acquired over the years detailing the Vietnam War. Even before I hit the light switch I knew it would be an exercise in futility to continue my quest. As extensively as I had researched that damn war, other than the mauling the 2nd Battalion, 4th Marines received at Con Thien, I had been unable to discover any mention of them. It was as if my brother Jeff's unit had never fought in Nam.

Nonetheless, I hit the switch and turned toward the bookcase to my left. I froze. Afraid to breathe. Goose bumps raced up and down my spine.

Coiled at my feet was an enormous king cobra.

The snake stared up at me, its head slowly moving back and forth. And then, agonizingly slowly, it raised its head. Higher and higher, expanding in size as it rose almost level with my face, seemingly daring me to move.

I glanced to my right and saw salvation. I have no idea where the M-14 came from, but there it was, a full magazine cranked into its belly, ready to rock 'n' roll.

In my mind's eye, it took me a full minute to reach out and take hold of the automatic weapon. Inch by inch, I extended my arm, wrapped my fingers around its lightly oiled stock, and then quickly turned the weapon toward the damn snake.

But as mysteriously as it had appeared, it vanished. Leaving only my terror in its wake.

From that moment on, the cobra visited me when I least expected it, appearing out of nowhere, sometimes causing me to piss in my pants. I would be in Van McKenzie's office, huddled with him and Gary Caruso as we planned that Sunday's section. McKenzie, as was his nature, would be sketching out pages in advance of the various games' outcomes, and Caruso would be playing devil's advocate, saying "but what if?" to McKenzie's preplanning. And just as I would start to make my case for one boss or the other, I would feel the goose bumps start racing up my spine. My words would be cut off in midsentence; coiled at my feet was the snake.

"Well, what do you think? Am I right or wrong?" McKenzie would say to me.

Surely Van sees the snake. How the hell can he miss it?

I would look at Caruso, whose only expression was irritation. *Jesus, he doesn't see it, either. What the fuck's going on?*

And then, just like that, the cobra would disappear, leaving my heart racing and my head aching, my mind ripped apart. Leaving me to cover up my mental lapse by saying something outlandish— "Hey, I think you're both full of shit. I know it sounds crazy, but Georgia Tech's gonna beat 'Bama." The room would echo with their laughter, then we would resume formulating our game plan.

I got away with the deception until the early morning hours of November 5, 1982, almost nine months to the day after the birth of our fourth daughter, JoAnne. Dead drunk, I was driving home from an all-night birthday celebration, sticking to the back roads to avoid the police. My tactics worked well until I hit the Duluth city limits. That's when the cobra raised its head from the floorboard on the front seat passenger's side, which literally scared the shit out of me. And in my panic, I swerved to the left, crossed the median, and almost ran head-on into a police cruiser. Blue lights flashed. I knew there was no getting out of the situation, so I remained calm—as calm as I could possibly be, what with the snake watching my every move.

I pulled the car over, then finished the beer I had opened moments before.

As expected, the two cops didn't understand, especially the one I cold-cocked when he said I was crazy as a loon.

Right or wrong, that's how I remember it. A few punches thrown and received, being roughly subdued and escorted to jail, where I had to take a Breathalyzer test, which I was told registered some sort of record. "Jesus," one of the police officers said, "according to this you should be dead. How long you been drinking?"

Since age fourteen, I told him; with great regularity since I was twenty-one.

The cop was not amused. "No, asshole. How long have you been on this here particular drunk?" Honest to God, I could not recall the last time I had gone a day without consuming at least a twelve-pack of beer. I remember being fingerprinted, but what happened afterward is gone. I awoke handcuffed to a steel bunk in an isolation cell. My head ached; my mouth tasted as if I had spent the night chewing on filthy gym socks. More than anything else, I was in dire need of a drink. But before I could protest, I was escorted out of the cell by a mirthless guard, then hauled to the Brawner Psychiatric Institute Recovery Center in Smyrna, northwest of Atlanta.

Only later did I learn that my wife had arranged for my being institutionalized. She had gone before a circuit court judge and pleaded with him that I had no control over my life, that booze was dictating my every action. The judge agreed, which led June to sign the paperwork that opened Brawner's doors to me, which necessitated my being locked behind those doors for the next seventy-three days—protecting me from myself.

I remember being escorted into a small room and introduced to a white-smocked young lady who handed me a set of hospital pajamas. She smiled. Standing behind me were two burly, humorless men positioned in front of the door. They said nothing. I could feel their eyes jabbing me in the back.

"Do you know why you're here?" the woman asked.

I nodded.

"What are you feeling right now?"

"Nothing," I replied.

She smiled again. "How do you feel about being here?"

The question seemed to bounce around in my head, echoing. My response was not immediate, but I finally said, "I need help."

Indeed. The next week or so remains jangled, a bizarre mix of snakes and scorpions that slithered and crawled over me as I slipped into and out of the fog of detox. I would wake up screaming—*was I really screaming?*—and there would be a counselor sitting beside my bed, a reassuring smile plastered on his face. I would frantically brush the scorpions off me, my eyes following the snakes as they slithered off my sheets, disappearing over the edge of the bed. The counselor didn't seem bothered by my antics, still smiling, even when I sat up and cowered, pulling the sheets to my chin, my eyes now locked on that damned king cobra. The sucker just sat there, coiled, its tongue darting in and out as it mocked me—daring me to make a stupid move, hoping I would get up and run so it could jab its fangs into my throat.

Jesus Christ, how the hell can that asshole just sit there smiling with that snake about to strike?

And then I would drift away, falling into a deep sleep. Not the fitful sleep of the past; it was devoid of nightmares. I ate three square meals each day, and before I realized it, the snakes and scorpions disappeared altogether. My hands no longer shook. I started noticing things I had never really noticed before, like the sun's rays breaking through the window in long, fuzzy, golden shafts. I heard words I had never heard uttered before—"Just concentrate on making it through today without a drink. Don't worry about how the hell you're gonna stay sober for an entire week, for a whole year. All you need to do is worry about today. We're going to teach you how to stay sober one day at a time."

Just like that, a great burden seemed to have been lifted off my shoulders. Granted, my mind was still a bit fuzzy. But I was actually feeling better, both physically and mentally. Although I had no real idea why I was being incarcerated with twenty-three other alcoholics and drug addicts, I accepted my lot without argument. Soon I understood that I was exactly where I needed to be.

Understanding began with Dr. K. Mundy Smith-Hamm, the facility's head shrink, and Gracelyn Franco, the psychologist who supervised my sessions. Both were kind and caring, never raising their voices, remaining cool and calm no matter how insane or inane my responses were. I asked why I was being locked up against my will. Was I under arrest? "No," said Dr. Smith-Hamm. "You are here because you need help."

"Help with what?" I asked.

Dr. Smith-Hamm smiled ever so slightly, then said, "Living problems, mainly. You have a tendency to hurt others."

Before I could protest, she and her sidekick began administering a battery of tests, most of which dealt with my memorization abilities. And then they showed me cards adorned with various inkblots, asking me what I saw. I laughed when Dr. Smith-Hamm showed me the first card. It looked like a vagina. I shook it off and got serious, studied the card at great length, and then told her it reminded me of a stomach wound. In fact, the first three or four cards all looked like stomach wounds. But when she showed me the fifth card, my hands started to shake. I felt sick to my stomach.

"What do you see?" she asked.

I hesitated, then took a deep breath and slowly released it. I told her that was a picture of me on a hill, sitting behind a smoking .50-caliber machine gun. And at the bottom of the hill, which was a sea of red, those were the gooks I had killed.

"And what are you thinking about? What are you going to do now?" the psychiatrist asked.

"I'm getting ready to walk down the hill with my K-bar, that's my Marine Corps combat knife, and then I'm gonna cut out the hearts of all of them gooks. And then I'm gonna eat 'em."

Next thing I knew, the room was very crowded with counselors, thick-necked security guards, and a few nurses. I felt claustrophobic as hands reached out and subdued me. I was being smothered, drowning in a sea of anxiety and nervous twitches, looking for a way to strike back. Every damn time I came up for air, a strong-armed goon shoved my head back underwater. I couldn't fight back because my arms overlapped each other, pulled tight crisscrossing my chest and encased in a tan canvas jacket with big straps that were wound behind my back and then back in front, secured at my waist by a big buckle.

What the hell's going on? "For Christ's sake," I yelled at the shrink, "all I did was answer your fucking questions."

Silence as I fought against the straps. "You have a death wish," said Dr. Smith-Hamm. "You are not going to feel whole until you get revenge, or failing that, until you die in the attempt."

Die? Hell, I wasn't gonna die. *Tougher dudes than you have tried to put me down, you mirthless bitch. All of them failed.* My mind calculated the situation, concluding that Dr. Smith-Hamm was just trying to scare the shit out of me, making me feel like Houdini, forced to dangle from a chain secured to his legs, upside down over a bottomless precipice.

I laughed.

"There is nothing whatsoever funny about this," said someone in the room. "It is obvious to all of us that you need help." Indeed. I needed someone to take off this confining jacket and assist me to the nearest tavern. I was in desperate need of a beer. And a cigarette wouldn't hurt, either.

"This is bullshit!" I yelled.

No, it was therapy. I was carried from the room and placed in bed, then sedated. When I awoke, it was as if none of this had happened. I ate breakfast, sat in on an Alcoholics Anonymous meeting, being force-fed sobriety. And then later that afternoon, I was escorted once again into Dr. Smith-Hamm's office. She handed me a notebook and encouraged me to keep a diary. "You don't have to write a lot," she said. "Whatever you're feeling, whatever you think was important that happened to you during the day will be fine. You don't have to work hard at it." Because she said it in a soft voice and with a pleasant smile, I gave it a try.

It was November 29, 1982. No way will I ever forget the date. I still have the diary in which I compiled my musings, my observations, my rants, and my rages over the next two weeks. Some of it was humorous: "Well, Lord, here I am back in Marine Corps boot camp, but at least the drill instructors here are smiling and not beating the shit out of me. No uniforms, just pajamas. No rifle, just some pills to clear my body of all the poison I've consumed over the past eighteen years."

Some of it was not: "I saw a glimpse of hell today. Came to realize how sick I am. I am a sick and very lonely individual. For the first time in my life I'm getting honest with myself. But I'm still not liking myself. I'm working on it, though."

And then, in mid-December, I was again summoned to Dr. Smith-Hamm's office. This time, however, I went without escort. It was as if I had earned trusty status on a prison farm, no longer being considered a threat.

The session began with honesty on my part. I finally gathered the courage to tell the shrink about the king cobra that had tormented me. I had avoided the subject in the past, afraid that she would think there was something seriously wrong with me. Being thought of as an alcoholic psychotic was okay. But I didn't think I could handle being labeled a complete Looney Tune. Much to my surprise, though, the psychiatrist didn't seem to bat an eye when I finally told her about the snake. In fact, toward the end of our session she told me that hallucinations of this sort, snakes and wolves and even rabid rats, were quite common occurrences for people such as myself—unfortunate souls with psychopathic, sociopathic, and narcissistic character disorders, who unwittingly compounded the problem with booze and dope. This information elicited from me a deep sigh of relief. I remember thinking: *maybe I'm not as crazy as I think I am.*

But my euphoria evaporated when she handed me the diary she had asked me to keep during our last session and said, "I believe I've discovered the core of your problem. It's right there on the pages in front of you."

I reread my entries and found nothing unusual.

"Look at the dates," the shrink said.

I read the dates at the top of each page and blinked, feeling the urge to cry but somehow finding myself incapable of doing so. The date on the first page was March 7, 1968. The dates for the next five days continued in that vein, then suddenly jumped back to the present, December 5, 1982.

"I know your brother died in Vietnam," Dr. Smith-Hamm said in a solemn voice. "And I know he died on March 7, 1968. As painful as his death continues to be for you, you are never *ever* going to get better until you release him."

If only she could have told me how. And how I would know when it was done.

10

Heaven's Door

Dear Dad: Well, it's Thursday and we shove off tomorrow at 0900. Just thought I'd write and let you know. I got promoted to PFC today. It's about time. I'm happy we get liberty in Okinawa. It should be fun. Thirteen months will pass soon and I'll be home. Don't worry about me. Take care of yourself and the family. Love, your son, a Marine—Jeff

—November 18, 1967

As soon as I got sober, I began to learn that staying sober involves a lot more than just not taking a drink. That journey, which I am still on, began with a question.

"Mind telling us what the hell's *your* problem?"

I stared at the questioner and hesitated. My gut flashed a warning. The humorless counselor sitting across from me was short, muscular, and defiant. His face was scarred from barroom fights, his eyes reflected some former lifestyle I didn't want to know about, and his forearms bore tattoos that were more like aimless inflictions than art.

I blinked.

"C'mon, enlighten us," Dave Andersen said. "Tell me why you decided to piss away your life. What was so traumatic that you said to hell with your wife and children, said to hell with living like a normal human being and started living like an animal?"

I opened my mouth but thought better of it. Moments before, I had listened to the tale of a doctor who had become addicted to his own painkillers. Pretty boring stuff until the doc told how, under the influence of drugs, he had killed a pedestrian in a hit-and-run automobile accident. Before the doc spoke, we had heard from the Vietnam vet who lost both legs and an arm to a mortar blast near the A Shau Valley. Strapped to a wheelchair and addicted to morphine, all the ex-soldier wanted to do was put a gun in his mouth and end his pain and torment.

"Ah, I'm just a little screwed up," I finally said. "Compared to some of these other people, my problems don't amount to much."

Andersen glared at me, then said, "Well, no shit. You've just made the first intelligent statement since you've been here." And then he smiled; his face lost its hardness, his eyes suddenly had a touch of warmth. "Nonetheless, we're not keeping score here; we're not interested in seeing whose drunk story is better than anyone else's. Everyone here has an obvious problem. Whatever happened to you in the past was enough to make you pick up a drink. My job is to make sure you don't do it again."

And that's exactly what Dave Andersen did. In the days that followed, we interacted in ways I had never before thought possible. Andersen became my father confessor; I opened my heart and soul to him, laying before him my hurts and my pains. More than anything else, though, I listened to Andersen's advice without rebelling. His message, for the most part, was the gospel according to Alcoholics Anonymous—a message devoid of religious doctrine, one built around the spiritual concept of a higher power.

"You won't hear me preaching no church message, although I do pray," Andersen told me early on. "Yeah, I pray for serenity: God grant me the serenity to accept the things I cannot change, the courage to change the things I can, and the wisdom to bury the bodies of those who pissed me off."

Andersen and I shared a lot of laughter. We were lost souls, brothers of pain, two divergent individuals who probably never would have given each other a second thought had we not stumbled drunkenly down the same path. Over time, we moved past the teacher-pupil hierarchy and became best friends. So different, yet so similar—two zanies who helped each other over life's trau-matic hurdles, identical nut cases on a mission of sobriety.

I slowly came to realize that our meeting wasn't accidental. My wife's prayers had been answered.

"*You're in Jesus' hands now.*" My wife's words seemed to drift over me, penetrating my consciousness each time I drifted back into the realm of reality.

"*You're in Jesus' hands now*"—words that hovered above the crush-ing anxiety that curled me into a ball of fear, my arms overlapped and tightly wrapped about my chest.

"*You're in Jesus' hands now*"—words that caressed me when I needed it most, easing the terror that gripped my heart, soothing the fear that came from a voice inside me that screamed a warning that something was sneaking up on me, preparing to attack.

I had been in treatment almost four weeks before June was allowed to visit me. While the horror of detox was still fresh in my mind, the warmth of my wife's hand in mine and the sincerity of her love were just what the shrinks had hoped for, although June did not need to be coaxed in that direction.

Her love has always been freely given, even when I did not de-serve it. And *that* is exactly what had started eating away at me as I entered my second month of sobriety. My mind cleared, then my conscience started to gain the upper hand. The AA message—that I had been powerless over alcohol, that I had been in the grip of a deadly disease—was reassuring at first; it lifted a burden of guilt. But just as soon as my physical and mental health were on the mend, guilt of a different sort began to suffocate me—the realization that for the greater part of my marriage, I had been a self-centered idiot, a devout atheist who thought nothing of drinking away my family's grocery money to numb my own misery. With this newfound aware-ness came the terror that I would lose my wife and daughters.

"You were an asshole, right?" Andersen asked.

Indeed, I was.

"So when we have the family session tonight, why don't you tell your wife that in front of the entire group."

Which I did. It was a tearful admission, in fact. In response, June embraced me and said, "You *were* an asshole—a total asshole for many, many years. But no more." And then she received a standing ovation.

What I did not share with Andersen or any of the other counselors was a vision I had experienced weeks earlier. Just as I feared what the presence of the king cobra might say about my mental health, I also feared that this vision, too, would only certify my insanity and leave me locked away forever.

But now, with my wife at my side, holding my hand and professing her lasting love for me, I gathered up my courage and told her what I had seen—how I had been embraced by the screaming, clawing-at-the-jugular DTs, when suddenly a strange calmness overtook me, and the big cockroaches and black scorpions were brushed off me by an invisible hand, a hand that surely must have been real because there, hovering over the foot of my bed and caught in a glistening, ethereal light, were unshod feet jutting from beneath a purple, fiery robe. Even in my state, which the doctors later explained to have been a near-death situation, I knew it had to have been Jesus, which I interpreted as a miracle of sorts.

"Don't know why He's giving me a second chance, hon, but I sure as hell ain't gonna screw it up," I told my wife. She replied, "Jesus has been with you all along, but you carried too much hatred and pain to see Him. You've never been alone."

And then I held onto her for what seemed like an eternity as we wept.

Getting released from Brawner's wasn't all that difficult. You attended daily classes that explained in blunt detail how addiction worked, and attended AA meetings each night. In between were group sessions and family sessions. Doctors monitored you day and night, looking for signs of physical and mental withdrawal. Treatment normally lasted twenty-eight days. Mine was much longer, mainly because I had difficulty dealing with the past, which led to my difficulties working AA's twelve-step program. Step One was a no-brainer, admitting to myself that I was powerless over alcohol— that my life had become unmanageable. Step Two, believing that a power greater than myself could restore me to sanity, wasn't that difficult to grasp, either. Once the booze had been flushed from my system, I immediately started feeling better. Even more remarkable, the cobra disappeared. And having seen Jesus at the foot of my bed, it was easy for me to accept Step Three, making a decision to turn my will and my life over to the care of God.

But Step Four, making a fearless moral inventory of myself, kicked me in the butt. I compiled a list, tore it up, then compiled another list and ended up tearing it up also. My sins, real and imagined, were staggering. But there was no avoiding the issue. Dave Andersen, who had agreed to be my AA sponsor on the outside, said that the odds of my holding on to sobriety were higher by completing Step Four. So I conned myself by doing a less-than-honest job of it. Even though Andersen was not fooled, I was released from Brawner's into my wife's custody on January 17, 1983.

Sober for the first time in nineteen years, I was free of most of the demons that had tormented me during that decades-long drunk; responsible and respectable, for the most part, and raring to confront life with solid footing—embracing sobriety with a fervency I had never shown for anything before. I appeared before a kindly judge, who also was a recovering alcoholic, and vowed that I had seen the light. He smiled his approval and said I had damn well better. He gave me a year's probation. If I continued to remain sober during that time, all would be forgiven and my criminal record wiped clean. One drink, though, would be enough to render the court's mercy null and void, and I would spend a year in jail.

I thanked the judge, shook his hand, and walked away a free man. Upon my return home, the first thing I did was pack away in an old filing cabinet all reminders of my brother Jeff. I saw it as closing a door on the past and committing to my new life. The reality was more literal. Jeff was filed away. I still had a lot to learn about letting him go.

Over the course of the next year I attended Alcoholics Anonymous meetings daily and followed its twelve-step program with the same unquestioned devotion with which I had once embraced Catholicism. Gradually reassembling the pieces of a shattered life, I gave my four daughters my complete attention; no longer were they second to booze. I even reached out to embrace my father, brothers, and sisters, something the shrinks said would do nothing but strengthen my new lease on life. Although Jeff's death in

Vietnam had driven a wedge between me and my family, I followed the shrinks' orders. I telephoned everyone, mumbled a few
nervous sentiments, then turned the phone over to my wife, who
went into great detail about what she called "the miracle of mira-
cles," my turning away from death's door.

June and I even repeated our wedding vows—in church. Shortly
afterward, I was baptized, my entire body immersed, symbolically
washing away the old me. It seemed to work, for there were no
more barroom brawls, no death wishes to play out. I became
healthy—physically, mentally, and spiritually. In the clutch of sobriety, I dealt with all of my demons face to face and purged them.

"All it's gonna take is one drink—one drink, and you'll die. I
don't know of any other way to put it," Dave Andersen had warned
me as soon as I took my first step toward freedom. "You start feeling like shit, you call me. You get the urge to walk back into a bar,
you call me." He embraced me, shook my hand, then gave me one
last piece of advice: "You stay away from those asshole buddies of
yours. Only way you're gonna make it is by completely changing
your lifestyle, your patterns."

That's easier said than done, of course. All of my friends were
coworkers at the *Atlanta Journal-Constitution*. And up till now, my
life had revolved around designing sports pages and drink. I knew
I could lick the latter, but I was too old to embark on a new profession. Glenn McCutchen, the paper's new managing editor,
made my life somewhat easier by allowing me to transfer out of
the sports department and into lifestyle, where I became an assis-
tant editor. Although my primary concern was the section's overall
design, I was allowed to write, which was a godsend. Although
none of the stories I wrote were that big a deal, for the first time
as long as I could remember I truly felt alive. The only uncomfortable moments were bumping into former drinking buddies, all of
whom blamed my wife for having me locked away.

"You're different now," they would say. "Heard you've got that
ol'-time religion. You're not gonna start preaching to us and shit
like that, are you?"

When I simply smiled, they would say, "Didn't mean anything personal. Why don't you join us after work. Hell, one drink ain't gonna hurt none."

My response was always the same. "I've never had just *one* drink in my life."

Their response was just as frightening. "Hell, you never drank that much; no more than me."

Indeed, this is why I kept my distance from them. And they from me. It was almost as if I had an incurable and transmittable disease, which I did when you get right down to it. Sobriety scared the hell out of my newspaper cohorts.

Nonetheless, I attended at least two AA meetings a day, worked without complaint, and concentrated on my writing, even volunteering to work weekends without pay in order to write stories that dealt solely with military issues. And much to my surprise, quite a few of these stories appeared on the newspaper's front page. As much as I would like to take credit for this occurrence, claiming I wrote and reported my way onto page one, the person responsible for my newfound fame was Jim Minter, the *AJC*'s editor. Minter was a Korean War veteran. More to the point, he had a good nose for news. He liked the fact that I had been a Marine, not to mention having fought my way out of the hell of alcoholism. "You've got guts," he once told me.

But most of all, I believe Minter liked my outspoken patriotism, which was an oddity in the newsroom. He also seemed to like, or at least not be offended by, how vocal I was about disliking the politics of my coworkers, almost all of whom were more liberal than I.

11

War Zones

Dear Mom & family: Time's flying fast, already I've been over here three months. Some guy has a portable record player, and right now I'm listening to Daydream Believer. If at all possible, I wish you could send me a couple of albums. Judy round up some 45s—Monkees and Beatles (but only the good ones). Till next time. Love, Jeff

—*January 12, 1968*

I was in Beirut covering the violence for my paper, and I was being interrogated by Captain Attrici and his minions. Attrici was pissed. The Lebanese intelligence officer's face almost brushed mine, his eyes ablaze, his voice rising in decibel with each question. Why was I going into the forbidden zones? Why was there a need to visit Martyrs' Square? After all, that was just inviting a bullet from the Phalange, Christian or not. And speaking of being a Christian, why was it necessary for me to speak with the Muslims? They are terrorists, are they not? Why would I visit the Marines at the airport, then be driven across the Green Line? Was I delivering messages? And what was I looking for in the Chouf Mountains?

"It is all very suspicious. Whose side are you on?" Attrici asked. His inquiry reminded me of a dog barking.

I sat in a hard-back chair, surrounded by an unhappy group of interrogators, all of whom worked for Beirut's defense ministry.

Having seen enough of this city to last a lifetime, I had concluded there was nothing left for Attrici's ministry to defend. Beirut was an open wound—a gaping bloody hole in the backside of humanity. At the best of times it was uncertain who controlled what; at the worst of times, like now, it was a lunatic asylum in which all the patients carried Kalashnikovs. When the seven or eight various Muslim factions weren't killing Christians, and vice versa, they were killing each other. Americans were killing Syrians and an occasional Palestinian and bombing the daylights out of the Chouf, which raised the body count in both Muslim and Christian villages.

As a journalist, my only crime had been a voyeuristic attempt to sift sense from the insanity, which was why I had received Attrici's scrutiny. He glared at me. To pass the time, I kept my expression neutral, taking my measure of him.

Only Attrici spoke; his minions merely thrust daggers into me with their eyes. Soldiers, armed to the teeth, came and went, advancing to the sound of the guns, I suspected. Outside the concrete and steel building, the twisted symphony of fighting reverberated: the dull explosion of a mortar shell, the dense staccato of heavy machine-gun fire, the sharp crackling of AK-47s. Business as usual in Beirut.

But that was not what concerned *AJC* photographer Calvin Cruce. Standing unguarded across the room, Cruce kept shaking his head, silently encouraging me not to be myself, to keep my sarcasm in check—to say nothing that might sway the gruff, humorless Attrici to put a bullet into our heads.

I smiled at Cruce, then gave Attrici my most innocent look and said, "Tourism."

The captain's jaw dropped. When he recovered his composure, he asked, "'Tourism'? What do you mean, 'tourism'?"

"*Tourism,*" I said. "You want to know what I'm doing. I'm simply checking out the sights, going around asking questions of your wonderful citizens, trying to figure out what the killing is about. That's *all* I'm doing—asking questions, then writing stories."

My honesty—naïveté, really—caught Attrici off guard. He glared at me again, shuffled through my press credentials, found what he wanted, then jammed my *Atlanta Journal-Constitution* credential in front of my face. "You are not a journalist. This says you are 'Sports.' There is no sport in Beirut. I give you one more chance to explain."

Oh, shit! That's when the fun really began. Momentarily forgetting to whom I was speaking, I fired from the hip, telling the good captain that before my arrival in Beirut, I had been the *AJC*'s deputy sports editor. But because that was not what I really wanted to do—I had no interest in baby-sitting a sports staff—I wanted to write, but not merely write about meaningless sports. Instead, I desired *real* action—to be a war correspondent. So, last month, when Islamic terrorists drove a truck laden with explosives into the headquarters compound of the 24th Marine Amphibious Unit, killing 241 Americans, I stormed into *AJC* editor Jim Minter's office and said, "I'm either going to go over there and fight those bastards or I'm going to cover that war."

"That's all I said," I told Attrici. There was no mention of Marines or Beirut, just my simple demand. In return, Minter had smiled and said he liked my spunk. Then he said for me to cool my jets and not to worry, because he would send me to Beirut.

"So like it or not, here I am," I told Attrici, which prompted him to shrug his shoulders and say, "You are not very smart."

Indeed. But at least I was being honest about it. Which surely counted for something, because Attrici immediately tired of the interrogation and let Cruce and me go. Cruce was free to take his prize-winning photos, and I was free to be me—a loose cannon skidding across the deck of a doomed warship; a threat to the perceived norm if not to myself.

Sober or not, I have always had problems controlling my tongue. If I truly believed it or felt it, I said it without thought as to the consequences. A conviction that I was right is all the justification I have ever needed. This doesn't work well in a combat zone or a newsroom. In fact, it's rarely welcomed anywhere.

My being sent to Beirut ended up being but one white-knuckled stopover on a roller-coaster journalistic journey in which I would battle all sorts of demons—some real, most perceived. The real ones were easy enough to identify: Hezbollah gunmen and Syrian snipers, to name but a couple of the threats posed by being in Beirut. There also was a troublesome shark off the coast of Key

West, Florida, a fearsome critter I would encounter during the summer of 1985 while reporting on the deep-sea adventures of treasure hunter Mel Fisher and his discovery of $500 million in gold, silver, and emeralds from the sunken seventeenth-century Spanish galleon *Nuestra Señora de Atocha*. And shortly thereafter the terror ratcheted up a notch as I cowered in a trench beside soldiers of an Eritrean People's Liberation Front battalion as the 3rd Ethiopian Army and its Soviet advisers attacked us atop an East African mountain stronghold.

But freely interspersed among these high points was chaos, most of which I brought on myself. And amid it all, not only was I constantly reminded that being sober does not necessarily guarantee sanity, but also, to use my wife's words, "The Lord takes us just the way we are, then He works on us."

I was forty, five years sober, and once again started stumbling down a familiar path called self-aggrandizement. Like all fools who take this fork in the road, I believed I had nothing else to prove or learn.

Lucky for me that God has always placed wonderful friends in my path.

One such guardian angel is Lloyd Burchette. A Vietnam vet, Burchette had prepared me both physically and mentally in 1986 for my extended stay in East Africa, where I reported on the Eritrea-Ethiopia war. An expert on all things military, he also knew more about my psychological makeup than I cared to admit.

As Burchette told me, "Once upon a time I thought I had dealt with all my demons—all the heartache I experienced in Vietnam. But I was only kidding myself. Only when I visited the Wall did I finally dump everything. I know you've been sober for a while now; I know you *think* you've experienced everything there is to experience. But you're wrong, my friend. Pay your respects to the Wall. You owe it to yourself, to your brother, to grab hold of its peace."

That opportunity came in November 1986, while I was in Washington, D.C., at the behest of the Eritrean government to help to raise money, food, and medicine for the embattled nation. Between speaking engagements I took a taxi to the mall, then hesitantly made my way up the path to the outstretched wings of the black-granite Vietnam monument, stepping lightly in the shadows of the names of the dead.

My tears began at the base of the three bronze grunts standing guard. Tears accompanied me the rest of the way—tears and a kindly veteran, who noticed that my emotions had gotten the best of me. In response, this guardian angel, whose name I never learned, placed a reassuring arm around my shoulders and guided me to the most hallowed place I had ever visited—Panel 43-E, Row 48.

A cold, stinging downpour that day had driven most of the visitors to the shelter of nearby trees. The raindrops splattering along the walkway echoed loudly in my subconscious as I slowly ran my fingers over each letter of Jeff's name, talking to my brother as if he were alive. I told him how sorry I was that we couldn't grow old together, how my lust for battle had evaporated in Beirut and Africa, how stupid and self-centered I had been—apologizing for neglecting my family, for neglecting my brothers and sisters, for embracing insanity.

And then I collapsed onto my knees, my head buried in my hands, and prayed for forgiveness. With this came a strange tranquillity, as if unseen arms were gently rocking me. With the tranquillity came relief and light-headedness, as if a great burden were lifted from my heart, which prompted more prayers of thanksgiving.

Evening eventually consumed an already dark day; the rain finally ran its course, moving elsewhere.

To say total healing occurred at the Wall would be an oversimplification at best. Although my desire for physical confrontations abated, I still had little control over the way I dealt with authority, especially when Jim Minter was replaced as the *AJC*'s editor. Always my own worst enemy, I voiced my opinions regarding his successors. And when management retaliated by saying I could better serve the newspaper by once again designing sports pages instead of covering major news events—two Pulitzer nominations notwithstanding—I jumped ship to become the sports columnist for the rival *Gwinnett Daily News,* owned by the *New York Times.* What followed were the four happiest years of my career. Having rediscovered my heart, which reignited my passion for writing, work became a joy—journalism was no longer just a job. Once again it became a career in which I thrived.

It proved to be short-lived, however. When the *Atlanta Journal-Constitution* bought the *Daily News* and closed it down, I was without a job for the first time in my adult life. After nine months of trying to raise a family of six on unemployment benefits, my options were minimal. When the *AJC* offered me a job as a page designer in May 1993, I accepted without complaint. The ground rules were clear: writing was not an option; it was design pages or work elsewhere.

Thus began a seven-year sentence in purgatory. Sobriety notwithstanding, I was miserable company. Having been able to call my own shots at the *Daily News,* now I had control of nothing, most of all my emotions. Not only was I working for a newspaper whose politics I detested, I also was rejoining it at a time when New Age mindlessness and diversity were at the height of popularity. If I raised my voice to protest the liberal party line, which I did without fail, I was reprimanded for "inappropriate behavior."

Of course, I thought there was nothing wrong with my antics. I was right, everyone else was wrong. And I didn't give a damn who knew it.

In truth, I went through seven years of what the knowledgeable folks in Alcoholics Anonymous call a "dry drunk"—sober, yet crazy as hell; acting out the same sort of idiocy I had while under the influence of booze. Paranoia was a constant companion. I dipped deep into the poisoned well of militant right-wing philosophy, delving in all the fashionable conspiracies of the day—the Clinton administration's perceived selling out of America, "Big Brother" ordering the assassinations at Ruby Ridge, and the mass killings at Waco.

I lived each day as if caught up in a never-ending episode of television's *X-Files,* like one of that show's Lone Gunmen characters, clinging desperately to its adage "The truth is out there." *But where?*

When my nonsense neared the break point in 1997, my wife once again rescued me from myself by escorting me to a psychiatrist. The shrink promptly talked me through the lunacy, restoring my peace of mind with sound advice and strong medications. Once the meds took affect, my world leveled out.

But as has always been the case, my salvation came mostly through the efforts of enduring friends who worked overtime trying their damnedest to pull me away from the abyss.

Where the hell would I be without guardian angels?

I continually asked that question of myself over the next three years, groping in the dark for answers yet smart enough never to let go of my wife's guiding hand. While unable to clearly see the light, I did see an occasional glimmer. Our daughters matured and married, and soon June and I had more grandchildren than we knew what to do with. And among the weddings and childbirth, my passion for writing continued to grow. It began with the dream of being a novelist, then shifted into the realm of biography when I coauthored Nevada circuit court judge and boxing referee Mills Lane's *Let's Get It On*. Soon afterward a friend encouraged me to write about my treasure-hunting adventures with Mel Fisher and his crew. When my agent agreed, the book proposal was completed, and she went in search of a publisher. By early February 2000, many publishing houses had rejected the query.

Thoroughly dejected and despondent, not to mention feeling as if, at age fifty-four, I were over the hill, I lay in bed one night agonizing over what the future had in store for me. As has always been the case, June turned to me and imparted her wisdom: "Instead of trying to do everything on your own, why don't you get down on your knees and turn everything over to Jesus."

So I crawled out of bed, got down on my knees, and prayed more fervently and honestly than ever before in my life. I told God I was a screw-up, that despite the urgings of my wife I continued to believe that I was in control of the universe.

For some reason, I slept like a baby that night.

* * *

Less than two weeks later, on a Friday night, February 18, 2000, I was sitting in front of my home computer—staring mindlessly at a blank screen, awaiting insight that I doubted would ever come—when the telephone rang. On the other end was my younger brother Joe, who was now a sergeant major in the U.S. Army and stationed at Fort Irwin, California.

"I've opened Pandora's box," Joe said. "Just received an e-mail from Jeff's best friend from Vietnam. Guy's name is Jim Arnold. He was with Jeff when he died. Anyway, he *really* wants to talk to you."

12

Revisiting Purgatory

Dear Bro: While I'm thinking of it, would you send me some of your writings? I'd really appreciate it. I have a buddy who writes also, and I told him all about you. Don't be bashful. With my outlandish tastes, if I like it, then he'll really like it too. I'm known as the flower child in our platoon. Take care of June. I'll be home soon. BAH! As a writer I always was a good plumber. God bless. Love you, Bro—Jeff

—*January 27, 1968*

J oe's phone call produced a flashback to Beirut, that of an incoming howitzer shell—a high-pitched, long-distance screech followed by gut-twisting moments waiting for the shell to impact. And when it did, I was numbed, my breathing coming in quick, sharp gasps. Years earlier, cowering in the war zone, I had been too scared to speak. Now, my only comment, uttered over and over: "Jesus."

When I failed to say anything else, Joe apologized once again and said he had been hesitant to call because he was afraid that the shock of finally finding Jeff's best friend might send me tumbling back in the direction from which I'd escaped so long ago.

"You've always been a crazy bastard," said Joe, laughing. "But at least now you're a *sober* crazy bastard."

It turns out that two weeks before, Joe had returned to headquarters amid a night operation, logged onto his computer, and visited the base's chat room. He watched mindlessly at the string of conversations that popped onto his computer screen, but then a bizarre thing happened: He saw two ex-Army buddies connect; the last time they'd seen each other was in Saigon in 1972. Joe immediately joined the conversation, identifying himself, and asking if the Marine Corps had a chat room such as this. He said our brother Jeff had been a member of Fox Company, 2nd Battalion, 4th Marines, and had been killed somewhere in Quang Tri Province on March 7, 1968. Could anyone out there help us?

Help arrived within minutes. Joe was directed to 2/4's Web page, where he left a message seeking information about our brother. Within three days, he was bombarded with messages, including the note from Jeff's best friend, Jim Arnold.

"I'm in the middle of a training exercise right now," Joe said, "so I don't have time to forward all the e-mails to you. But I can tell you this: Arnold is legit. He knew all about Jeff; his love of the Monkees, that Dad was a schoolteacher, Mom was a telephone operator. Hell, he even sent me pictures of Jeff. I'll be back in from the desert in three days or so. I'll send everything your way then. But you've got to promise me one thing, bro. Don't you be going nuts on me again. Keep it cool, hear?"

I set the receiver down. My hands were shaking, my heart screaming; a deep roaring blasted my ears. I tried to recall Joe's conversation word for word, comparing the recollection with the page of notes I had taken. Staring at my scribbling, I tried to recall the sound of Jeff's voice. Failure to do so deepened my anguish. A single tear formed in each eye. No more. And then I felt my wife's hand on my shoulder. I had not heard her enter the room, but there was no mistaking her crying. She hugged me, her hand resting on my notepad, her fingers brushing the underlined notation: "Found Jeff's best friend from Nam!" We held onto each other, neither of us speaking, and then June finally said, "The Lord has answered your prayers."

Indeed, He had. But I was too numbed by Joe's call to pray or even consider doing so. That would come days later. For now, I tried to arrange the jumble of disjointed thoughts that passed through my mind. At June's suggestion, I pulled a few of my Vietnam reference books from the shelf and stacked them on my desk; then we got a flashlight and scrambled outside to the storage shed to an old filing cabinet. In the glare of a flickering beam of light, we searched one drawer after another, extracting several file folders and a large manila envelope containing the mementos I'd squirreled away—the nine letters Jeff had written to me from Vietnam, four glossy pictures that the *Rockford Morning Star* newspaper had taken of his funeral, and the red ribbon emblazoned "United States Marine Corps" that had adorned the wreath standing beside Jeff's casket. June continued to sob throughout the ordeal and offer up her prayers, none of which made any sense to me. My heart had instantly hardened as soon as Joe had revealed what he had discovered. Rage returned, as did the maddening desire for revenge.

"You sure you're all right, hon?" June's soothing words. "Please don't allow the devil to tear you apart. This is all part of God's will."

I glared at her, yet said nothing. My hands started shaking again when I reached into the bulky envelope and extracted the letters of condolence from President Johnson and other government officials, and the Western Union telegram from Marine Corps commandant Leonard Chapman. My eyes drifted over the messages; something squeezed my heart. All I could think of to say was, "I never found the sonofabitch."

June's tears were hot on my neck as she embraced me; then she silently led me back into the house. Her parting words that night: "Remember what Jeff told me—revenge solves nothing." And then she left me alone with my demons.

I was still rereading Jeff's letters that morning when June greeted me with a hug and a cup of coffee. She stayed at my side for much of the rest of that day, leaving me only to fix lunch and dinner. Reading my brother's words was as cathartic as it was frustrating. Not once had he referred to any of his friends by name. He wrote about his squad leader being "a kick-ass combat Marine" on his third tour. He said his best friend was from Ohio, and that another buddy had willingly agreed to thirteen months in Vietnam in return for the government taking care of two years of college tuition and books. Jeff mentioned Con Thien, but only in reference that the 2/4 had been bloodied there months before he joined the unit. He mentioned Khe Sanh, saying his platoon would probably take a position south of it. In other passages he said he was "guarding a bridge" or was setting "ambushes in front of our position at C-4," which was on the coast about two miles south of the DMZ.

The letters were so damn vague, yet were my most treasured possessions.

Equally frustrating, I had no pictures of Jeff taken in Vietnam; my only picture of him was his framed graduation photo, which I had put away upon my release from Brawner's. I took it out of the envelope and positioned it next to my computer. Staring back at me was a picture-perfect seventeen-year-old without a care in the world. The image that I had carried around inside my heart, though, was a much younger version—my constant childhood companion on the playing fields. When I closed my eyes I could still see Jeff's silly Huckleberry Finn grin.

But as far as the nineteen-year-old version of my brother was concerned, that of the hardened combat Marine clad in green fatigues, flak jacket, and helmet, and carrying an M-16? I had no idea what *that* Jeff looked like. In my mind's eye, that version of my brother was strictly government issue, a chalky face inside the casket.

My rage finally burned itself out late Sunday afternoon, when I collapsed in exhaustion. Hours earlier, I had frantically reassembled the jagged pieces of a fractured family. It, too, was an exercise in frustration because it finally dawned on me how little I knew of my brothers and sisters. I kept seeing them as little kids running about the house and seemingly always underfoot; little kids I had to babysit, or budding teenagers who certainly weren't as world-savvy as I. They were nuisances who never aged—their biological clocks were frozen at March 1968. This only heightened my guilt, because now, thirty-two years after the fact, I realized just how absolute had been my grief in the wake of Jeff's death, how self-centered I truly had been. I had erased my siblings as efficiently as they had erased me.

Granted, much of the blame for this was due to my alcoholism. But even when I sobered up after being institutionalized in
1982, so clear-cut had been my determination to put my life back
together that I still gave little thought as to what degree my brothers and sisters had suffered. There were so many questions I wanted
to ask them, so many apologies I wanted to extend, but I resisted
the temptation to telephone them. In truth, I really did not know
what to say other than that I had been a selfish idiot. But surely
they knew that already. Besides, why dump my guilt on them when
I did not have all the facts from Joe? Why raise their hopes of
being able to communicate with Jeff's friends when I did not have
all the information in front of me?

No, I told myself, all I could do was wait. Just as I had been
waiting all these years. Alone with the same maddening questions
that had nagged at me for decades: How, exactly, had Jeff died?
What had his final days been like? What were his buddies like? Did
Jeff talk a lot about his family? How brutal had life been near the
DMZ?

My mind raced. Guilt once again consumed me. Did I really
want to hear the answers? Or had I truly mastered the art of deceiv-
ing myself? I even questioned my manhood, knowing I was paralyzed by fear—afraid what I might find out. Fear of the unknown—
afraid of what Jeff's best friend might say, afraid of finding out
what *really* happened on the day Jeff died.

Christ, I was even afraid of learning what his last words might
have been.

The headaches returned, pounding away without letup. And
my gut quivered, just as it had on the day we buried Jeff. I finally
sought relief through prayer, even though I did not know what
to pray for other than peace of mind. But I prayed nonetheless:
"Lord Jesus, I pray for your wisdom and serenity. Embrace me
and protect me from doing anything stupid. Give me the strength,
courage, and patience to endure the days ahead. Allow me to
focus on all that is good, not the evil. Again, I apologize for all my
sins, for hurting so many others. Please take away this guilt, Lord.
Please take away my anger, my hatred. I love you, Lord; I *do*
love you."

And then I sat back and waited for Joe to contact me again. Three days grew to a week. A week grew to two. But finally, on the evening of March 4, Joe telephoned. He apologized for the delay, saying that he had been in the field evaluating the troops. He was stationed at Fort Irwin, at the National Training Center in California, but I had no idea what his job entailed because I had never asked until now.

"Believe me, it would take too long to explain. But thanks for asking," Joe said. "Besides, I've got something *really* important to run by you. I've had a lot of time to think things through, and what I'm thinking is you've gotta write about this. After all, that's what you do—you write. It's your therapy."

The hell with therapy, I told him. I told him that all I wanted to do was get hold of Jim Arnold. I needed to speak face-to-face with him, find out exactly what happened over there.

"Ever stop to think that finding out, then putting everything into words might help someone else?"

I asked if he meant Dad, Jude, Jim, and Jane.

"Plus you and me, not to mention all the others," Joe said.

I asked him what others.

"How about the families of the rest of the guys on the Wall? I can give you fifty-eight thousand reasons why you've got to write this book. We're not the only ones who've gone through this shit. Ever think about that?"

I hadn't. I was thinking only of myself, seeking closure without a thought to the thousands of other families scarred by that war. Some of them were probably coping in the same confused, self-destructive manner that our family had for thirty-two years.

I glanced across the desk, my eyes locking on the picture: Christmas 1951, the Smith family's Three Musketeers sitting in front of a Christmas tree: baby Joe in the middle, supported by Jeff's right arm. I'm at Joe's right shoulder, leaning on him, seeking support. Relying on him, just like now.

I released a deep sigh, then said, "I'll have to think about it, bro. I don't know if I can handle it."

"Yeah, I know what you mean," Joe said. In the meantime, he told me he was going to send me the stuff he had in his computer.

He said that since his last call he had received a bunch of messages from three more Marines, guys who were in the same company but didn't know Jeff. Arnold also contacted him again; he
lived in Ohio and said he was at Jeff's side when our brother had
been killed. He also sent some pictures of Jeff taken in the Philippines and Nam; Joe would attach them to the e-mails. "You okay?"
he asked.

"Not really."

Joe laughed. "Hey, no sweat, you'll be okay. Thirty-two years
without shit, then everything falls out of the trees. Don't want to
overload you too much, but I've got another surprise for you. Jeff's
company gunnery sergeant made it out alive. Lives up in Oregon
somewhere. He also sent me a message, and I gave him a call last
night. He's one hell of a great guy. He also was there when it happened. He wants to speak to you, too. Anyway, everything will be
downloading in a few minutes. You're still sober, right?"

"Just barely."

Joe laughed again. "You're gonna be okay, bro. Just keep doing
what you've been doing since they locked your ass up, okay? What
do they tell you—one day at a time? So you just do what you do
best. I'm dumping all this shit in your lap now, downloading everything I've got. You take it from here. All I ask is that you keep me
posted. Semper Fi, bro."

The e-mail messages were transferred to my computer one by one.
I hesitated before I read them. It was as if I were approaching the
scene of an accident, seeing the blue flashing lights and the medics
scurrying from the ambulance, knowing that if I slowed down and
looked hard enough I was going to see something horrible.

13 February 2000—Joe: Are you aware of the 2nd Battalion, 4th
Marines home page for the Vietnam era? I am deeply sorry for the
loss of your brother. If you are planning to go to Vietnam, may
I suggest going with Military Historical Tours. I just returned in
April '99 and they did a great job of going to our areas of opera-
tion. Semper Fi: Ken

14 February 2000—Joe: Jeff was killed by incoming rockets just outside a village called Mai Xa Thi (pronounced My See Tie). But in some of my reading I see it called Mai Xa Chanh—I don't know why the discrepancy. You will find it on the map a little bit northeast of Dong Ha city, northwest of Quang Tri city, right on the Cua Viet River. Strangely enough, I have been communicating with Jeff's best friend lately. His name is Jim Arnold. It might comfort you to know that "Smitty" lives on in Jim's memory and he recalls him fondly. As a favor to me, I might ask you to approach him slowly because I haven't told him of finding your message yet and I don't want to startle him. Jim was with your brother when he was hit and the memory is still quite tender to him. You might also try leaving a message on the 2/4 message board. You should be aware, however, that most of the guys who knew and served with Jeff were themselves KIA at a place called Dai Do a couple of months later. So don't be surprised if you don't get a lot of feedback. If you have trouble finding the village, I have a map I can copy and send to you. Good luck in your search and I pray God will bring you peace concerning the events surrounding your brother's tragic death. Semper Fi: Steve Klink

14 February 2000—Sgt. Maj. Smith: According to a list I have, there is an Association for 2nd Battalion, 4th Marines. Call this number and maybe they can help in your search for some of the guys from Fox. Hope you find closure. Jeffrey rests among the heroes. Semper Fi: Kevin

16 February 2000—Joe: I have the daily diary for the 2/4 for March, April, and May of '68. I have the map grid numbers where the fight took place (YD280667 Bac Vong). That's on the north bank of the Cua Viet River. Take care: Jim

16 February 2000—Joe: My name is Jim Arnold and I was with your brother the day he was killed. I was his fire-team leader, and we were good friends. He and I were lying against a mounded-up gook grave when we started getting hit with 122mm rockets. I was hugging him from behind with both arms wrapped around him.

I was burnt by some hot shrapnel and asked your brother if he was okay. He said "No, I'm hit," looked down at his wounds, and never said another word. I helped carry him back to the LZ. Your brother and I were close. I remember him saying that he played in a band. And while we were on ship (BLT), he had a record that he played all the time. It was "Daydream Believer" by the Monkees. Every time that song comes on the radio, I remember. I have a couple of pictures of your brother that I would like to pass on to you, and will do that the next time I write. Semper Fi: Jim

20 February 2000—Joe: More from the log of Fox Company. "Company F would sweep southwest, and then move to the final objective at YD280667 (Bac Vong). Company F started to sweep generally south and running parallel to the Cua Viet River. At 1000 hours the third platoon of Company F came under heavy enemy small arms, mortar, and rocket fire as it pushed south to the blocking position established by Company H. Eventually all of Company H became engaged in this action, and at 1045 hours Company H assumed operational control of the third platoon, Company F." Log goes on from there to say how Company G also got involved. It tells how they went back to Ma Xa Chanh (operations CP) after last medevac at 1815 hours. Log says: "Casualties for the day were 10 Marines killed and 35 wounded and medevacked." Good luck and if I can help, yell: Jim

23 February 2000—Sgt. Maj. Smith: I was Company Gunny for Fox, 2nd Battalion, 4th Marines and was with J. Smith the day he was killed. I carried him to the LZ and put him on the chopper. Give me an address. I have a story to tell you about him. Semper Fi: Gunny Brandon

1 March 2000—Sgt. Major Smith: I am Sgt. Maj. Bob Herndon USMC (retired). I was in the same battle as your brother, but in a different company and location. I was in Hotel Co., 3rd Platoon Machine Guns. Your brother's company was attacking Objective Delta. It was a burned-out village that was full of North Vietnamese soldiers. I was 500 meters away from your brother's company.

We lost 7 in our platoon that day. Sorry, wish I could help more. Semper Fi: Bob

4 March 2000—Joe: Ray Meadway here. I was in Hotel Company from Oct. 67 to Nov. 68. On March 5, we started on the Cua Viet River Campaign. It ended around May 29. On the seventh, Fox Co. assaulted Objective Delta. Hotel Co. assaulted the village of Vihn Quan Thuong. Neither attack was successful. Hotel Co. had eight wounded and two dead. Two days later, Hotel went to Objective Delta and picked one body up from Fox Co. Objective Delta was about one-third of the way to Dong Ha from our Battalion CP, which was in the blown-up village of Mai Xa Chanh, which was located right on the river. This was sand and hedgerow country. Every action was basically frontal attacks. These were very determined enemies, they did not mind paying the price. In the three months on the river, we had over 800 wounded and 243 KIAs. On April 30 to May 2, we engaged elements of three regiments of the 320th NVA Division. Hope this is some help. Semper Fi: Ray

I had trouble turning off the computer. My hands were shaking and my fingers were numbed almost as much as my mind. Sleep was impossible. I spent the rest of the night sending e-mails, then praying.

Dad and Ma in 1944

Dad in 1944

Two cowboys at play, 1950—Jeff pointing a toy gun at me

From left: Me and my brothers Joe and Jeff, Christmas 1951

Counterclockwise from left:
Joe, my sister Jude, me,
and Jeff mugging for
the camera, 1953

From left: Jeff, Joe, and me after a good day of fishing at Pike Lake
Resort, 1956

Me *(at left)* with my best man, Jeff, at my wedding, 1967

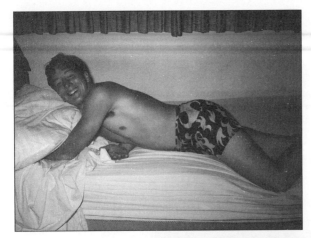

Jeff, the morning before leaving for boot camp, 1967

Jeff with a friend in the Philippines

From left: Jeff, Jim Arnold, and Ken Watkins at Quang Tri, Vietnam

Scenes from the funeral of PFC Jeffrey E. Smith, USMC, 1968

Jeff's grave, 1968

Ma laying a wreath on Memorial Day, 1972

My youngest siblings,
Jim and Jane,
Christmas 1968

My wife, June, holding
our daughter Julie,
1971

Me in my drinking years

My sister Jane with Jeff's guitar, 1979

Jeff's name on the wall of the Vietnam Memorial, Washington, D.C.

My sister Jude with Ma's ironing board, 2000

Jane in 2000

My brother Jim the treasure hunter, 2000

My brother, Sergeant Major Joe, 2000

From left: Me, Joe, and Dad at Joe's retirement, 2001

Ho's celebration, Hue City, Vietnam, 2001

Jeff's buddy Jim Arnold with villagers in a Vietnam market, 2001

From left: Mr. Anh, Gunny Brandon, and Ed Garr with map in Vietnam

Gunny and Anh

Gunny, a valiant
old Marine

At the memorial for my brother Jeff

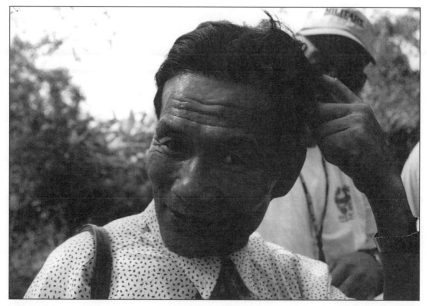

Mr. Anh

From left: Ron Dean, Dave Leverone, Gunny Brandon, and Steve Klink

13

Opening Eyes

You don't know me but I'm Jeff Smith's older brother. I just got off the phone with my brother Joe, a Sgt. Maj. in the Army, and he said you had information concerning Jeff's death in Vietnam. Enclosed are my phone number and e-mail address. I sure would appreciate hearing from you. I thank you ahead of time for any assistance you might be able to give me. Semper Fi—Jedwin Smith

—March 7, 2000

A s much as I wanted to contact Jim Arnold, Steve Klink, and Gunny Brandon, I hesitated in order to compose myself, to regroup. Receiving their messages had produced a joy I hadn't experienced in ages—the ecstasy of seeing Ernie Banks hitting a game-winning home run; of hearing June saying, yes, she would marry me; and learning that June had given birth to yet another healthy and beautiful baby girl, all rolled into one. I was a nut case—a happy nut case, this time—literally bouncing off the walls, shouting to the heavens, and thanking God for knocking down three decades of barriers, all of which elicited a continuous smile from my wife and the question "Have you taken your medicine today?"

Indeed I had.

But the antidepressants seemed to have done too good a job. If I had been physically capable of doing backflips, I would have been cartwheeling across the living room. Instead, I simply shouted and smiled—waiting patiently for the euphoria to abate, to drop me back down to earth.

At the same time, I was terrified. Did I really want to know the circumstances surrounding Jeff's death? If so, could I handle returning into the darkness from which I had escaped? Getting to know Jeff's friends would be like excavating his grave. Why would anyone want to do that?

Guilt also played a role in the delay—I didn't want to stir up bad memories, assuming Jeff's Marine buddies had suffered more than enough already. Alleviating my agony was not worth rekindling it in others. Also at play was my sense of history. Timing was everything, so I wrestled with my joy and sorrow, my empathy and pain, and then finally moved forward. On the morning of March 7, the anniversary of Jeff's death, I awoke with cold determination and immediately fired off the e-mails.

Klink's response was immediate. He said he grieved not only for my family but also for all of the families of all the men with whom he served in Vietnam. "After thirty-two years, the pain is just as real for me as if it was yesterday," he wrote. Klink said he knew Jeff, but nowhere near as well as did Jim Arnold, whom he said had been lying beside my brother when he was killed. Because Arnold still had not come to terms with Jeff's death, Klink reiterated that I approach Arnold with care and not push too hard concerning the details of my brother's last moments. Klink also said that he had started to write a book about some of the events from long ago, and was going to send the manuscript to me in hopes of clarifying Fox Company's role in Vietnam.

In closing he said, "My prayers are with you on this night. Jeff is gone. But while we live he will not be forgotten."

Jim Arnold's e-mail response touched me even deeper. Life's ironies abound, he said, because he had received my message on the "day that you lost a brother and I lost my best friend." Arnold said he had a difficult time dealing with Jeff's death because, as his fire-team leader, he felt as if he had failed to do his duty—protecting Jeff. But as the years passed, he said his guilt subsided. Nonetheless, Arnold was still kicking himself for failing to get in touch with our family.

"Thank God for the computer age," he wrote, giving me his phone number and attaching three pictures of my brother. In closing, he thanked me for allowing him "to get some of this off my chest," and said I should feel free to telephone him.

I opened the attached files containing Jeff's pictures. According to the caption information Arnold provided, the first picture had been taken in the Philippines when the unit was being refitted in January 1968; Jeff's left eye is bandaged, the result of a barroom brawl. The second picture showed Jeff standing next to Arnold and Ken Watkins, another of their close friends; it was taken at a forward post called C-4, at the juncture of the South China Sea and the DMZ. Arnold said that Watkins had been killed in action on March 12, 1968. The third picture, also taken at C-4, was a close-up of Jeff smiling back at the camera.

I was crying when I showed the pictures to my wife.

Later that evening I received an e-mail from Percy Eugene "Gunny" Brandon, Fox Company's gunnery sergeant. The message was to the point: "I live in Oregon. Here's my telephone number; call me, buddy." Which I did, without hesitation. Brandon answered on the first ring, we exchanged pleasantries, then he told me to call him Gunny and not Percy because who the hell can respect a Marine named Percy? That cleared up, he spent almost an hour leading me down a horrific memory lane.

Brandon, who was sixty-six when we spoke, began the reminiscences by apologizing for his memory lapses. The days of his Vietnam tour now all seemed to run together, he said, pointing out that, at age thirty-three, he was "an old fart" when he finally landed in that country, and that all of the riflemen in Fox Company were just kids, no more than nineteen or so—"less than a year away from dancing with Mary Sue at the senior prom." And then, without giving me a chance to respond, he started highlighting the tragedies of his combat tour, which began in December 1967 and ended seven months later, when he received the last of his six wounds—waking up in a body bag at Graves Registration.

"Can you believe that? Some asshole thought I was dead. What a crazy war, huh?" Brandon laughed but did not elaborate.

Gunny went on in this vein for a long time, recounting his version of hell while inundating me with a plethora of names of dead

Marines and battles for villages with unpronounceable names, which only added to my confusion. In an hour I went from knowing nothing about my brother's tour in Nam to information overload. As difficult as it was to grasp all the details, it was impossible to place them in an orderly sequence. As if sensing this, Gunny said somewhere in one of his old seabags was a map he had taken off a wounded lieutenant named Sisk, who got shot through the throat.

"Sisk was the first one to get hit the day your brother died," Brandon said. "I'll make a copy of the map and send it your way."

Before I had a chance to ask about that tragic day, Gunny said that he didn't hold out much hope of me hooking up with anyone else who might have known my brother. Even on its good days, Fox Company could muster only sixty-five riflemen; six were lost on March 7 at Mai Xa Thi, another sixteen were KIA five days later at Lam Xuan East, and "just about everyone else" was killed at the end of April in the battle for Dai Do. Gunny said he knew of only two other survivors, Lonnie Morgan and Richie Tyrell, and had already contacted them, giving both of them my address and telephone number. And then he shifted the conversation back to Mai Xa Thi, elaborating on Lieutenant Sisk's neck wound; how he stemmed the bleeding by inserting his forefinger into the wound, then ordering the radioman to call in an evacuation helicopter. And then he moved on to the events of the battle for Lam Xuan East, then to Dai Do. Agonizingly repetitious depictions of death and destruction, never varying from his original accounts, rattling off the names of so many young men he had fought beside, almost all of whom he saw ferried away from the battlefield via evacuation choppers.

As much as I wanted to steer the conversation solely to Brandon's reminiscences of my brother, I patiently waited him out—allowing him to unload without interruption. Be patient; Jeff's day will come, I told myself.

To help clarify what he had been rambling about, Brandon said he would send me a copy of his book, a memoir highlighting his nineteen years in the Corps—tours in Hawaii, Japan, and Cuba, plus a stint as a Parris Island drill instructor, then on to Vietnam. He joked about the book being his reclamation project, something he had compiled during therapy and self-published shortly thereafter.

Brandon explained that he had suffered through several years of post-traumatic stress syndrome, which led to his being hospitalized by the Veterans Administration.

"Not to worry, though. I'm okay now. I'm not a wacko," he said.

But there had been a time, long ago, when he found it impossible to sleep. Every time he closed his eyes, the faces would visit him—the faces of all the young Marines who had died during his tour. But once he was hospitalized, one of the VA psychiatrists encouraged Brandon to keep a journal, composing all of his nightmares. When sleep was still impossible, when the faces continued to plague Brandon, the doctor asked if Brandon remembered the names of these dead men haunting. He did, with the exception of one Marine. To make an excruciatingly long story short, the doctor told Brandon that when the faces materialized, he should say hello to them, calling them by name, telling each of them that he would never forget the sacrifices they had made for their country.

"What really bothered the shit out of me is that I was right there beside your brother when he was killed," Brandon said. "But I could never connect the right name to the face because we had a couple of Smiths, both of them killed. So Jeffrey keeps on visiting me. But now that I'm talking with you . . . shit, talking about your brother is like lifting the lid of a coffin. I sure as hell don't want to do it, because of all the bad memories. But it's something I *must* do because I'm still a Marine, and I owe it to Jeffrey."

There was a prolonged silence. I did not know how to respond, and it was obvious that Brandon was groping for the right words. Finally, he said that if it were at all possible, he would like to sit down with me face to face because there was so much he had to get off his chest.

"Geez, now I know that that face belongs to Jeffrey," Brandon said, "I'm gonna sleep like a goddamn baby tonight."

I wrote a letter to the Marine Corps commandant that night, asking General James L. Jones for his assistance.

Sounds silly, I know. But General Jones was a special breed of Marine, part of the old "can do" Corps that had been so prevalent before Vietnam. Equally as important was the fact that General Jones had actually experienced combat, having served as a platoon and company commander with Golf Company, 2nd Battalion, 3rd Marines during the same period that Jeff had been in Vietnam.

I gave General Jones a brief rundown of our family history, emphasizing our Marine Corps heritage, and told him that thirty-two years of silence were enough. Our family wanted answers. I tried my damnedest to be polite and not too demanding. I thanked the general for his sacrifice, for serving our country in time of peril; I thanked him in advance for trying to shed light on our family's darkest moment. I closed by sharing this remembrance of Jeff: "Sir, my brother hated war. He was a long-haired peacenik who played guitar in his own rock band. Then one day he cut his hair and announced at the dinner table that he had joined the Marines. Never have I been more surprised, sir. And never had I been so proud of my little brother."

I sent the letter on its way, convinced that it was a waste of time. After all, I had written identical letters to two other commandants almost twenty years earlier, receiving only silence in return.

I spent the next few days in euphoric meltdown. I would be in the middle of a conversation, or in the middle of doing design work at the newspaper, when the electric tingle passed through my body. I would hold onto it for as long as I could, then release a deep sigh. It sounds a bit weird, but deep inside I knew I was expelling the residue of decades of hatred and loathing, dumping the buildup of vile waste that had accumulated—the shit that had been killing me.

And then came the realization that after eighteen years of sobriety, I had finally started getting honest with myself. Peering deep inside the abyss that had once been my soul, I saw the ironies to be endless—how, despite my best efforts, I came to emulate my father: disdaining all forms of authority and constantly being at odds with my bosses, moving for less money or a small economic boost under the guise of enhancing my career, which proved to be merely an excuse for burying the past. And just like my father, finding it impossible to bury it deep enough. So I had kept on the run. And by elongating the miles between the past and present, I stretched the memories to such a degree that they were obliterated.

But what had I done to my brothers and sisters?

Granted, throughout the years there have been brief moments of disguised family unity. In 1977 I took my wife with me to California to cover Super Bowl XI and spent a few drunken days with Joe and his first wife at Oceanside. Jane moved to Atlanta in 1983 shortly after I returned from covering the civil war in Beirut, Lebanon. Dad and his wife, Darlene, also moved to Atlanta shortly thereafter, arriving in time for Jane's wedding to an Alabama boy with little work ethic. Jude flew down to be the maid of honor; we spent a few days together, discussing little of the past.

Dad and Darlene moved to Florida a year later, after Jane's troubled divorce. Jim drove down from Madison, Wisconsin, in 1991 to see the Braves play the Minnesota Twins in the World Series. And Joe, now married to his second wife, Pam, spent a week with us in 1996, recuperating from his military travails in Haiti. Everyone except Jude spent three days at our house during Christmas 1997. It was a tense reunion in that all of us *wanted* to talk about Jeff. But after a few minutes of seeing just how tender the wounds still were, we chose less pressing memories: our days at Pike Lake and our excursions to Wrigley Field to see the Cubs.

Deep, meaningful conversation in the past thirty-two years with any member of my family, either in person or on the telephone, was nonexistent. I had difficulty remembering the names of Joe and Pam's five children; I kept getting Jim's wife, Mary, mixed up with Joe's first wife, Mary; I couldn't remember the state senator for whom Jim worked; and I couldn't recall the exact year of Jane's divorce or the name of her ex-husband. It was also hard for me to believe that Dad had been married to Darlene longer than he had been married to Mom.

And now I was about to embark on the most treacherous of all historical journeys, groping blindly for points of reference. It was a frightening place to be because ever since Joe planted the seed that I should write a book about our brother's death and how it had destroyed our family, I had come to realize that I had few memories of our family left.

Mending our family's fences was a starting point. As my brother Joe said: "If Jeff's death tore us apart, maybe the act of trying to piece together his final days in Vietnam would bring us back together."

It sounded easy enough. I would telephone Dad and my brothers and sisters and explain to them the mission I was about to undertake, that I planned to link up with Jeff's best buddy in Ohio and his gunnery sergeant in Oregon, hoping that neither would mind if I flew out to visit with them in hopes of reconstructing Jeff's final hours in Vietnam.

Eliciting my family's cooperation would be the tough part. The initial peace offering would be to ask their forgiveness and apologize for being a self-centered, selfish asshole for the past thirty-two years. I could only hope and pray that they understood where I had been coming from in the past, hope and pray that they knew without doubt where I was coming from today.

I planned to emphasize to them that this wasn't going to be my book—it was going to be Jeff's story, our family's story, right or wrong. There could be no healing unless all of our demons were exposed. We had carried the excess baggage for too long. It was time to get on with our lives.

I knew that is what Jeff would have wanted.

My first call was to Joe. After all, if indeed a book was completed, the credit would be his. He had done all the legwork, finding the Fox Company survivors, plus encouraging me that I had an obligation to our family to move forward on this mission. Joe was out in the field, however, so I left a message on his answering machine, telling him that I would soon be telephoning Jim Arnold, Jeff's best friend, and hopefully making arrangements to fly up to Massillon, Ohio, to meet him face to face.

Next I called Dad in Phoenix, Arizona. It proved to be the strangest conversation I've ever had with him. I told him what Joe had accomplished, that he had found not only Jeff's best friend but also the company's gunnery sergeant. "Oh, my God," is all Dad could say. I hesitated, screwing up the courage to tell Dad that I was going to do a book on Jeff and our family, that I wanted to sit down with him and everyone else and have them tell me in their own words the grief they had endured, how Jeff's death had destroyed our family.

Dad surprised me by interrupting and asking if I was going to write about it. When I told him I planned on writing a book, he said, "Good, it's about time. What do you need me to do?"

Again I hesitated, then told him there would be nothing easy about such an undertaking, not for him or anyone else; that I wanted to lay everything on the line—our upbringing, the divorce, the good with the bad. I wanted to cover everything.

Much to my surprise, Dad agreed. In fact, he would make it easy for me. Darlene and he would be vacationing in Florida in April; they would stop in Atlanta for three days.

"I'll try my best to answer all of your questions," he said before cutting short the conversation. "Gotta warn you ahead of time, though. I'll never read the book."

I telephoned Jim in Key West, Florida, and Jane in Rockford, Illinois, and received their blessings. Both said pretty much the same thing: they had no problem sitting down with me and talking about how they had made a mess of their lives. The problem was they didn't know what they could tell me about Jeff because they had little recollection of him. Other than all of the pictures of Jeff that Mom had on the Wall, it was as if they never had a brother named Jeff.

Joe and I played phone tag for a couple of days. Finally he sent me an e-mail saying that he was still out in the field watching the troops do the operations order for a defense in sector and evaluating the battle and the performance of the unit's noncommissioned officers. He wrote: "One thing, bro—don't go crazy on me in regards to Jeff's book. We both kind of went nuts for years. I'm glad you told June about what you're about to do. She, like Pam, is the buffer between craziness and reality." Joe said that he would help me all he could, that he still had Ma's personal belongings packed away in a storage box and would send everything my way.

In closing, Joe gave me absolution. "Our lives were so different than Jeff's. Yes, we all picked the Corps! Yes, maybe we felt *that* was a way to get closer to Dad. But it is not Dad's, yours, or my fault that Jeff went into the military. He, as we all remember him, picked his own path, as did we all. This book will just be a simple putting together of the puzzle pieces. Although the questions that will eventually be answered won't change reality, they will clarify what happened thirty-two years ago."

Emboldened by Joe's sentiments, I screwed up my courage and telephoned my sister Jude. Of all the children, she carried the most hate—for both Dad and Ma. She disliked my politics, which were too right-wing for her to stomach; she thought little of my attempts to be a Marine; and she despised me for running out on her, Jim, and Jane when I moved my family from Illinois to Florida. Yet I hoped that Jude would approve of my doing the book, agreeing to share her story with me.

"I think it's time we finally put this to rest," Jude said from her home in Madison, Wisconsin. "As for all of that other stuff, you being what you are . . . well, I can't believe I'm going to quote a Clint Eastwood flick, but in *True Crime* someone refers to Clint as an asshole, and James Woods says, 'Yes, he is. And like a lot of other assholes, he just happens to be very good at his job.' So keep on being good at what you are, okay?"

The ice had been broken and we laughed together at the expense of my shortcomings. Then Jude said that although she knew there was nothing she could say that would change my mind, she felt as if Jeff had no business joining the Marines and being sent to Vietnam.

"That war was political bullshit," she said. "I still have trouble coming to grips with that. I still have trouble, period. But I think the book's a great idea."

We shared a pleasant conversation for the next half hour; then Jude shifted gears and said she was still upset about our parents' divorce, that she still wondered where Dad was when she needed him most.

"And our mother—are you also going to write about her?" Jude asked. When I joked that there was no way to write about our family without mentioning our mother, Jude snapped back, saying that Ma was just a drunk.

I hesitated, trying to figure out how to respond. When I asked her if she was all right, Jude said, "No, I'm not." Without another word, she hung up on me.

I wanted to throw the telephone through the nearby window. Instead, I pounded my fists on the desk until they were numb. Only then did I close my eyes. I wanted to pray for my sister but found it impossible. I was too angry.

Just like old times, I told myself. Jude's way of handling stress was to give you a sharp shot to the gut, then stomp on your heart.

In that instant, I had no regrets about having walked away from my family.

14

Guardian Angels

Dear Bro: In our fire-team we have some pretty cool heads. Our team leader's been over to Nam three times. He's been in the Corps four years and one month. He gets out this summer. He doesn't like the Crotch that much. Who does? We have a 27-year-old reserve (called up) and another guy from Ohio, who's my best buddy. . . . Love, Jeff

—January 28, 1968

I was still fuming over Jude's parting shot when the telephone rang. The voice on the other end said, "You don't know me, but my name's Richie Tyrell. I was with your brother in Vietnam. . . ."

As Tyrell spoke, I could feel my heart racing as I fought to regain my breath.

His pleasant, compassionate voice on the other end of the telephone line kept asking, "Don't you have any questions?"

I did. Hundreds of them. But I was too numbed to communicate. Once Tyrell identified himself—telling me that he knew Jim Arnold, Steve Klink, and, of course, Gunny Brandon—he said he remembered Jeff as an easygoing guy. And then Tyrell apologized for being unable to remember a lot of the specifics of what he did over in Nam because, like a lot of the veterans who saw heavy combat, he had been plagued for years by post-traumatic stress syndrome.

"But whenever I close my eyes I can still see Jeff's smile," Tyrell said. "Your brother was always singing and smiling, even when there wasn't anything to smile about."

And that's when the rush of tears startled me. There was no noticeable wailing, no embarrassing sobs. Instead, my heart was lodged in my throat as a steady stream of tears rolled down my cheeks, blinding me at the same time they made it impossible to speak.

Tyrell told me not to feel embarrassed about the tears; thinking that Marines don't cry is bullshit, he said. So I cried, my heart screaming in silent supplication as Tyrell recounted that horrid day at Mai Xa Thi—how Fox Company was pinned down by a hardcore Viet Cong unit, how he and his fellow Marines were peppered by small arms and mortar fire, then bracketed by rockets.

What time of day was it? Time is always a funny concept when you're lying on your stomach in the middle of a rice paddy and people are trying to kill you, he said. Tyrell's main memory of the ambush is that he was scared out of his mind, hearing the bullets zip past his head, hearing the rockets come screaming in. Worst of all, though, were the screams of his buddies, those who had been wounded. And that's why moments seem like hours, and hours can be like moments.

"But even now," he said, "looking back on it at fifty years of age . . . considering the horror and confusion that warfare is, we must have shared some small joys together for me to remember Jeff's smile and his humor. To me, in my heart and mind, your brother is one of us who remains forever young, with all the greatness and joy of youth."

Silence on both ends of the line, then Tyrell said he knew what I was going through, why I was so damn shell-shocked and unable to articulate what my heart wanted me to say. He said there were a lot of people out there, those who have never sacrificed one ounce of themselves for anything throughout their entire life, who believe that those who died in Vietnam were sacrificed for nothing. Tyrell disagrees with that line of thinking because when you're in the middle of a firefight, the most important thing in the world is the man at your side.

There was little sleep in the days that followed. Even if I had wanted to, it would have been impossible because I was too busy purging my soul. One moment I was staring at a blank computer screen, agonizing over how little I remembered of Jeff's and my childhood; the next, I was typing furiously. Before I knew it, pages became chapters. Between bouts of tears and rekindled animosities, June and I prayed for clarity, for forgiveness.

And between the ups and downs of that first week of remembrance, Steve Klink stood guard over the process, inundating me with e-mails, providing just the right touch of pathos or hilarity to keep me going. In return, I shared my progress with him, sending the respective chapters his way. I also kept my priorities right, telling Klink that I considered him to be one of my guardian angels. This, despite my ignorance of precisely *where* he was coming from; hell, he could have been a member of the Aryan Nation or a devout atheist, for all I knew. But I just *knew* he had been sent from God.

In response, Klink fired off a missive that carried me back to 1964, to the day I had enlisted in the Marines. "Having been allowed to glimpse inside your soul," Klink wrote, "it has been pressed upon me that I doubt if there's ever been a Marine who was raised in a sane household."

Klink said it was the nature of the beast that those who have been slapped around, told they're worthless, and who have failed in one form or another—whether it be in sports, academics, or with the opposite sex—become Marines. And the moment of revelation that causes us to enlist seldom varies. Convinced that we're useless, we stumble upon a bull-chested recruiting sergeant wearing dress blues adorned with a chest full of ribbons. Of course, this dude tells us that while being a Marine isn't for everyone, if we *do* make the grade we'll be a man among men, a member of the greatest fighting force on the face of the earth.

"And, by God, son," the recruiter says, "I'm convinced you've got what it takes to be one of us. All you have to do is sign this piece of paper." Which we do, without hesitation, because we like what we're hearing—how the Corps will feed and clothe us and teach us everything we'll ever need to know about survival. We'll learn hand-to-hand combat, plus the use of a plethora of weapons. And once we've graduated from boot camp, we'll wear the uniform of a Marine. We'll walk down the street and people will step out of our way because we're Marines. And because we're Marines, no one will ever again push us around. From that moment on, no one will *ever* again be stupid enough to give us any shit.

Klink's manuscript and Gunny Brandon's book arrived the next day. My writing was put on hold as I committed Klink's *Tail-End Charlie* and Brandon's *Gunny—Mostly a True Story* to memory. Both texts were filled with the horrors of war, Brandon's more so than Klink's simply because Gunny's began and ended with my brother's death.

"The 2nd platoon commander had been shot through the neck; another Marine was also hit, three times by the look of the bandages on him," wrote Brandon, who then went on to explain that as he started to race across a rice paddy to locate a radio in order to call in a medevac chopper, he paused beside a Marine who was smoking a cigarette as he hunkered down behind a mounded-up Vietnamese grave.

"Funny how you remember such minute details," Brandon wrote. "I had just taken a few steps when I heard rocket rounds coming in. I dove for a bomb hole when I heard a Marine scream that he'd been hit. I looked back at the Marine who had been smoking the cigarette . . . he was dead; the round had landed on his legs."

Jesus! I had not been prepared for this. While Brandon had shared with me that Jeff's death had impacted him deeply, I had no idea as to what degree. As I would discover, Jeff was the first fatal casualty under Gunny's watch. Even more startling was that although I had long suspected that my brother's death was far from clinical, the realization of him having been blown to hell ripped my heart out.

When I shared my grief with Klink via e-mail, his response was almost immediate: "My understanding is that your brother died almost instantaneously, in the arms of one who was able to give him the comfort, and strength to lean on, that you would have given him, had you been there—his best friend, Jim Arnold."

While going to great lengths not to disparage Brandon's account of my brother's death, Klink said it was impossible for any two men to recall with any sort of precision the horror both experienced. It made sense, so I accepted Klink's observation on faith. But then he startled me by saying that he was a minister in Eaton Rapids, Michigan, a profession that was far removed from the lifestyle he endured upon his return from Vietnam—a life filled with drugs, booze, barroom buddies, and professional counselors in his quest to regain mental stability.

Learning that Klink was far from being flawless was reassuring, but then I was overwhelmed with the knowledge that he was a man of the cloth. Whoops! My previous e-mails to him had been filled with profanity. I immediately apologized for my ignorance, which prompted Klink to tell me not to worry. After all, he had been there, done that. He also said, considering the circumstances that had brought Arnold, Brandon, him, and me together, it was obvious that a higher power's fingerprints were all over the situation. No way could this be brushed aside as either coincidental or happenstance.

"Sometimes, the hand of God is so apparent as to not be denied," Klink wrote. Then he chided me about my last e-mail, how I had praised him for allowing God to use him to assist in my "heeling," an inadvertent misspelling on my part. Klink said the typo was quite profound because, according to the dictionary, heeling is defined as "to follow closely at the rear of." He reminded me that the most important lesson we learn in the healing process is heeling—to stop taking things into our own hands, to stop making plans without checking them out with God first; in essence, to stop getting out in front of God.

"When Jeff died in combat, you chose to blame yourself," Klink said. "Your mother blamed the Marine Corps and your father. I don't know whom your father blamed, but I suspect he blamed himself." As for my sister Jude, Klink surmised that she was blaming everyone and everything. All that was important is that I continue to love my sister and that I continue to pray for her healing.

"As you surely know by now," he said, "God is in the business of answering prayers. He answered your prayers once, and I suspect He'll answer them again."

Klink closed by telling me that, having just spoken to Jim Arnold, it was obvious that neither Arnold nor I would have peace until we had spoken with one another. So why delay the inevitable?

Why indeed. I immediately telephoned Arnold. I thanked him for being there when Jeff needed him most, then apologized for the statement because it might be interpreted as me laying a guilt trip on him. Truth is, I told him, no one in our family felt as if Arnold was responsible for Jeff's death. But guilt's a bitch, and no one is immune from it.

There was another prolonged lapse of silence; then Arnold said that most of his time in Vietnam remains a blur. He said that as soon as it was confirmed that Jeff was dead, he remembered very little of what happened next. Next thing he knew, it was March 12 and he was moving with the rest of Fox Company into the bombed-out village of Lam Xuan East, where he was seriously wounded. When he finally regained consciousness, he was at Bethesda Naval Hospital in Maryland. Only then did the somberness leave his voice, saying that he traded Marine green for U.S. Postal Service blue, having been a letter carrier for the past twenty-six years.

When I asked if he had a problem with me flying up to see him, he said he didn't. There was no need for me to book a hotel; I could stay at his place. He started to say something else, then paused and started laughing. "Whoops," he said. "My wife is giving me that *look*. She's always giving me hell when I do something like this. You're not a serial killer or anything like that, are you? Good; then you can stay with us. Next month would be best for me."

Arnold told me that he and his wife, Cheryl, lived in Massillon, which is a few miles outside of Canton. I conveyed this tidbit to June, who kissed me on the cheek and left the room. We talked for another twenty minutes or so; then June reentered the room and handed me a sheet of paper. On it was my flight information.

"Ah, Jim, I don't know how things are run in your household, but here my wife is the commanding general. Anyway, she just informed me that I will be flying to Canton next weekend," I stammered. "You got a problem with that?"

He didn't.

Jim Arnold views himself in simple terms: He is principled, yet shies away from preaching the moral gospel; patriotic, yet not hesitant to lambaste the military hierarchy; friendly to those he trusts, yet not overtly outgoing in the presence of strangers. He deeply loves his family and friends and grudgingly has come around to loving God. Above all, he is traditional. His memory, although not as sharp as he would like it to be, is long and unwavering.

At first glance he also is replete with oddities, which at times have caused his neighbors to wonder why he does what he does.

He has a number of American flags, yet they fly from a simple flagstaff above his garage door and are on display only on certain days. This flag-waving is not something he brags about. Instead, his actions are guided by humility and reverence. Each of Arnold's flags was obtained from his congressman; each flag has a certificate that attests to its authenticity, that it flew over the White House on a specific day. November 10, the Marine Corps birthday, and March 12, the battle for Lam Xuan East, are just two of the six dates he honors in his special way. He flies the flag on the Corps' birthday for obvious reasons, and on March 12 to honor the memories of Ken Watkins and Thomas Fleming, fellow Fox Company buddies who died at Lam Xuan East in 1968. Another flag is flown on February 8 to honor Jerry Buckhead, a friend who volunteered for Vietnam at the same time as Arnold did, and who died at Quang Tri during the 1968 Tet Offensive.

Other flags honor slain warrior friends, but the date that causes Arnold the most distress is March 7. At the crack of dawn he runs the flag up the flagpole, says a silent prayer, then snaps to attention and salutes. And then he enters his home and quietly makes his way downstairs to his den, where he pops the top of a can of Natural Ice beer and then approaches the antique Wurlitzer jukebox next to his bar. Moments of quiet reflection, then he punches a special selection. Seconds later, the Monkees are singing

"Daydream Believer." This is the only time that Arnold plays the song—Jeff's song.

None of this information was easy for my brother's best friend to convey.

Arnold and his wife, Cheryl, have been married for thirty-three years. Their children, Brenda and Shawn, are grown and gone. Thirty-year-old Brenda is married to Mark Volkert, and they have a year-old son, Alan. Twenty-nine-year-old Shawn is engaged to Teri Newton. Arnold has been a letter carrier since 1974, a job he finds solace in because it keeps him from getting fat and lazy. He said this with a grin, as well he should. Standing 6-feet, he weighs no more than 190; unlike others his age, there is no pudginess. His demeanor is serious, almost professorial, complete with a short salt-and-pepper beard and a receding hairline.

But his most striking feature is his eyes. They're spring-water blue, which I imagine to be cold in either winter or summer. Not that Arnold is humorless. Far from it, for he knows how to laugh with others and at himself. It's just that he doesn't find much to laugh about, which probably is the result of almost three decades of government service, first as a Marine, now as a postal employee.

It was only after a pork-chop dinner that night, when we retreated to Arnold's downstairs den—where I nervously chain-smoked and he downed one beer after another—that we got to the business at hand. Arnold began by saying the mind is a weird-working oddity, that he had thought about Vietnam every day for the first ten years after returning to the civilian ranks. Then, to his great relief, the memories vanished.

But then I had suddenly walked into his life, carrying with me the specter of Vietnam. Once again Arnold was reliving the nightmare that is combat, reliving his final six days in-country—the day a rocket-propelled grenade blew out a portion of his back, which necessitated him being medevacked to Bethesda; reliving the events of five days earlier, when the rocket landed and my brother died in his arms.

"Smitty was there 107 days. I lasted 113," Arnold said, pointing out that the events surrounding my brother's death have raced through his mind every day for the past thirty-two years. "But as angry as I was over Smitty dying, the war didn't end. We still had to fight our way through that village. We still had to run the gooks out of there. Except that's where everything goes blank."

What he does remember remains somewhat fuzzy. It was a day or two later that the 1st platoon was sent to secure another nameless village, looking for NVA and weapons. It was obvious as they neared the hamlet that the enemy was not using it as a staging base. Nonetheless, Arnold entered one of the bamboo-and-thatch huts. There was an old man inside, a very old man wearing glasses. Arnold first busted the old man's chair and his bed, then snatched the glasses from the elder's face and broke them. Snapped the glasses in half, then dropped them into the dirt and ground them under the heel of his combat boot. A senseless act of revenge, he said. His best buddy is killed, and then he lashes out at a defenseless old man. It's not as if there was a Lens Express down the road where that old man could get another pair. Arnold agonized that the old man probably saved his money for a year or so to buy those glasses. And that chair and bed of his were probably made by hand, a long labor of love.

"And then, just like that," Arnold said, "I've destroyed everything that poor old man owns. It's crazy. But that's what that war did—it made you crazy."

Now, thirty-two years after the fact, he would give anything to be able to go back and apologize to that old Vietnamese gentleman. He didn't start that damn war, he just got caught in the middle of it.

Ever since Arnold had been discharged, he had wondered about the fate of his fellow Fox 2/4 Marines. But more than anything else, he had been looking for a painless way to reach out to the families of those Marines he had known who had been killed in action—especially Jeff's family. He discovered the 2/4 Web page.

Cheryl was cooking dinner when Arnold read my brother Joe's message. He screamed. She found him, drained of color, staring blankly at the computer screen, as if he had seen a ghost. When Arnold showed her the message on the screen and asked her what he should do, Cheryl remembers that she silently thanked God for answering her prayers. She had known all along that her husband's healing would not start until he finally spoke with a member of Jeff's family. She told him that he had no choice—he had to respond.

"It took me two days to build up the courage to answer your brother Joe," Arnold said. "What was I supposed to tell him? Jeff was dead, I was alive. That's always torn me apart. I've had to live with that every day since March 1968."

I told him that apologies were unnecessary, that I was every bit as scared as he was. Ever since we had clasped hands at the airport, I had been trying to screw up the courage to ask about Jeff's final moments. Instead, I was avoiding the subject, asking what the weather had been like, or how many hot meals he and Jeff had eaten—everything but what I *really* wanted to know. "Why? Because sometimes knowing is worse than not knowing," I said. "I'm afraid to ask."

Arnold cleared his throat and grabbed another beer. He took a deep breath, then slowly released it. His eyes held onto mine for the longest time; then his heart reached out to mine. Once the connection had been made, he related the events of March 7 as best he could recall:

Fox Company moved out early that day, at first light, moving south of the bombed remnants of Mai Xa Thi, paralleling the Cua Viet River. They weren't expecting trouble. When the enemy opened fire on the lead platoon, Arnold's fire team—himself, my brother, and another Marine he remembers only as Barry—bunched up, taking cover behind a mounded-up Vietnamese grave. He has no recollection of the time of day. He remembers it being hot, that the backs of everyone's fatigues were soaked through with perspiration, and that he and Jeff were hungry. Then someone ran up and told Arnold that the 2nd platoon was getting hit hard and that Arnold's fire team needed to spread out; one of them needed to move off and cover their flank.

"Because Jeff was my best friend, I wanted him to stay with me," Arnold said.

So Arnold ordered Barry to cover the flank. And then Jeff reached into his pocket and produced a can of fruit cocktail, which they shared, eating the fruit with their fingers. Time passed. How much, Arnold does not recall. He does remember the confusion. A madhouse of people scurrying about, yelling and screaming, and the dull thumping of helicopter blades. Arnold said it was just another typical day in Vietnam—attempting to clear a village that didn't even have a name, searching and destroying, and getting fired upon by an enemy they couldn't see, let alone pinpoint.

"It was like a game," he said, "and it went on for hours."

And then, sometime in the late afternoon, just when he and Jeff decided to have a cigarette, the enemy turned up the heat, blanketing the area with 122mm rockets—six-foot-long finned monsters as thick as a man's thigh and packed with high explosives.

"Believe me, those rockets scared the living shit out of us. They've got this high-pitched scream and . . . Jesus, if you hear one coming, you're okay; that meant it was going overhead. Even then, when they impacted, the ground shook. The explosion would knock you off your feet, even a hundred meters away. All you could do was hug the ground and pray."

When the rockets came screaming in, Arnold and my brother had no place to run, no time to dig a hole to protect themselves. Their reaction was one of instinct. They buried themselves in the side of the grave, Jeff face-first in the loose soil, Arnold on top of him, his arms wrapped about Jeff's legs, holding on for dear life.

Arnold did not hear the fatal rocket, which impacted in front of them, on the reverse slope of the grave. He has no recollection of an explosion. But he does remember the numbness. Then he felt a burning sensation on his right arm. Hot shrapnel. He brushed it off, and then asked Jeff if he was okay.

"All Smitty said was, 'No, I'm hit,'" Arnold said. "And then we rolled to our left and your brother looked at his wound. I'm sure he immediately went into shock because he just closed his eyes and never said another word."

That's when Arnold screamed for a corpsman, the Navy medical personnel who accompany Marines into combat. And then he disregarded a golden rule of combat, jumping up in the face of enemy fire and deserting his post as he ran across the battlefield, looking for a corpsman. By the time he located one, nothing could be done to save my brother's life.

In this instant, Arnold's memory was crystal clear. He could still see the corpsman's face; thin and emaciated. He had blond hair and no-nonsense eyes. Arnold couldn't recall his name other than Doc. But one thing is for certain—Arnold is still pissed at him. He believes the corpsman did nothing to help my brother. While conceding that Jeff's wound was horrible and most certainly untreatable, Arnold says the corpsman could have at the very least *pretended* to do something.

Arnold paused, crushed the empty beer can, and then looked away. A deep sigh, a blank stare, a cold moment of silence.

"It was my job, as fire-team leader, to keep your brother alive," he said. "If I'd sent Smitty to protect our flank, if I'd had Barry stay with me at that mounded-up gook grave . . . dammit. I thought we'd be okay where we were. It seemed safe enough. . . . I failed; I failed."

And that is when I reached out and hugged this remarkable man. Neither of us spoke. We merely held onto each other as if our lives depended on it.

Arnold cleared his throat, and then apologized once again for his memory lapses. He said there was so much he wanted to tell me if only he could somehow remember it all. Some of it remains—them arriving in Nam a day apart and becoming fast friends; smoking marijuana together at C-4, a base camp near the DMZ; Jeff getting into a bar fight in the Philippines; bunking together on the USS *Cleveland,* and Jeff finding a 45-rpm of the Monkees' "Daydream Believer" and playing it over and over, "driving everyone nuts." With the exception of those few memories, however, everything else is gone.

"We share the fruit cocktail, smoke a cigarette, and then the rockets come screaming in," he said. "Next thing I know, Smitty's dead."

From that point on, the day was covered in gauze. Arnold remembered helping someone place Jeff's body into a poncho, then carrying it through knee-deep rice paddies to an evacuation helicopter. He remembered the journey as the longest trip he has ever made, sinking deep into the paddy, trying to keep Jeff from slipping out of the poncho. He had no idea what time of day it was, nor does he recall what happened in the village after my brother's body was evacuated. It's all gone.

"I want to believe Smitty was still alive when we got him to the LZ. But I knew he was gone. I've just blocked out the rest of it," Arnold said.

I spent the rest of the weekend trying to do the same.

Arnold had to deliver the mail the next day. I sat at the dining room table and drank coffee with Cheryl.

She said, "Even though Jim says he only knew your brother for three months, he's carried that friendship around with him for thirty-two years. Jim's *never* let go of it. In his mind, your brother is still alive."

We talked for hours, Cheryl and I. She relived those nightmarish months in Maryland as her husband hovered so close to death— he and so many other grotesquely wounded Marines. When she entered the ward each morning, she was greeted by the screaming. The loudest came from the young man in the bed right beside the nurse's station. He kept screaming for water. It angered Cheryl that no one would help him. But then she saw his stomach. It was torn open; water would have killed him.

"And just about the time I started feeling so sorry for Jim and the pain he was going through," she said, "I saw two Marines in the corridor. The young man in the wheelchair had no legs; the young man pushing the chair down the corridor had been blinded. But together they were each other's eyes and legs, and they were smiling."

Cheryl thanked me for the copies of the letters Jeff had written me. She said Jim had scanned them briefly, all except one, which he had read over and over. It was the letter in which Jeff wrote a simple message: ". . . and another guy from Ohio, who's my best buddy." No name, no mention of a town in Ohio.

"When you mentioned that to Jim, did you notice that he cleared his throat and left the room?" she asked. "That's his way of covering up the grief. He's never cried; he's never let go of his hurts from Vietnam."

The kitchen telephone interrupted her. Cheryl answered it, but did not return to the living room for a long time. When she returned, she said that the telephone call had been from Jim. She said that when he had arrived at work, all his buddies surrounded him. Everyone wanted to know how my visit had gone, what was I like, was I anything like my brother Jeff?

Cheryl said her husband told his coworkers that our visit was going very well, that he had been able to help me quite a bit. Then he turned to his best buddy, another Vietnam combat vet, and asked if it was okay to share something with him. He told his buddy that Jeff had written me thirty-two years earlier, telling me that his best buddy was from Ohio.

Arnold had known all along that Jeff was *his* best friend. But to finally find out after all these years that Jeff also considered Jim to be his best friend finally took him over the edge.

"Jim says he was so embarrassed," Cheryl said, sobbing. "There he was, crying like a baby, but not knowing *why* he was crying . . . hugging his buddy, apologizing for the tears, and crying and crying for almost a half hour."

The man she had married had finally returned home from his war.

15

Heroes Forged
in Granite

Dear Dad: Who's who in the Big Ten? Haven't heard much about it except for Purdue's Rick Mount and Dale Kelly of Northwestern. Send me some newspaper clippings if you get a chance. Received a lot of letters from friends of yours at school. You have a lot of nice folks working for you. I'm doing OK, and hope you are too. God bless you. Love, your son—Jeff

—March 3, 1968

When I returned home from Massillon, Ohio, on Sunday evening, March 26, 2000, there were several messages from my brother Joe, Steve Klink, and Gunny Brandon on my answering machine, none of which my wife would let me answer until I had relived with her my experience with the Arnolds. Once I had, she was saddened by the guilt my brother's best friend still carried with him.

"What is it with you guys that you believe you're in control of the universe?" she said, hugging me. "Jim Arnold is no more responsible for Jeff's death than you are; or your father, or even the men who sent Jeff to Vietnam."

And then we prayed together, something I no longer felt uncomfortable with. That completed, she gave me a mysterious smile and told me to make my telephone calls.

When I phoned Gunny, he said he had already been in touch with my brother Joe and everything was moving forward according to plan—that once I had spent a few days in the desert reacquainting myself with my brother Joe, I would then head north to Oregon and spend a few days with Brandon and his wife, Shirlie.

"Everything's set," Gunny said. "You'll be staying with us. We've got a lot to talk about."

Dumbfounded, I stared at the telephone and tried to decipher Gunny Brandon's comments. June chose that moment to enter the room, gave me another big hug, and held up the airline tickets.

"Here's your early Christmas present," she said, handing me the ticket to Bakersfield, California, which, on May 15, would put me within driving distance of Fort Irwin. "And this is your birthday present," June added, handing me the ticket to Portland, Oregon. "First you fly out to see Joe, then you meet with Jeff's gunnery sergeant. Indeed, God works in mysterious ways."

It took a while to catch my breath, and then I telephoned Joe, who promptly told me that he had cleared my arrival with his commanding officers. He said I had been approved to participate in the base's next operation, working with the 1st Cav out of Fort Hood, Texas. We would be in the field for ten days, moving rapidly through the desert alongside lots of Abrams tanks and Paladins, the army's tracked artillery, getting the troops ready to fight the next war.

"It'll be just like Beirut and East Africa for you all over again; smelling cordite, breaking things, and seein' shit go up in flames," Joe said. "Except one major difference—no one's gonna be tryin' to wax your ass this time."

When I attempted to get a word in edgewise, telling Joe about what I had learned from Jim Arnold, he told me to hold that thought, that we would have plenty of time to hash it over when I arrived in May.

I looked once again at the airplane tickets and noticed that my hands were shaking every bit as fast as my mind was racing. Thirty-two years of agonizing silence and now everything was moving at blinding speed. I kept seeing Jim Arnold's face, kept hearing his words as he agonized about having survived while his best buddies died. And then I sat back and closed my eyes.

On Monday night I spoke with Steve Klink, who, along with my brother Joe, had started this runaway train rolling. Klink laughed when I told him that my wife had taken complete control of the operation, making arrangements for me to connect with Joe and Gunny Brandon.

"She sounds like every good wife of every good Marine I've ever known," he said, then quickly moved on to a more somber topic, that of compiling a list of the Fox 2/4 Marines who had died during my brother's tour of duty. If, indeed, a book was written, I wanted to dedicate it to their memory and sacrifice. Although Klink believed this to be a noble gesture, he viewed it as nearly impossible. While he personally had recorded the names of the company's twenty-two KIA from the Battle of Dai Do—but only because he was still recovering from the wounds he sustained at Lam Xuan East, which found him serving as the Fox Company clerk—tabulating the rest of the Fox dead would be hindered not only by the passage of time and forgetfulness but also because, in some instances, Klink never bothered to learn people's real names.

In the meantime, Klink suggested that I log on to the Internet and visit the Vietnam Veterans Memorial Wall Web page. Maybe I could get some insight from it.

I've always been fascinated by war, reading voraciously on the subject. For reasons I cannot explain, I had always received a thrill from delving into the heroics of others, allowing my mind to wander and picturing myself side-by-side with Davy Crockett or Alvin York, J.E.B. Stuart or Audie Murphy.

I would read about a glorious Civil War battle and scan the casualty reports, unmoved by the countless thousands of dead and wounded, then quickly move to another battle that occurred during a different war. One moment I would be Ulysses S. Grant, ordering his Union regiments into the suicidal frontal assaults at Cold Harbor; the next I would be the immortal Chesty Puller trying to extract his Marines from out of the freezing hell of the Chosen Reservoir.

Odd that I had never imagined myself storming the beaches of Tarawa with my father, had never asked him who his Marine buddies were, had never had the courage to ask him what his battles had *really* been like.

It was also odd that I had never imagined myself going on patrol toward some nameless village in Quang Tri Province with my brother Jeff. Maybe that would have made war too personal. Maybe it would have put faces to casualties, thus depriving me of some vicarious thrill.

Once Klink figuratively pushed me toward the Vietnam Wall's Web site, I scanned through its pages with the usual historical fervor. Within minutes, however, the headache began.

Nothing prepares you for the Wall's Web page. You're greeted with "Taps," then somber images of war's remembrance. And once you've filled in the blanks on an electronic search engine, which is capable of directing you to a specific casualty or one of the monument's 140 panels, you're overpowered by the names. It is a mind-numbing blur of names, from Captain Leo Bert Abramoski, the first name on Panel 1-East, to Private First Class Ted Oland Brazzeal, the last name on Panel 70-West. Officers and enlisted alike: Army, Navy, Air Force, Coast Guard, and Marines; men and women of all creeds and color—a diverse glimpse of American dead from the 1960s and 1970s. A total of 58,178 souls.

I searched the Web site until I could no longer endure the headache, scanning down the list of the 8 nurses who perished there; scanning the list of the Medal of Honor recipients, discovering that of the 244 men who were honored with our nation's highest military award, 152 of them did so at the cost of their lives.

Sobering statistics: 13,085 Marines were killed in combat, as were 5 members of the Coast Guard. Twelve generals perished, as did 17,995 lance corporals. Four of the men on the Wall were

American Samoans, and 57 were from Alaska. But the state that suffered the greatest was Arkansas, which gave up 4,572 of its sons. The first American death occurred in 1957, the only one that year. The deadliest year was 1968, when 16,589 servicemen perished.

I also learned a little about my brother Jeff's and Jim Arnold's two fire-team buddies, Kenneth Maurice Watkins and Thomas Ryan Fleming. Watkins, a nineteen-year-old black Protestant, was from Washington, D.C. Fleming, a twenty-seven-year-old white Roman Catholic, was from Arlington, Virginia. Both died side by side in the same fighting hole in the same instant on March 12, 1968. Yet eight lines of names separate them on Panel 44-East—a separation that has always bothered Jim Arnold.

I also learned that 67 other American servicemen died on the same day as Jeff. Somewhere out there were other families who grieved on that date. And if they are anything like our family, which I'm sure they are, they continue to grieve.

16

The Wisdom of
Wolf 40

Little Bro: Looking forward to track season? You should do
pretty well in vaulting this year. I guess you know by now that I'm
homesick as hell. You wrote me a lot in boot camp, so I hope you
write a lot now that I'm over here. Started picking out a college
yet? Don't get any wild ideas about the Marines. School comes
first. You may have one beer for me: Big Bro, JES

—*December 5, 1967*

I t was May 23, and Joe and I were talking softly at the rear of a
military Humvee, cooking bratwurst on a portable grill at nine
o'clock in the evening. For now, the fire support trainers' headquarters was at rest, preparing for a night attack by the 1st Cav
that would begin in approximately five hours. So, with time to kill,
Joe—no longer "Little José from Pike Lake," but instead "Wolf 40,"
his radio call sign among the FST command—brought me up to
date on his life, which was embarrassing at times because, for the
most part, we had been strangers since 1968.

From my standpoint, the remarkable thing about our get-
together was my discovery of my brother's intelligence. Ten days
living in the Mojave Desert with the command element provided
me with more than enough evidence as to why Joe had been able

to overcome all obstacles in becoming one of the Army's top enlisted men, a sergeant major—remarkable under normal circumstance, extraordinary considering that Joe's first tour of duty, as a Marine, had been somewhat flawed.

Like everyone else in our family, Joe's life was a roller-coaster ride that went spinning out of control when Jeff became Boone County's only Vietnam fatality.

"In essence, Jeff's death gave me a license to be crazy," Joe said.

He did so with anonymity, much in the same fashion by which he navigated high school. He was an all-conference wrestler at ninety-five pounds his freshman year, yet no one in our family saw him perform. When Jeff cleared the bar while setting the school record by pole-vaulting twelve feet, three inches, it was Joe who caught the pole. All eyes were on Jeff; no one gave Joe a second thought. Never mind that Joe was a stellar track star in his own right, consistently high-jumping six feet, even though he stood only four-feet-eight. Never mind that Joe was a star pole-vaulter his senior year, destined to break Jeff's record—if only his family would cheer him on. Instead, Ma could never attend Joe's events because she worked. And our father, for reasons Joe can only surmise, wouldn't attend because of the divorce, errantly thinking that Joe didn't want anything to do with him.

"Whatever, I just lost interest in everything, including track, so I quit the team," Joe said. "Bottom line? Jeff dies and my life turns to shit."

Joe adapted by playing our parents off one another. Dad didn't want Joe to have a motorcycle, so my brother talked Ma into signing for it. Dad was patriotic, so Joe drove into Chicago and joined the protest movement during the 1968 Democratic National Convention. Then he did an about-face, realizing that protesting the war didn't make sense because it was an admission that Jeff had died for nothing. Yet when Dad refused to sign Joe's Marine Corps enlistment papers, it was Ma's signature that assured my seventeen-year-old brother's entrance into boot camp.

"I was like Switzerland; I was the neutral country, the new breed that Mom and Dad didn't know how to deal with," Joe said. "As for Mom, she wasn't about to lose anything else to Dad. Whatever I wanted, I got—especially the freedom to experiment with drugs. Then again, I never had to go through the crap that you and Jeff went through."

His sole reason for enlisting in the Corps in 1970 had been the same as mine the year before: he sought to avenge Jeff's death. But when Dad and I signed waivers that exempted Joe from being sent to Vietnam, the Marines made him a cook—degradation for someone who wanted to go off and kill. Joe was pissed at me, pissed at Dad, and pissed at the Marine Corps. In retaliation, he got involved with drugs and went AWOL, was court-martialed, reduced in rank, and spent thirty days of hard labor in the Marine Corps brig.

Joe refused to allow his heart to be hardened. He got married in 1971 and eventually had two daughters, Jenny and Rhiannon, and a son named Jeff. He was honorably discharged with the rank of corporal in 1973. He and his wife, Mary, moved to Belvidere, then back to California in 1975. But when our mother was diagnosed with inoperable lung cancer in 1978, Joe and his family returned to Belvidere to care for her.

Joe was pissed at Jeff for dying in Vietnam, he was pissed at Dad for getting remarried in 1970, pissed at me for signing the document in 1970 that kept him from being sent to Vietnam, and pissed at Ma for not only getting sick but also for erecting the Wall in her dining room.

As soon as he stepped into Ma's house, he once again came face-to-face with the Wall, the pictures of Jeff from the crib to Vietnam. While the Wall was meant to honor Jeff's memory, instead it was a source of constant, endless intimidation for all of Ma's sons and daughters.

Joe said it was bad enough that there was no avoiding the visual reminders of our slain brother. But the worst part was our mother's constant needling when one of her children screwed up, her saying "Jeff would have never done that to me." No matter where they turned, Joe, Jude, Jim, and Jane were constantly being measured against Jeff, being held accountable to a vision only our mother never tired of seeing.

"Don't get me wrong; I loved Ma, love her to this day. And while a lot of people thought she was a drunk, she worked her ass off day and night. When she worked, she never drank. But when she had a day off, she was drunk all the time. I guess that never bothered me because I was right there alongside her, pumping the beers," Joe said. "But what *did* bother me was the Wall."

Joe still carries a burden about our mother's sickness. It was his idea for our mother to undergo chemotherapy. He said he did so out of selfishness, hoping to prolong her life. And subliminally it was Joe's idea to place Mom's hospital bed in the dining room instead of in her upstairs bedroom, thus making it impossible for her to avoid seeing Jeff's face.

"I wouldn't call that being vindictive because that's all she talked about, Jeff and death," Joe said.

On October 1, 1979, our mother died with Joe at her side. He felt her pulse, found none, then closed her eyes. Before making any phone calls, he got a big cardboard box and took down all those pictures of Jeff.

But as much as he hated them, he kept two of the pictures for himself.

In 1981 Joe went into the regular army as a thirty-year-old private. Despite his age, he chose to become a 13 Foxtrot, a forward observer for field artillery—in essence, the point of the army's spear, which resulted in his being an integral part of combat operations in Beirut, Haiti, and Desert Storm. Warriors are defined by their decorations. Joe's dress uniform has seven rows of service ribbons and combat awards adorning its left breast, including an Air Medal and a Bronze Star for heroism during Desert Storm.

Joe and Mary divorced in 1983, when Joe was getting ready to ship out for Germany. Shortly thereafter, he was sent to Beirut. Unknowingly, our paths crossed at thirty-two thousand feet. While

I was on the last civilian plane to leave Beirut International, departing in January 1984 as the city fell into the hands of Druse and Shiite militias, Joe was landing en route to helping the French Foreign Legion call in air strikes from the array of international peacekeepers.

It was ironic that amid the hellfire of a war zone his life started on the upswing.

Redemption began with rejection. With his marriage falling apart, Joe telephoned our father, looking for support. Instead, he received awkward silence. This was understandable, considering Dad wasn't exactly an expert when it came to the reconciliation of failed marriages. And when Joe shifted gears, telling Dad about the mission he had just completed in Beirut, all our father could talk about was what a fantastic job I had done reporting on that war.

"But before I could beat myself up any more about that, I met Pam," Joe said. "We started dating, and then got married on July 26, 1984. Just like that, I embraced sanity."

Coming under enemy fire in Lebanon was Joe's military wake-up call. From that moment on he threw himself into the job, attending every combat school the army offered, volunteering for every hazardous job that came along.

"Believe it or not," Joe said, "I'd found a *real* home. The military had destroyed all of our lives, yet it was the military that saved mine."

His Air Medal, he said, was justifiably earned for flying combat missions and recording "kills" against Iraqi tanks. He wears it with pride because it is the rarest of combat decorations for those not directly attached to the military's air wing. It is an award he doesn't wave in anyone's face, mainly because the army decorated its Iraq vets in abundance. It was not uncommon for the rank and file to receive five or six combat decorations for that short-lived war.

But what really embarrasses Joe is his Bronze Star. As he summarized it, the war kicked off in January and he was home by April 1. All he did was do the job he had been trained to do—nothing more, nothing less. He will tell you that he did a superb job against the Republican Guard, but certainly nothing worthy of a Bronze Star.

"Basically," Joe said, "that was the ninety-six-hour war. But Jeff goes off to Vietnam, spends four months over there, fighting every day for his life in constant combat against hardcore NVA, and for this he gave his life. So what does he get out of it? A Purple Heart for dying. To me, that's bullshit."

No, my brother said, Iraq was light-years removed from being Vietnam. This is why, three years after the medal was pinned on his uniform, Joe made it a point to visit the Vietnam Veterans Memorial in Washington, D.C. There were moments of tearful reflection; then he attached the Bronze Star to an American flag and placed it at the base of the black granite panel beneath Jeff's name. He also left a letter that he had written to Jeff the night before:

Brother, I am leaving this flag and medal in your memory. No one deserves this medal more than you, Jeff. I am proud of your service and sacrifice for your country. I would be less than honest, though, if I did not say that I am still angry that you died. I did what I did in war willingly, but I still have my doubts about your willingness to fight in Vietnam. War was always against your nature, Jeff. Nonetheless, you stepped forward when your country needed you. I love you, bro. You were, and always will be, my hero.

Joe stared into the vast darkness that lay outside our perimeter, covered by an endless blanket of stars. We did not speak for the longest time, content to wrap ourselves in the chilled silence. Somewhere deep in the desert's shadows, coyotes yelped. Finally, Joe said that psychologically he had no idea how burdensome that Bronze Star had become. But once he laid it at the Wall, symbolically awarding it to a brother who truly deserved it, an incomprehensible weight was lifted off his shoulders, off his heart.

"Getting rid of that medal—damn, I honestly never felt so relaxed in my life. Just like that, my mission was over."

And now, he said, mine was just beginning.

17

A Marine's Marine

Dear Dad: I've enclosed a map out of *Newsweek* and marked the route of our operations. 1) C-4, where we were in November and December; 2) where we made our first operation on January 27; 3) where we are presently, guarding a bridge on Highway 9, near Camp Carroll and the Rockpile. Something big will obviously come of the Khe Sanh situation, but who knows when? God bless. Your son Jeff

—*February 28, 1968*

I had a fairly good idea of what would be waiting for me as I got off the plane at Portland International on that Friday evening. Gunny Brandon said he would be easy to recognize: "I'll be the ol' fart wearing a Marine Corps T-shirt, the big guy held together with duct tape."

I thought he was joking.

Percy Eugene "Gunny" Brandon is the face of war. Shrapnel pocks his cheeks and forehead; four fragments embedded in his right eye cause him double vision. Shrapnel fractured his left wrist on March 4, 1968, and an enemy mortar round blew off his left thumb on March 12. He received a concussion from an NVA artillery blast on March 30, and two days later another enemy artillery round again knocked him out. When he finally regained consciousness, he coughed up blood for three hours.

Being in charge of sixty-eight riflemen, he joked that everyone shied away from him because he was a magnet for enemy fire.

"Of course, everyone knew the body bag hadn't been made that could hold my sorry ass," Brandon said as he and his wife, Shirlie, escorted me out of the airport to the parking lot. "Well, almost."

On June 28, the day before his thirty-third birthday, Brandon tripped an enemy claymore mine—what his Marines appropriately called a "Hellbox"—an explosion with such horrible consequences that Brandon was left for dead inside a rubber body bag. When he regained consciousness eleven days later, he was told that his body had been punctured forty-three times—in both eyes, both arms, both legs, and the right testicle. The right side of his face was sliced open in three places, and his left eardrum and right lung were punctured. The worst of the wounds were to his stomach, which was ripped from breastbone to groin, exposing his intestines. Brandon said he would have bled to death within that body bag had it not been for a Captain Turley, who was asked to make the final identification of Brandon's body at Graves Registration. Turley noticed that Gunny was still breathing, which resulted in Brandon's being immediately medevaced to the hospital ship USS *Sanctuary*.

Gunny recounted this near-death experience with a burst of laughter as he patted his wife's hand. Shirlie looked at her husband, then at me in the backseat of their van. She raised her eyebrows, failing to see the humor. She only remembers the horror and helplessness as she prayed at Gunny's side in August 1968 as he drifted in and out of consciousness, screaming all the while, from his bed at Bremerton Naval Hospital in Washington.

Brandon spent less than seven months in Vietnam, his tour beginning in December 1967. He was discharged after twenty years in the Corps, the last four of which were spent on medical leave as he underwent a seemingly endless series of excruciating bone transplants and skin grafts. That should have ended his ties to the Marine Corps. But it didn't.

"Gene has never *really* taken off the uniform," Shirlie said as we made the forty-minute drive southwest to their home in McMinnville.

Whenever there is a Marine who needs help, no matter what part of the country he is from, Shirlie said her husband is quick to lend a helping hand. Even now, approaching age sixty-five and recovering from prostate cancer surgery, he has opened up his home and his heart to a complete stranger.

Well, almost a complete stranger, Shirlie concedes. After all, I am the brother of one of her husband's young Marines. "And Gene has never stopped caring for his men," she said. "He's never stopped being a gunnery sergeant."

Gunny and Shirlie live in a quaint ranch home on a sprawling farm. The local chamber of commerce calls this part of the state "Oregon at its best," which is not a stretch. This is wine-producing country, nestled in the Willamette Valley. Downtown McMinnville, with its many buildings built in the 1880s, feels like it is in a time warp. The locals aren't hesitant about boasting that this is an old-fashioned community with old-fashioned values and that Gunny Brandon is one of its heroes, its heart and soul, the embodiment of the community's patriotism. Gunny and Shirlie grew up here. They were married in 1956, three years after Gunny's enlistment.

At their kitchen table, shortly after we arrived from the airport, Gunny was busy sorting through his memorabilia—combat maps, souvenirs taken off the enemy dead, and snapshots he had taken in Vietnam—laying everything in his semblance of order, of fractured time and place, which he admitted without embarrassment was a bit jumbled. His memory lapses are due to the combination of concussions sustained in combat and post-traumatic stress.

"Damnedest thing," Gunny said. "I'd be out working somewhere, and then all of a sudden I'm back in Vietnam, watching someone die. It's sort of troublesome, driftin' in and out like that. I lost something like fifty-six of my sixty-eight riflemen killed in such a short time, between March 7 and May 2. I see too damn many faces."

There was an uncomfortable silence, then Shirlie said that her husband has no recollection of being sent home from Vietnam in May 1968, shortly after his fourth wound. She said he played with the children, mowed the lawn, and drank a lot of beer with friends and neighbors, acting quite normal. But then the guilt started eating away at him; he was kicking back and enjoying himself while his young Marines were fighting and dying far, far away. So Gunny signed a waiver, which allowed him to be sent back into combat.

"The next thing he remembers is being back in Vietnam," Shirlie said. "In Gene's mind, he hadn't been at home at all." Shirlie gave me a hug, then excused herself, cautioning her husband not to stay up too late embracing the past.

I tried my best to make Gunny heed his wife's warning, yet failed. And much to Gunny's credit, he kept pace with me until we both were hoarse. In truth, I learned more than I cared to about the hell Brandon and his Foxtrot Marines endured along the DMZ, mainly because the majority of it was gut-wrenching and nauseating. As Brandon summarized his Marines' version of the war, they were surrounded at all times by hardcore NVA and VC.

"We'd hit them, and then they'd hit us. That was our war, simple as that," Brandon said.

At 6 feet 2 and 276 pounds, Gunny Brandon is a big man.

But what is impressive about Brandon is that he has in full measure that elusive and indefinable quality called "commanding presence" that ambitious lesser men, especially generals, aspire to but rarely acquire. In a room full of other 6-feet-2, 276-pound men, Gunny would seem the largest of them all.

He is not particularly articulate or well educated. He quit high school midway through his sophomore year in January 1953 to fulfill his ambition of being a Marine, which was a matter of honor— tribal honor, the blood mix of his Rosebud Sioux and Cree Indian warrior tradition; military honor, because his older brother, Howard, was killed at Iwo Jima while helping pin down Japanese snipers as fellow Marines and Navy corpsmen raised the flag on Mount Suribachi.

That Brandon achieved the most honored and respected rank within the Corps—gunnery sergeant, which is the closest thing to being God among enlisted men—qualifies him to be called a Marine's Marine.

But even Brandon has a weakness. Although haunted by what he has seen, what bothers him most is that perhaps he wasn't good enough. And while he thinks nothing about making light of all the "zippers" that decorate his body, those horrid surgical scars from hundreds of stitches, the worst of these are only visible during the ghastly remembrances shared with trusted friends as Brandon fights back the tears and exposes the scar tissue around his heart.

And that's exactly what he did as we sat face to face at his kitchen table, with only his memorabilia separating us, as the clock on a nearby wall slowly advanced toward midnight, and Brandon's mental clock spun wildly in reverse to Vietnam 1968—jumping from combat in June to incidents that happened in February, then to his surgeries in Japan in August and then back to battles that happened in May. And in the course of his recollections, I remembered my brother Joe's warning not to press Gunny too hard and realized just how insightful he was. For it was clear that Brandon's physical injuries, horrific as they were, were second or even third to the guilt he felt as a survivor and especially as a gunnery sergeant who survived when so many of his young charges died.

Because I had read his book three times, it was fairly easy to follow Brandon's lead as he slogged through the debris of the war, from Dong Ha to Camp Carroll, from the Rockpile to Mai Xa Thi. So I listened, the sponge that soaked up Gunny's agony—listening to stories that all had a sameness, a profound sadness, the closeness only those thrown into combat feel; men of various faiths and race with little in common except the circumstances in which they were trapped, becoming brothers in blood, terror, and anguish.

"The hardest part," Gunny said, "was moving back down the line to one of my Marines and having to tell him that his best friend just got killed. They'd say 'Can't be, Gunny; we just had a cigarette together a few minutes ago.' That's the way it was with Jim Arnold; he really took your brother's death real hard. He just didn't . . ."

Gunny looked away, his fingers unconsciously moving around his war souvenirs before pausing at the combat map in front of him, the map once carried by 2nd Lieutenant Richard Sisk, the commander of Fox Company's 2nd Platoon. Sisk was the first casualty, suffering a gunshot wound to the neck during the battle in which my brother was killed. The map still bears traces of Sisk's blood.

Silence, for I felt guilty putting Brandon through this once again. Before I could summon the courage to ask about my brother, Gunny told me about the night Jeff and his fire team were attacked by three-foot-tall apes while manning an observation post near the Rockpile. Damnedest thing you'd ever want to see, said Gunny, getting the call on the radio that monkeys were overrunning Jeff's fire team.

"So I tell 'em to throw some fuckin' bananas at 'em, thinking they were pulling my leg. Then they call back and say, 'Hell with the bananas, Gunny. They're throwing rocks at us.'"

When Brandon checked on their position at daylight, sure enough, there *were* apes nearby, screeching and jumping up and down on the rocks. Indeed, Jeff and his mates had been attacked by the critters, displaying their cuts and scratches to Gunny. In retaliation, Brandon fired a few rounds at the apes and they scurried away.

"Believe me, it was a weird war," Brandon said.

Our laughter was short-lived because as the night wore on, Gunny's depiction of Vietnam took on a darker tone. His visual aids enhanced this darkness—pictures of enemy dead, letters and family pictures taken off the bodies of slain NVA and VC. And there were pictures of some of Brandon's own men, who proudly mugged before the camera before the assault toward Bac Vong on March 7, smiling Marines with their weapons poised for combat.

He stared at the pictures for the longest time, seldom blinking. And then he said that ever since we had first spoken on the telephone, he found himself wondering if his memories really happened. "Vietnam was so damn crazy," he said. And there were so many mistakes made in that war. But at the time, no one could convince him that the Corps' tactics were flawed. His country, right or wrong; his Marine Corps, right or wrong. So he would be ordered to assault a specific area, and his men would assault it—capturing a village, staying a few days, and leaving, and then being ordered to assault that same village a week or so later.

"And we lost Marines, lots of good Marines," Brandon said, unable to stop the tears. "They were like family. It hurt so damn much . . ."

Whenever Brandon closed his eyes, the faces of those young men haunted him. This went on for years after he left Vietnam.

Gunny's sleep was fitful, if he slept at all. He would lie down and close his eyes, and David Bingham would visit him. Bingham, whom everyone called "Gunny's Shadow," the kid who was captured by the NVA at Dai Do, his hands bound behind his back with barbed wire, and executed. Gunny would close his eyes, and Skip Schmidt would visit him. Schmidt, who was a hero at Lam Xuan East, survived Vietnam and killed himself four years later.

Faces, an endless parade of faces darting in and out of Brandon's subconsciousness—David Rogers, Richard Bartlow, Thomas Fleming, James Bettis, Jeff Mead, Gary Hill, Walter Cleveland, Adolph Martinez, James Burke, Robert Weeden, John Malnar, and Ken Watkins; faces with only nicknames attached: Giant, Frenchy, Rat, Baby Doc, and Feather Merchant; and faces without names.

Gunny stared at the map in front of him for the longest time. Finally he said that once he returned home, the greatest pain he has ever experienced had nothing to do with the NVA, who had tried to kill him, or the military surgeons, who eventually saved his life by slicing away the spread of gangrene. Instead, it was the pain he inflicted upon himself—his futile attempt at burying war's horrors by drinking, which allowed the ghosts of his young Marines to haunt him even more. When the faces of his dead men would never go away, Gunny got behind the wheel of his automobile and steered it onto an isolated stretch of highway. And then he would close his eyes, praying that the pain would go away.

"I would wake up the next morning, the car in a ditch, its front end caved in, and me not knowing if I'd been playing around with suicide or not," Gunny said. "All I knew for certain was that my head hurt, my heart hurt, and that I'd have to spend another goddamn day with the pain. But then I got help from the VA; they screwed my head back on properly."

He paused to laugh at himself, then added, "Don't worry. I'm okay—now."

Quiet reflection, then Brandon said that he had spent his first twelve years in the Marines preparing himself for war, then the next three preparing young boots for war. And when it looked as if Vietnam would pass into history without him having had an opportunity to prove himself, he called in all the favors he had accumulated over the years and eventually found himself in combat. He said it didn't seem right being a Marine and never having tasted war.

"So I saw it and survived it. And now," he said, pausing, "and now here I am, knowing I shouldn't be thinking about that shit anymore, but being unable to stop myself—lifting the lids of a lot of coffins and looking in."

And what Gunny saw when he lifted the lid was my brother. Not Jeffrey or Jeff, but Smitty. He saw the yellow-orange muzzle flashes coming from my brother's fighting hole on the night of March 5, saw Jeff overcome the terror of combat, never wavering as he helped eliminate a reinforced company of NVA regulars who tried to overrun the battalion headquarters at Mai Xa Thi. And at first light, when Gunny carefully checked the enemy dead in front of the 1st Platoon's position, he felt so damn proud of what his men had accomplished.

"Everyone in your brother's platoon had at least one kill," Brandon said. "I counted twenty-six dead gooks in front of our position alone. Shit, they kept coming at us in waves, yelling and screaming. Not that this bothered Jeff. Your brother was really cool under fire, not excited in the least."

And once the attack was over, the men of the 1st Platoon stripped the dead, emptied out their pockets and took souvenirs, and then snapped a lot of pictures. It was a pretty big deal, Brandon said. In some instances, it was the first time some of his young men had actually seen the enemy face-to-face.

Brandon leaned back in his chair, closing his eyes, then smiled and said, "No doubt about it—Jeff was one hell of an outstanding Marine. One of the best."

My chest swelled with pride over Gunny's praise. I wasn't ready to release Gunny, wasn't ready to allow him to walk back into the darkness, taking his memories of my brother with him.

But just as soon as I gathered the courage to press him further on the details of my brother's final moments, he told me we had best grab a few hours' sleep. We would need it because in the morning we were making a four-hour drive to the northeast, up along the Washington border to a little town called Hermiston. Seeing my confusion, Gunny apologized for taking matters into his own hands. He had made a few phone calls before I had arrived, hoping to locate one more missing piece of a tragic puzzle.

"There's a guy up there named Ken Fickel, the corpsman for the 1st Platoon," Brandon said. "Fickel's pretty much a loner, but he'd like to talk with you. Says he's been trying to track you down for ages."

It was Fickel whom Jim Arnold was still pissed at, the corpsman who was unable to save my brother's life.

18

Corpsman Up!

Dear Mom & family: On March 28th I'll have one-third of my time done over here; June 2nd one-half and August 8th two-thirds. Yes, I'm already anxious to get out of here, but if the other Marines can do their 13 months then so can I. God bless and take care. My prayers go out to you all. Love: Jeff

—March 2, 1968

There was a day when the rockets kept coming and coming," Ken Fickel said, his fists clenched in his lap, his eyes downcast. "Rockets were an absolute terror . . ."

He paused, biting off the words. He took a deep breath, then said, "I'm not proud of this, but I actually considered shooting myself just to get out of that place. But I didn't because . . . ah, I don't know. All we ever had over there was each other. Your most valuable assets were your buddies, your Marines."

We were seated on kitchen chairs in the Fickels' front yard, the chairs arranged in a semicircle so everyone—his wife, son, and grandchildren, plus Gunny Brandon and I—could hear Fickel relate his memories of my brother. It was a rare moment for his family; he had never before shared with them his Vietnam experience. All were mesmerized, tape-recording and taking notes of the session, as the former corpsman revisited the anguish he had kept bottled up for thirty-two years.

Corpsmen are the guardian angels of combat Marines. They accompany their grunts into the thick of battle, carrying compress bandages, IVs, morphine syrettes, and other medical gear. They are lifesavers, not life-takers, yet their chances of being killed are often greater than those of the warriors with whom they serve. When the fighting is fiercest, when self-preservation dictates moving to safety, that is when corpsmen spring into action, moving *forward* to take care of the wounded.

Not that Fickel believes he did anything out of the ordinary. His job was to keep his Marines in the field and combat-ready by tending to their physical well-being, making sure minor wounds were continually cleaned and dressed; administering aspirin and foot powder; and, when the fighting was fast and furious, "baffling them with bullshit; assuring them that they were gonna be all right, that the wound wasn't as bad as it looked; convincing them to hold on until the medevac chopper could get them to the rear, where a real doctor could save their life."

Fickel said this without emotion, his jaw locked in determination, his hands clenched at his side. He said that after working twenty-four years as a state engineer, he had left with a medical disability due to chronic back pain—his back had been broken decades earlier. Experiencing excruciating pain the year before, he had passed out on the job and was rushed to the hospital. Only when the doctors showed him the X-rays, telling him that surely he must have fallen from a great height to have such a massive compression fracture, albeit one that had calcified over time, did it all come rushing back to him.

"On March 7, 1968; the day your brother died, the day I broke my back trying to get to him," Fickel said, nodding to his family.

He paused, then turned toward me and said, "Ever since Gunny called and said you were flying in from Georgia, I've been trying to sort it all out. I remember the monsoons and freezing my ass off sleeping in water, and I remember those bamboo vipers being everywhere. Our equipment was shit, especially the radios. But all of the firefights and battles are a blur."

What remains, he said, other than the frightening sounds of battle, are isolated vignettes. The courage—a nameless Marine staggering back to the rear under his own power, his face and hands charred, his uniform in tatters after an NVA mortar blast. The stupidity—a new second lieutenant reenacting a scene from a war movie, charging a bunker with a grenade in each hand, and getting killed before he took seven steps. The horror—seeing an armored personnel carrier returning from the Dai Do battlefield back up to the cement building housing Graves Registration, and lower its tailgate to let bodies roll out amid gushing blood. And the pathos—the serene face of the kid he knew only as Frenchy, whose father had died fighting for the French at Dien Bien Phu; Frenchy shot through the heart, yet still managing to say, "Doc, I'm dead."

Fickel stared far, far away, and then blinked. "I'm not going to lie to you," he said, his voice sounding as if it were coming from the bottom of a well. "I suffer depression. It's been that way for quite a while now. I've spent a lot of my time removing myself from those days. I came home and went about the business of living. I don't go to reunions, and I'm not too good about keeping in touch with the guys."

Silence as Fickel focused on something beyond the distant tree line. For a moment I feared that unlike my being flooded with information by Brandon, Fickel might dry up on me rather than revisit the battlefields of long ago. I turned to his wife, Vicki, and she responded by quietly nodding and placing a finger to her lips.

Fickel raised his head, looked me directly in the eye, and said, "Enough about me; you've come looking for answers about Jeff. I remember him well. He was stern and focused, and he appeared frail because he'd lost a lot of weight. Of course everyone had because the last hot meal any of us had had was in January, back in the Philippines; we'd been living on C-rations for about seven weeks. Out there, you had to learn fast; learn the different sounds of weapons, learn how to survive. Most of all, you had to learn that it was simply stupid to do some things—like being too curious; you didn't want to see too much of what was going on around you in combat, seeing people get hit. You just stayed low, popped a few rounds, and ducked."

Fickel stared at me. He bit his lower lip, then grabbed my notebook and silently sketched a map, marking Mai Xa Thi with a circle

with an X through it. The Cua Viet River angled southwest from
the Fox Company base camp toward Bac Vong. Between the two
villages lay a series of rice paddies broken only by a fifty-meter ex-
panse of trees and a couple of pagodas.

"What we didn't know," Fickel said, "is that a main-force VC
unit had moved into the tree line during the night. They were
waiting for us."

Thursday, March 7, 1968, dawned clear and hot, as usual, as
the Marines in the forward listening posts returned from their
fighting holes, carefully passing through the perimeter wire. Fox
Company was up at first light. Breakfast was a cigarette and a cup
of tepid coffee. There was no time to eat; there never was. The
priority was checking weapons, making sure they were cleaned and
functional. Canteens were filled, extra bandoliers of ammunition
and grenades were distributed, and then the troops moved out of
the loose fortification at Mai Xa Thi by platoons, in single file,
their destination Bac Vong, approximately twenty-two hundred
meters to the southwest.

"I was back with your brother and the 1st Platoon. We'd just
cleared the west gate when the 2nd Platoon got hit hard," Fickel
said. "I sort of hesitated because the last time I acted on instinct,
jumping up to help a wounded Marine, Sergeant Rogers threatened to shoot me if I ever again acted like John Wayne. But this
was different; the entire lead platoon was getting nailed, so the
rest of the company charged forward—running right into a hail of
small-arms fire."

Lieutenant Richard Sisk was the first to get shot, an enemy
round ripping through his neck. Three other Fox Company
Marines sustained minor leg wounds while, farther to the west,
Hotel Company also was pinned down in the opening volley, and
five of its Marines were killed. Ignoring the intense enemy gunfire,
Gunny Brandon raced to the head of the column and was the first
to reach Sisk. Brandon inserted his forefinger in Sisk's wound and
slowed the bleeding. Within minutes an evacuation chopper landed,
and Sisk was medevaced to a field hospital in the rear, accompanied by Fickel.

By the time field hospital personnel had unloaded Sisk, word came from the battlefield that casualties were mounting; evacuation helicopters were desperately needed. When a resupply chopper landed, Fickel and fellow corpsmen ran to it and dumped all the ammunition, mortar shells, extra C-rats, and all of Fox Company's mail, and commandeered the chopper for medevac. Fickel remembers the return trip to the battlefield as hectic, especially when they neared the tree line. That's when they took enemy fire, bullets ripping through the chopper.

"About that time is when the rockets started coming," Fickel said. "This must have been around two o'clock in the afternoon. The gooks always pinned us down with small-arms fire, then waited for the helicopters to arrive; that's when they started firing the rockets. Those 122mm rockets followed us all the way in."

Amid this chaos, the pilot of Fickel's chopper told him it was impossible to land, not with the rockets slicing through the battlefield. Undaunted, Fickel screamed at the pilot to make a low pass, which he did, and then Fickel leaped from the chopper—landing on his back, sustaining the compression fracture that would plague him decades later. Dazed by the fall and the concussion of rockets nearby, Fickel pulled himself to his feet and started moving through the rice paddy toward the rocket explosions.

"I don't know how far I traveled because this is where everything starts to blur," Fickel said. "I could hear those rockets exploding. Those damn things were fierce; the concussion alone was very severe. If you were within ten meters, you were dead."

With the blur and chaos of battle whirling around him, Fickel pressed on, moving east, toward the bank of the Cua Viet. But then he stopped dead in his tracks, mesmerized by the nightmarish howl of a rocket impacting right in front of him. For reasons he has never understood, the rocket did not explode.

"But just up ahead, one did. That's the rocket that killed Jeff," Fickel said. "It was the last rocket fired at us that day. It landed right between his legs. He was busted up pretty good. He was . . ."

We looked into each other's soul, Fickel searching for the right words, knowing I wanted every detail, knowing the details would shatter me. When I nodded, he rose and turned his back on his family, then slowly walked to the front door of his home. I hesitantly followed, my emotions every bit as fragile as they had been thirty-two years earlier when I first learned of my brother's death.

"Are you sure you want to know?" Fickel asked.

I took a deep breath and said yes. Ken placed his arm around my shoulder, and in a hushed voice told me the devastation of Jeff's wounds. I choose not to share the details; some things are better kept to oneself. What Fickel told me took away my breath. Too stunned to scream, I sat down on his front porch before my legs gave out on me. I felt numbed and nauseated.

Once we had returned to the family circle, Fickel spoke in solemn tones, saying that there was nothing he could do to save my brother. Jeff was cyanotic. When Ken could find no pulse, he filled out a wound tag and attached it to the laces of Jeff's left combat boot, the leg that was still intact. All the while, Jim Arnold screamed at Fickel to do something to save my brother.

"That was always the worst part, knowing one of your Marines was dead or he was so damn busted up that there was nothing humanly possible that *anyone* could do to save him," Fickel said.

He paused for what seemed an eternity, then in a hushed voice said, "I know Arnold took it hard, and I'm sure he's still pissed at me to this very day. But you've got to believe me—there was nothing I could do for your brother except cover him up with a poncho."

Approximately twenty minutes later, Brandon and Arnold carried my brother's body, using that poncho as a stretcher, through the paddy's waist-high muck and a hail of enemy gunfire, to an evacuation helicopter. So intense was the enemy fire that as soon as Brandon secured my brother onto the chopper, it lifted off so suddenly that Brandon did not have time to clear the hatchway. Hanging by his fingertips, he lost his grip and fell onto his back into the paddy—greatly winded and bruised, but intact enough to continue fighting for another two hours.

At four o'clock, the fighting ended as unexpectedly as it had started. The enemy vanished from the battlefield. Fox Company gathered the rest of its dead and wounded, then returned to Mai Xa Thi.

"That's about all I can tell you, except that I'm truly sorry," Fickel said. "Your brother was a good Marine and . . . well, those of us who made it out of there still live with a sense of guilt. There's not a day goes by that we don't ask ourselves why we lived when so many others didn't."

Ken Fickel and I embraced. There was nothing left to say.

19

Epiphanies

Dear Mom & family: Sorry that I didn't get to send you anything on Valentine's Day, but I want you to know you still are my favorite Valentine. If you send me stuff, send fudge, cookies, canned stuff like ravioli and spaghetti, and soups. Also lemonade Kool Aid will come in handy. Thanks for lighting a candle for me at church, and thanks for the prayers. God bless you all. Love: Jeff

—February 16, 1968

I departed Oregon with excess baggage—raw reminiscences and new nightmares.

For the first time in my life I realized I had not been alone in my grief for Jeff. I also realized how stupid, how selfish I had been to think otherwise. I had a fairly good idea now of just how destructive was war's aftermath; that the bullets and bombs were the least of the survivors' worries, for the guilt of having lived while others died was carried with them to the grave.

A couple of weeks after my return from Oregon, the telephone rang as I was preparing to leave for work. The woman on the other end informed me that she was calling from the Department of the Navy's Judge Advocate's Office in Washington, D.C. Marine Corps commandant James Jones had been touched by my letter of a few months ago, she said, and he had instructed the JAG to put together and send me a packet of declassified materials pertaining to the months my brother had served in Vietnam.

"General Jones passes on his heartfelt condolences, Mr. Smith," the Navy officer said, "and he apologizes for the lack of communication from this department in the past." She said documents were en route that hopefully would answer some of my questions.

Sure enough, on June 7, 2000, exactly three months after writing to the commandant, I received a package that contained command chronologies of March–April 1968 for the 2nd Battalion, 4th Marines, accompanied by a letter from Colonel K. H. Winters, deputy staff judge advocate to the commandant of the Marine Corps.

"Due to the nature of the issues involved, the Commandant asked me to respond on his behalf," the letter began, then went on to say that the Corps' official records indicated that Jeff died at approximately three-thirty on the afternoon of March 7, 1968, as a result of shrapnel wounds to his abdomen and right thigh inflicted by enemy mortar fire. At the time, Fox Company was taking part in Operation Fortress Attack/Saline II in the vicinity of Quang Tri Province. Colonel Winters said the Corps had no information that identified Jeff's platoon commander, fire-team members, or friends. It did, however, determine that First Lieutenant M. H. Gavlick was Fox Company's commander at the time of my brother's death. Gavlick later rose to the grade of colonel and retired from the Marine Corps on May 1, 1992. Winters said that the Corps had contacted Gavlick and provided him with a copy of my letter, and that Gavlick had assured the commandant he would review his historical records and contact me with any additional information he discovered.

"Finally, please accept my deepest condolences as to Jeff's loss while in service to our country," Winters said in closing. "As you well know, even the passage of thirty-two years doesn't begin to ease the pain of losing a family member before his time. I trust and hope, however, that our efforts herein will help to explain—if only in a small way—the dangerous circumstances confronted by Jeff and his fellow Company F Marines during February and March 1968."

The enclosed command chronologies put a name on the enemy (elements of the NVA 320th Division and the 164th Artillery Regiment), and provided exact locations of Fox Company's movements before the assault on Mai Xa Thi (the two bridges my brother helped guard near Camp Carroll were at map coordinates YD 026562 and 043566); the Rockpile was near the village of Ton Son Lam. Once Fox Company was airlifted southwest to the Cua Viet River, the face of the enemy changed (270th Independent Regiment, 3rd Battalion of the 27th Regiment, 6th Battalion of the 52nd Regiment, the 1st and 2nd Battalions of the 803rd Regiment, and the K-400 local force company). I also learned that the village Steve Klink, Gunny Brandon, and Jim Arnold knew as Mai Xa Thi was called Mai Xa Chanh (map coordinates YD 280667) by the Marine brass. From strictly a strategic standpoint, 2/4's primary mission was "to keep the Cua Viet River open to Naval boating by controlling the north bank; to deny the 'Jones Creek' drainage system [a known infiltration route] to the enemy; and to conduct search and destroy operations in the assigned AO [area of operation]."

The action in which my brother was killed was summarized: "Company H and the 3rd Platoon of Company F became heavily engaged during a battalion search and destroy operation. Friendly casualties were ten KIA and thirty-five WIAE [wounded in action, evacuated]."

Michael Gavlick's letter arrived three weeks later. He wrote that he would be happy to share with me all that he remembered, but also pointed out that his memory of his combat tour in Vietnam was vague and that he had no specific recollection of my brother's death. In an effort to stimulate his memory, he said he had been in contact with Gunny Brandon, and "while I cannot specifically recall the things that Gunny remembers, his recollections sound remarkably accurate to me." In closing, Gavlick extended his belated condolences and urged me to contact him.

When I telephoned, I was moved by Gavlick's sincerity and compassion, but most of all by his sadness at being unable to recall much of the tragedy he witnessed in Vietnam. Although he did not say he was ridden with guilt at being unable to keep all of his

Marines from being killed, he did tell me that he has spent much of his time in the years since "trying to forget that war."

We promised to stay in touch, even though we knew that would not happen.

Jim Arnold telephoned in August and said he had made contact with Ed Garr, a former Marine Corps captain who served with the 2/4 and was now a tour guide for Military Historical Tours, which specialized in tours to Vietnam. Long story short, when Arnold told Garr about my brother and my desire to visit the exact spot where he had been killed, Garr said he could arrange everything.

When I told Arnold to give Garr the go-ahead, he laughed, saying he had anticipated my approval and that we would be making the trip next March. In fact, Garr had already cleared the trip with the Vietnamese government, which was supplying a special guide who could take us to Mai Xa Thi.

"Garr says he's familiar with the guide, a Viet Cong who actually fought against us," Arnold said. "Sort of mind-blowing, isn't it? Guess the war's really over if one of the bad guys is actually going to lead the way," he added, pointing out that the trip would cost each of us less than $3,000, which included airfare, room and board, and most of the incidentals. We would leave Los Angeles International on March 18, 2001, with a short stopover in Japan, then fly into Bangkok, Thailand. We would arrive at the Danang airfield on March 20. Our itinerary would include China Beach, Dai Loc, An Hoa, Hill 43, Hue, and the Forbidden Purple City Palace complex. After that, we would navigate the Hai Van Pass, then head north to the DMZ, where we would visit Lang Vei, Khe Sanh, Dai Do, Lam Xuan East, and then conclude our trip at Mai Xa Thi, where Jeff was killed.

When I asked Arnold what he thought about us inviting Gunny Brandon along, he said he couldn't think of anybody else he would rather have covering our rear.

Emboldened by Arnold's enthusiasm, I telephoned Gunny and invited him to join us. "I've been expecting this call," Brandon said, pointing out that he would like nothing more than to be with us. In fact, his VA doctors thought it would be good therapy. His wife, Shirlie, however, suspected it would only rekindle his nightmares. When he began compiling a long list of reasons why he should not return to Vietnam, I told him I thought I understood his reluctance. But if he changed his mind, I would be honored to have him accompany us.

Two days later Gunny called back and said he had sent in his deposit.

"No matter where you go, no matter what you do over there," he said, "I just want you to know I'll be guarding your flank."

I felt better already.

20

The Truth

Dear Dad: Sorry I didn't get a chance to call you from the Philippines. I'll catch you next time I'm on R&R, probably from Australia or Bangkok. Right now we're getting ready to pull a major operation, probably at Khe San. We're just waiting, that's the worst part. I really look forward to your letters. Love, Your Son: Jeff

—*January 25, 1968*

I made arrangements in September 2000 to visit my sister Jude, who lived with her daughter and son in Madison, Wisconsin. I had seen Jude only twice in the past thirty-two years—in 1978, shortly before my niece Morgan was born, and the last time in 1985, at my sister Jane's wedding. We have never been close, and although we had telephoned each other on occasion, Jude always seemed to get pissed whenever I asked if there was anything I could do for her.

"I've always been distrustful of men. It's been that way ever since Dad divorced Mom," Jude said when I called to update her on my search for Jeff's Marine buddies. When I told her about meeting Jim Arnold and Gunny Brandon, and that we were going to Vietnam in March 2001, Jude asked for all the details. I told her she would have to wait until the end of the month, when we could sit down and discuss everything face-to-face.

Her scream almost knocked me over. "You're *really* going to come up here to see me?" she asked. Indeed I was, I assured her. She proceeded to talk virtually nonstop for the next forty-five minutes, occasionally allowing me to get in a word edgewise. For the most part, it was a great conversation—a Smith family rarity. We relived our shared experiences from days at Minnesota's Pike Lake to the circuses we held in our backyard in Wethersfield, Illinois.

But then the conversation took on a somber tone as Jude reminisced about our mother. Especially when she said, "You know, Mother always thought that she was living on borrowed time."

When I pleaded ignorance, Jude told me that Ma had lived with abandon in the belief that she would die young because of the injuries from the car accident. Mom first shared this with Jude in early 1977 at our Belvidere home on Union Avenue. They were sitting in the coffee nook—memorable because of the matching curtains, tablecloth, and tablemats, all of which were decorated with an Italian flair: red and white checks. On special occasions, Ma would change the motif to Hawaiian, with its matching curtains and tablecloth. We were never told why except she did say that Hawaii was about as close to heaven as anyone could get to here on earth. For as long as any of us could remember, Mom always talked about Hawaii. So convincing and elaborate were her stories that we took it for granted that once upon a time she had actually lived there.

"But she didn't," said Jude, sharing for the first time a secret that Ma had revealed only to her. "Mom never really came out and said so, but I got the impression she held it against you and Dad that she never got to Honolulu."

Jude said that as she was driving with our parents one day, Ma was drunk and began to rant and rave at Dad, and then attempted to grab the steering wheel. That's when Dad backhanded Ma, which prompted her to scream, "If we hadn't shacked up, I wouldn't be in this mess."

In 1977, when Jude finally found the courage to ask Ma about that outburst, our mother said that in May 1945 she was working at the telephone company in Oceanside, California, and was in the process of being transferred to Hawaii. All that stood in the way of Ma's dream-job-come-true was completion of the standard government physical. And that is when she discovered she was pregnant. Whoops! Mom, who had already proven the doctors wrong by living three years longer than expected, had had a miraculous conception. Meaning?

"You never bothered to do the math, did you?" Jude said.

No, I had not. Like the rest of us children, I also never questioned anything that was said or done in our home; I learned early on to shut up and follow orders, being a good Irish Catholic and adhering to blind faith. I knew without doubt that Dad's love of Mom was not subject to debate. If any of us children so much as questioned our mother's behavior, which usually was something she said or did while drinking, our father quickly and severely disciplined us.

According to Dad, the facts of my parents' marriage were that it took place on October 10, 1944, in Champaign County, Illinois. Although I had wondered about the fudge factor, that he had been fighting the Japanese halfway across the world on Saipan and Tulagi as recently as July of that year, I never raised the issue. But given the combative nature of our parents' marriage, the *facts* as told to Jude by our mother seemed more realistic—that Ma had "shacked up" with Dad, gotten pregnant, and then reluctantly agreed to be married on October 10, 1945, less than three months before I was born.

"So the rest of us kids weren't wrong," Jude said. "We always thought of you as a war-loving Marine Corps bastard. Now *you* know it as fact."

This shouldn't have bothered me but it did. On one hand, it explained a lot of the upheaval—the shouting, slapping, screaming, and crying, the plethora of accusations endlessly tossed back and forth—that seemed to be a large part of everyday life in our home. On the other hand, my conception out of wedlock was just another heavy stone of guilt that I found myself lugging around; that I was, in large part, the cause of so much of my mother's misery.

I spent a week of fitful sleep. Finally, knowing nowhere else to turn, I telephoned my brother Joe at Fort Irwin, California. "I'm a bastard," I told him.

"Shit, bro, we've known that for years," said Joe, laughing.

In no mood for laughter, I repeated everything Jude had told me, sharing my doubts and my all-consuming guilt. Joe immediately quelled my fears by saying he might be able to clear up the matter once he returned home to El Paso, Texas, the next weekend. When Ma had died, Joe had packed away all her personal belongings, most notably everything that was in her cedar chest, which was the one place in the house that was sacrosanct with Mom—forbidden territory for all of us kids. Joe said he had not bothered to examine the cedar chest's contents closely because it was too painful—that it would have been like opening a coffin.

"You know how it was with Ma—she could be pretty vindictive at times. None of us was spared; all of us ended up being collateral damage," Joe said. "I think she was probably having one of those moments, feeding Jude a load of shit. And because you weren't around—out of sight, out of mind halfway across the country working at some newspaper—you just happened to get caught in the crossfire."

Joe said that as soon as he returned home to El Paso, he would check out the box in which he had packed away Ma's possessions. He would call me as soon as he found the marriage certificate. Until then, he said, another week of being a bastard wouldn't hurt me none.

Joe telephoned the day before I was to fly to Madison, Wisconsin, to visit Jude. He had located the box containing our mother's prized possessions, which included her marriage certificate, complete with all the official seals. It was dated October 10, 1944—not 1945, as Ma had indicated to Jude.

But what would eventually give Joe and me greater peace of mind was other items that Ma had squirreled away in that cedar chest: her letters to Jeff while he was in Vietnam; Jeff's letters to her and our younger brothers and sisters; a telegram from the commander of Dover Air Force Base in Delaware that Jeff's body had arrived from Vietnam and would be transported that day to Chicago; letters of condolence from the commandant of the Marine Corps, the personnel office of the Navy, and various state senators; plus a couple dozen pictures that Jeff had taken in Nam, some of which were of his closest friends.

"If only Mom had shared this with us years ago," Joe said, "maybe there wouldn't have been so goddamn much confusion, maybe we wouldn't have had to wait so damned long for the answers."

But that just wasn't Ma's way of doing things.

21

Taking Sadness

Dear Jude: I got a chance to listen to some music lately and I'm
in pretty good spirits. I've got a radio and can pick up some popular music late at night. Write me and give me some scoop on
the music scene. Are you still digging the Monkees? I heard they
got a new album out. Is it very good? I know it probably is. Write
if you get a chance. Love: Your Bro, Jeff

—*January 22, 1968*

The Monkees' reunion tour stopped at Madison, Wisconsin,
during the summer of 1998, but my sister Jude chose not
to attend. There was a time when she would have done
whatever it took to see the zany 1960s rock group. After all, Jeff
used to call her "Davy," after the Monkees' lead singer, Davy Jones,
a nickname Jude's friends also adopted. But that was before Jeff
was killed.

Ever since March 7, 1968, Jude's outlook on life has been col-
ored by dark hues. There is little joy; what laughter escapes her
lips is forced. And music—a means of escape for all my brothers
and sisters—is a curse, a melancholy and agonizing ordeal, just as
it had been with our mother.

"When Jeff died," Jude said, "the Monkees died with him."

It was September 2000, and we were seated on the screened-in
back porch of my sister's second-story apartment. Her home is like

many we lived in as children—clean and tidy, yet quite cramped. And no matter where I looked or what I touched, everything was cloaked in and choked by the past. Jude and her children, twenty-two-year-old Morgan and eleven-year-old Madison, ate off the dishes our mother used at her getaway cabin at Lake Ripley, Wisconsin, the cabin Ma purchased with Jeff's government death benefit. The silverware was Mom's, as were the plastic salt-and-pepper shakers. Earlier, my sister gave me a tour of her apartment, showing me Ma's tap-dancing shoes, our mother's collection of Connie Francis records, and Mom's ironing board; then we had moved into the dining room. It was dominated by Jude's Hollywood shrines: Pee Wee Herman and Marilyn Monroe, and her favorite movies, *The Wizard of Oz* and *Gone with the Wind.*

On a nearby table were family pictures: our brother Jim's wedding, Morgan's high school graduation, Mom with the Army Air Corps wings on her left lapel, and Jude as an infant. As I admired the pictures, Jude picked up her baby picture and gazed at it, then said, "Whenever my friends are around, I ask them if they want to see a picture of me the last time I was happy. This is it, at age one."

I didn't know what to say. I never have when talking with Jude. Even her name has elicited her wrath toward me. In my mind's eye, she has always been Judy, the little girl dancing around the living room with Ma. It is one of those pleasant childhood memories I cling to. But it is a memory that does not sit well with Jude. Because I'm the only child in the family not fixated on music, I overlooked the Beatles' *White Album* recording session that produced "Hey Jude" in August 1968. I forgot the riotous evening shortly after the Beatles released the song as a single, when I sang along with Jude and Joe at Belvidere's B&A Tap—harmonizing as best I could in my drunken state. If I had taken better care of myself, no doubt I would remember that from the moment my sister first heard "Hey Jude," her birth name vanished. She became Jude; end of discussion. Or, if she was in an intellectual state of mind, it was Judith. But never *Judy.*

Our differences go way beyond music. Not only are we a generation apart, we also have very little in common other than shared misery. Jude is a pacifist and a liberal, whereas I am a conservative

Republican. If that were not bad enough, I've never known when to hug my sister, or even if such behavior is appropriate; never known when to say I'm sorry, for when I have expressed that sentiment, seldom has it come out right.

More often than not, I just tend to piss Jude off. Not by choice; it just happens.

She continued, "Mother was just half a person after Jeff died. Other than Jeff, the only person she *really* loved was Jack, her fiancé. Even that went to shit because he died when his plane crashed into that mountain. Wars ruined our mother—first she lost Jack, then Jeff."

When I maintained my silence, Jude said that although she was sure there was passion in our parents' marriage, without doubt our father never had enough time for any of us—especially our mother.

My sister is hurting, yet has trouble coming to grips with it. She is sentimental yet spiteful, mirthful yet suffers prolonged bouts of deep depression. She probably is the most intelligent member of our family, a straight-A college graduate with a major in theater, yet at the moment she is unemployed. Until a few months ago, Jude worked for the state lottery system, but she quit when her boss verbally berated her in front of coworkers.

"I've always thought of our father as a barking dog, always growling at us," Jude said. "So, when my boss yelled at me, I lost whatever serenity I had and quit. Dumb of me, yes. But I couldn't handle the abuse; too many bad memories."

She paused, as if to gauge my reaction, then said, "I don't do very well being bossed around, especially by men. I'm scared and intimidated by you guys."

Jude stared at me with a quizzical expression, then chuckled and apologized for calling me a bastard, qualifying her regret by saying I certainly acted like one at times. She was just repeating what Mother had told her, she said. When I hugged her, I expected a rebuke. Instead, she made another admission—she didn't hate our mother because she had always known how damaged she was. "So I hated our father instead. Even though until I'd read that chapter you'd written about his childhood and the war, I didn't know how *damaged* he really was."

Jude ran her fingers over the chapters I had sent her, each stacked neatly in front of the dining room mirror. She said she was thrilled to read about Jeff's childhood years because she had never heard the stories before. And even though the chapters concerning Jim Arnold and Gunny Brandon dealt mainly with the war, Jude said reading about Jeff's Marine Corps buddies somehow made his death less painful. When she asked if I had interviewed anyone else who had known Jeff, I lied. I wasn't ready to tell her about Ken Fickel yet.

And then Jude turned away, took a few steps, and stopped. She glanced back at the mirror and said, "This will probably freak you out, but do you know what I see when I look into the mirror? I see my mother staring back at me."

The ensuing silence drove me to the back porch. Jude followed, and then I sat without speaking and listened to my sister's monologue as she slowly flipped through the pages of an old photo album. There was a picture of her tap dancing at age six, another of her performing in another dance recital at age eight, and pictures of her in high school as the athletic teams' mascot, a Belvidere Buccaneer. I listened to her reminiscences, crying inside.

In my mind's eye, Jude has always been a beautiful lady, a budding Judy Garland for whom she was named, a budding Marilyn Monroe, whom she always wanted to grow up to be. Instead of realizing those dreams, she is now a forty-nine-year-old single mother of two. In her own eyes, she is overweight, a problem that has plagued her since age ten.

"I still remember the doctor shrugging and saying that if I could just eliminate the candy bars I wouldn't be so fat," Jude said. "The trouble is, I never ate candy bars, never ate any sweets at all. And I kept getting fatter and fatter and . . . so, what did it take? Thirty years later I'm diagnosed with a thyroid condition. If only . . ."

My sister's life is a seemingly endless series of *if onlys,* all of which began on a long-ago Saturday morning when a green government car pulled up in front of our house and two Marines climbed out. Jude was fourteen at the time; she remembers that day vividly. She was returning from school, where she was practicing for *South Pacific.* It was ironic, she said, that she should be costarring in a production about war and race relations, because the Vietnam War killed Jeff and, shortly thereafter, race hatred would lead to Martin Luther King Jr.'s assassination.

"All of us had been inundated with all the Marine Corps bullshit—mother laughing off our father's problems by saying he was 'nervous from the service' and how the Marines could take care of any problem. But then I walked in the front door that day and saw Mother crying, I saw the Marines and knew right away that Jeff was dead. Now, *there's* a problem the Marines couldn't solve."

Indeed. But then Jude supplied a piece of the story that I did not know—that once Dad and I departed to drown our sorrow at the VFW, our mother left shortly thereafter with Betty Brenner to get drunk at the American Legion Club. At the most crucial moment in her life, Jude was forsaken again, left to babysit Jim and Jane, our youngest brother and sister.

"My *best* brother is dead, and I get to play caretaker." Jude released a deep sigh and shook her head in frustration. "That's my life story. Mother didn't raise Jim—I did. I truly believe Mother was jealous of all of us kids, all except Jeff. There was never enough love to go around, or anything else. Mother drank, and in order to keep the house functioning I had to take over all of her duties. But I lost interest in everything after Jeff died. I lost interest in being a surrogate mother, lost interest in school."

Her most vivid recollection of Jeff's death involved one of her closest friends, Debbie Anderson, who telephoned and said she had just heard that we had lost Jeff in Vietnam. "Don't worry, Jude, they'll find him," Debbie said. "And when they do he'll be okay." Jude said it broke Debbie's heart when she told her that Jeff wasn't lost—he was dead.

She had another vivid memory: Jeff's wake, his looking so perfect in his dress blues. "I touched his hand in the coffin; it was so cold."

From my sister's viewpoint, she was abandoned—first by Jeff, then by Dad, and finally by our mother, whose sole purpose for adorning the dining room wall with Jeff's pictures was really her way of blocking out the rest of us children from her life. Ma did this, Jude believes, because she never wanted to be hurt again.

"But Mother never considered what those pictures did to the rest of us," Jude said.

What it did to Jude was push her deeper and deeper into depression. Seeking an outlet, she joined the anti–Vietnam War movement during her sophomore year—"protesting against the war, not the soldiers." When that provided little relief, she admittedly gave up on herself and barely made it through high school, graduating in the lower third of her class. Still clinging to her desire to become the next Janis Joplin, Jude enrolled in the Patricia Stevens finishing school in Chicago. That lasted one semester after the school closed its drama department. She remained in Chicago, working in the makeup department at Marshall Field's.

"Mother used to get pissed because I loved everyone," Jude said. "Then again, it seemed like she always got pissed at everything."

I cannot speak for my brothers, but not once had I bothered to seek out Jude's perspective. Until now. This was both comforting and agonizing, for although I now realize I was never alone when it came to doubting my parents' love, it is painful to see what the uncertainty of affection has done to my sister. Since childhood she has believed she has been ignored. Despite our mother's having been dead for twenty-one years, it still bothers Jude that Ma never once told her that she loved her. Despite Jude's having eliminated our father from her life for thirty-two years, she contends Dad wanted nothing to do with her because she was a girl—that all of Dad's attention went to us boys.

"I worshiped our father, even though he hardly ever talked with me," Jude said.

That adoration turned to hatred shortly before Jeff died, during a family outing in which Ma had had too much to drink. As was her habit, our mother started screaming at Dad, blaming him for Jeff's having joined the Marines. And when Ma's hollering and repetitious accusations got to be too much, Jude told her to shut up.

"Father slapped me full in the face, defending her," Jude said. "Although this was the only time he ever laid a hand on me, all

I could think of was, How could he hit me when he *knew* she was a drunk?"

Jude's lasting memory of our mother is equally as painful. It occurred at my sister's high school baccalaureate. "Mother was in the audience, sitting all by herself. It was so sad, because she was *really* drunk this time and she threw up on herself."

Jude's great escape provided little joy. She moved to California in 1973 and joined a Christian cult. When that experience proved unfulfilling, she worked at a San Diego strip club in 1975 as the master of ceremonies, introducing the strippers. When she tired of that, Jude moved to San Francisco's Haight-Ashbury district. But happiness always seemed to be out of her reach. Even the joys in my sister's life have been tinged with darkness. When she discovered that she was pregnant with her first child, Morgan, in 1978, Jude moved back to Belvidere. Everything was on the upswing until Morgan, at age twelve, was diagnosed with Hodgkin's disease, which went into remission after two years of chemotherapy. In the years since, Morgan has given my sister hope, something to live for. The same can be said for Jude's son, Madison, who was born in 1989.

"He's a natural," my sister said. "Everything he tries to do, he excels in." Her eyes brightened as she said this.

But then the dark cloud returned when she shifted the topic back to our brother's death, reminiscing about living in Belvidere and how she always visited Jeff's grave. Without fail, she was always finding "stuff there—beer cans and roaches; you know, you always have a drink or a toke with your dead friends." One time she said she found peonies in a peanut butter jar, and another time she found that miniature Bronze Star that our brother Joe had buried in a flowerpot. She also has visited the Vietnam Veterans Memorial, taking the train to Washington, D.C., and then crying her heart out before laying a white rose at the base of the monument.

Jude gazed into the distance, her mind locked onto something I could not see, holding on to the silence for what seemed like an eternity. Her hands shook, and tears ran down her cheeks. She took a deep breath, slowly released it, and echoed the anguish embraced by our entire family: "I miss Jeff so much."

And then she apologized for burdening me with her sorrow, saying that she truly wanted her life to turn around, that she continues to look for her dream job—hoping someday to be a schoolteacher, or a caretaker of pregnant teens and their newborn children. What's baffling, she said, is that she doesn't know how to get there from here.

I love Jude too much to hurt her further, which is why I hesitate to tell her that the only way she can reach that dream is by moving forward—leaving the past behind, allowing the dead to bury the dead. But then again, what the hell did I know? I had been trying to do this myself for the past thirty-two years.

We hugged, shared a few more tears and a few more memories, and then it was time for me to move on.

I departed for the airport with only one regret: I wished Jude would join me.

22

Collateral Damage

Dear Mom & family: How's the Lady of the house, the 4 kids, puppy and parrot doing? Does Jimmy like school? I guess that's a stupid question. I hope you can send me some pictures, Mom. I love those of Jimmy & Jane. In a few days I celebrate 3 months over here! On March 1 I celebrate that great moment in history (ha, ha) when I enlisted in the Corps. God bless you all. JES

—*February 18, 1968*

For Jim and Jane, the youngest members of our family, the Vietnam War has nothing to do with fire and brimstone, of body counts or dustoffs, of political sanctuaries or lines of demarcation, of battles won or a generation lost. Instead, they will always view that war as an enigma wrapped within a mystery, a solitary date of emptiness and loss that generated our mother's unfathomable stares mingled with tears.

Jim was six when Jeff was killed, and to him Vietnam's specter appears in the form of a one-legged, one-eyed Marine who stood guard at the funeral home's front door during Jeff's visitation, a kind yet unyielding sentry who grabbed Jim around the waist and prevented him from viewing his favorite brother lying in the open casket.

"I just didn't get it—not then, not now," Jim said. "One moment Jeff's a long-haired rock 'n' roll dude who's playing catch with me in the backyard. Then he's gone, which is bullshit. Know what really pisses me off, though? Sometimes I feel as if I never had a brother named Jeff."

Jane echoed that sentiment. She was a month shy of her fourth birthday when Jeff was killed. For her, the war is represented by our brother's scarred guitar, which she still strums, and a pile of sheet music from the 1960s, the chords and lyrics that she knows by heart from Bob Dylan, the Mamas and the Papas, and the Monkees.

It was her rebellion that gave her Jeff's music. She grew up with the unwritten rule that no one touched anything of Jeff's—not his uniforms, not his medals, not any of the stuff Ma had hidden away in her cedar chest. And certainly not his guitar. But at age seven, Jane picked up Jeff's guitar and started strumming on it. Instead of our mother being upset, she smiled at my sister and asked if she would like to take guitar lessons. Jane did, which is how she first connected to our brother.

"Until that moment," Jane said, "he was just that smiling kid looking back at me from all of those pictures that Ma had on the Wall—Jeff smiling back at me in silence. For three years no one ever told me anything about my brother. But then I picked up that guitar, strummed it, and that's when Ma started talking about how Jeff loved his music. Just like that, Jeff was alive again."

For the longest time the only picture of my youngest brother and sister that I chose to display was of them decked out in their GI Joe outfits and roughhousing on the front porch. The picture was taken in 1973 shortly after President Nixon declared an end to the Vietnam War. The picture was a constant reminder of life's irony, if not its cruelty. It was a picture of innocence and guilt. Jim—long-haired, carefree, and flashing his ever-present smile—has always reminded me of Jeff; and Jane—her facial features tense, her body a coiled spring, and her fists clenched—has always reminded me of myself.

Jim was thirty-nine and lived at the mythical end of the road, in Key West, Florida. From his perspective, this was as far away from life's accepted norms as the law allowed. My youngest brother, still the spitting image of Jeff, was a treasure diver for the Mel Fisher family, and spent most of his time at sea in search of gold, silver, and emeralds from the legendary Spanish treasure galleon *Nuestra Señora de Atocha.*

Jim finally agreed to share his thoughts with me in November 2000, yet even then it took him six days to agonize over the impending ordeal. Seated at a metal table on the cement patio of the home he housesat for Wisconsin owners, Jim shrugged and said he really didn't have that much to say.

He unscrewed the top of a bottle of beer, took a deep drink and sighed, then spoke nonstop for almost three hours.

By default—Dad was gone via divorce, I was married and raising my own family, Jeff was dead, and Joe was in the Marines—Jim became the man of the house by his seventh birthday. Living in a house full of women, he raised himself and became self-sufficient. He developed what he calls a gypsy mentality with the aid of disenfranchised teenagers, marching alongside them and our mother in antiwar protests.

"I set my own example, which was pretty cool," Jim said. "I was an eight-year-old hippie."

Over the years Jim has made ends meet by a variety of means. He bused tables at age twelve, worked with food services at an automobile assembly plant four years later, then promptly quit school during his junior year and, in 1978 at age seventeen and shortly after our mother died of cancer, set up residence in Rockford, experimenting in the drug culture. When he eventually tired of that lifestyle, he moved to Wisconsin and lived with our father and stepmother, and eventually graduated from high school at age twenty. As a student at the University of Wisconsin-River Falls, his campus jobs included writing editorials for the school newspaper, working as a DJ for the campus radio station, and delving into school politics, which he discovered he had a knack for. That's the path he took upon graduation, eventually helping run the state senatorial campaign for Russ Decker, who surprised Wisconsin's voters by winning the 29th District race. Jim stayed with Decker for nine years, steadily building his 401(k), then walked away from the job at age thirty-seven.

Jim's priorities were discovering seventeenth-century gold and silver at the bottom of the ocean, baseball, and rock concerts, especially Aerosmith. He prided himself on the fact that his politics leaned to the extreme left, that he was the only son "who wasn't a mental retard" by enlisting in the Marine Corps, and that he no longer participated in the corporate rat race. Key West suited his lifestyle. It was a good life—there was plenty of sunshine and the bars stayed open late into the night. Great companionship in a fantastic community without a care in the world.

Well, almost no cares. Life would be absolutely perfect if someone would appropriately answer the one question that has bugged him for the past thirty-two years: why did the government send our brother off to die?

Jim had two pictures of Jeff in his mind. In one, he was playing his guitar shortly after graduating from high school, and then went off to California for a few weeks with his buddies Wes Dobbins and Terry Gamlin. And when he returned, Jeff had gold streaks in his hair. The other picture was of Jeff returning home after boot camp. Jim hardly recognized him. Jeff was so grown up, a Marine wearing dress blues.

"And then—what? Maybe three months later he's dead," Jim said. "Just like that, Jeff's gone before I could *really* get to know him. That sucks."

Jim was outside playing ball when the Marines informed us that Jeff had been killed. At first, Jim didn't give much thought to the steady stream of cars that pulled up in front of our house. He figured something was up when the parish priest arrived. When Betty Brenner, our mother's best friend, rushed from her car and sprinted up the front steps, it finally dawned on Jim that something *big* had happened, so he, too, ran into the house.

"Yeah, something big happened, but no one would tell me what it was," Jim said. "Everyone ignored me. No one said shit."

Jim's next memory of our brother was when his body arrived at the funeral home. Mystified as to why he would never see or hear Jeff play the guitar again, never get to play catch with him, all Jim wanted to do was say good-bye to Jeff in the casket. But the one-eyed, one-legged Marine Corps sergeant standing guard at the door wrapped his arms around Jim, refusing him entrance into the sanctuary.

"To this very day I can still see that son of a bitch," Jim said. "I was pissed then, I'm pissed now. I didn't get to see my brother, didn't get to say good-bye. Know how that affected me? It's like Jeff didn't even exist."

Jim didn't get it. No one, including myself, would tell him what happened to Jeff, why it happened, why our family was self-destructing. In protest, Jim took crayons and Ma's lipstick and wrote on the walls, the refrigerator, on anything he could pen his message: "I DON'T GET IT!" The family doctor dismissed Jim's actions as being harmless, that he was simply a confused child who would eventually settle down and walk away from his grief, his anger. But Jim never has.

To this very day, he still doesn't get it. For thirty-two years he has been waiting for someone to sit down with him and tell him what Jeff was like, what he was doing over there in Vietnam, who Jeff's friends were. Jim's questions were endless: What was it like fighting a war that couldn't be won? Could Jeff see his death coming? Was it like a Chinese water torture?

Jim paused and angrily downed his beer, then opened another. Finally regaining his composure, he said, "I think about Jeff all the time, wondering what it was like for him in Vietnam, what happened on the day he died. I've thought about that from age six."

And as the years passed and he matured, Jim came up with his own conclusions. He said he finally realized how stupid we were as a nation—gullible, buying into that bullshit domino theory. The Vietnam War came down to a simple fact: we didn't like the way Hanoi spent its money.

"Hell of a reason to get fifty-eight thousand Americans killed, huh?" Jim said. "And then to lose the stupid war on top of it."

He grabbed another beer, his bitterness mounting, and then made a confession: He entered the political world not because he thought it was cool; he hated politicians. After all, he said, it wasn't the NVA or the Viet Cong who killed Jeff—it was the U.S. government.

"All I've ever wanted is a say; never again, never another Vietnam," Jim said. "If we have another war, I'm all for letting the senators' sons go fight it first. Man, that would stop that war-mongering bullshit."

Jane was thirty-six. She was diabetic and suffered radical mood swings, the result of depression. In many ways, she resembled our mother— the reddish hair, eyes that seemed to dance whenever she was in a musical mood and flashed her sardonic smile. This is no small wonder because Jane and our mother were best friends, soul sisters in spirit, singers of songs who shared each other's laughter.

But more than anything else, Jane had the capacity to sit in silence while our mother reminisced about her life, sharing ambitions realized and those that were not.

"I had the greatest moments of my life at Jeff's cabin," Jane told me in September 2000 during a visit to our sister Jude's apartment in Madison, Wisconsin. Every bit the loner that she has been during the past thirty years, Jane took a Greyhound bus from Rockford because she had no automobile of her own.

She said she was content to let others do the driving, just like when Jim and she were kids, jumping in the backseat of Ma's ratty old car and driving through the night to Lake Ripley—singing and laughing for the most part. She remembered our mother as working ten straight days with little sleep, working around the clock so she could get a few days off to take her children to Jeff's cabin. And once there, she and Ma would sit on the front porch; Ma in her favorite chair with Jane sitting on the floor at her feet, holding Ma's hand and listening to the endless stories about Jeff. They had an agonizing sameness to them—Jeff playing guitar and writing his own songs for his rock group, "The Rubber Band"; Jeff being the greatest pole-vaulter in Belvidere High School history, topping the bar at twelve feet, three inches; Jeff driving the convertible that carried the Buccaneer cheerleaders in the annual homecoming parade; and then Jeff doing the stupidest thing anyone could ever do, cutting off his beautiful long hair and volunteering to be a Marine, a mindless sheep following other mindless sheep and marching off to his death.

"Ma always told me that Jeff just *knew* something terrible was going to happen to him," Jane said, "and that when it did, Ma was supposed to use his money and do something nice for the family. That was the cabin."

And it was there that our mother first told Jane about her dream, her vision—she had seen Jeff on a battlefield, and there was an angel walking toward him ready to take him away to heaven. Ma never saw Jeff die in that dream—just the angel of death coming to take him away. But she did say that Jeff walked into her bedroom a few nights later and told her that everything would be okay because he was no longer in pain. Ma said Jeff came to her in her sleep the night before he was killed.

"Every time she told me that story, Ma's hands were shaking," Jane said.

The first time our mother shared that vision, Ma opened her cedar chest to let Jane look at all the letters Jeff had written to her, letters that always asked about the well-being of his brothers and sisters. Jane said she must have read those letters hundreds of times before our mother died—letters that breathed life into lifeless pictures. And amid this resurrection, she wrote a song about Jeff, the chorus of which goes like this:

> Why did he have to fight that war?
> Why did he have to go to Quang Tri?
> Why don't I know my own brother?
> Why can't he sit here and tell me?

"Of course, Jeff couldn't tell us why," Jane said. "What's worse is that no one could—not Mom or Dad, not anyone."

Jane's world came crashing down upon her at age fourteen, in February 1979, when our mother was diagnosed with cancer. When Mom died seven months later, Jane moved in with our father and stepmother.

"It was always me and Mom and Jimmy, then all of a sudden it was just me. I was all alone," Jane said. "I rebelled against everything, against everyone—including you and June when I lived with you for those two years."

We reunited in 1983 when Jane, at age nineteen, moved to Atlanta. As strange as it may sound, she said she moved south to be near my family and me. By that time I had sobered up and was just beginning to make amends. Jane said that she thought some of this good fortune might rub off on her; drugs were her gods. More than anything else, she needed to distance herself from the bad memories associated with Belvidere. But all she accomplished was to exchange one nightmare for another, marrying within three years of moving to Georgia. Because her husband had trouble holding a job, Jane worked two. Finally, the physical and mental abuse took its toll, and she was granted a divorce, then moved back to Illinois.

A decade later, we sat side by side, reunited in our shared grief, our smiles forced, our laughter feigned as we took a stab at reconciliation. For the most part, I was at a loss for words, so I merely listened. For almost two hours Jane laid before me her sorrows, her disappointments, and her failures. And then she took a deep breath, slowly released it, and told me she really didn't have anything else to add. That's when we hugged, our tears falling on each other's shoulders.

As I turned away, intent on refilling my coffee mug, Jane said, "First Jeff is killed, then Mom dies of cancer. And now . . . well, I know I've spent a great deal of my life screwing up. I'm not concerned what anyone says about me, but I am bothered when someone starts bad-mouthing Mom. I don't remember her as a drunk. She was my best friend, my teacher, and provider of everything we needed. She was my life, a powerful, awesome woman. She was my idol, just as Jeff is your idol."

There was a glint of steel in Jane's eyes as she said this, but then they softened as she stepped forward and gave me a hug. She smiled and told me that there was no need for me to worry about her. She had put her yesterdays behind her. She had faith in God, faith in her friends. And even though she occasionally smoked a little dope and drank a few beers, she said she was no longer jumping off the deep end.

Her life seemed to be getting better—one bittersweet day at a time.

Less than three months after we spoke, just before I was to travel to Vietnam and hopefully visit the spot where our brother was killed, Jane hit bottom. Under the influence of both alcohol and drugs, she stepped off the curb into traffic—right in front of a police vehicle. Jane was hospitalized.

When I was finally allowed to speak with her, she said, "You know, I always connected to Jeff through his music. But even then, he was always in the past tense; it was always 'Jeff died in Vietnam.' Hopefully, now that you're going to Vietnam, you can put your own grief into the past tense. And hopefully, now that I'm here, now that I'm where I should have been a long time ago, I can finally put my problems into the past tense."

23

Across the Pond

Dear Dad: Sometimes I seem like a chessman on a chessboard. Not getting our mail and slacking off on chow tends to piss us off. You know how it goes; you went through the same thing. I guess I'm just blowing off steam, because I know our outfit ain't the only one like this. My squad leader rotated back to the States. I can't wait for that day when I rotate back home. Until next time—God bless you.

—*February 16, 1968*

The first leg of my journey to Vietnam—the flight from Atlanta to Los Angeles—was disconcerting because my mind would not stop playing games with me.

Was I scared? Hell, no. I was petrified. Not of the people I would encounter in Vietnam, not what I might learn from the battlefields I would visit. What ate away at me as I sat in the window seat of that Delta flight whisking me away from home to the unknown were my doubts. What exactly was I searching for? More war stories? Anecdotes to fill some soon-to-be-written travelogue? Adventure? Personal gratification? Satisfying my morbid curiosity? Being able to shout at the world: "Hey, look what I did?" There was no answering my doubts and questions, which made me feel worthless.

But more than anything else, what accompanied me to LA was my youngest brother Jim's anguish; his demand—the demand of a heartbroken generation, really: "Find out what's so special about that damn place that it cost us our brother."

By the time my flight touched the LAX runway, I was more confused than at any other time in my life. Anxiety pulsed through me as I checked into the Hilton, the angst accompanying me as I entered my room and threw my luggage onto the bed, then made my way to the hotel's coffee shop. There it vanished immediately once I saw Gunny Brandon and Jim Arnold. I no longer felt alone.

Handshakes, hugs, and coffee filled the next hour, not to mention a running commentary from Gunny. More stories of Nam: blow-by-blow accounts of his numerous wounds, reminiscences of Marines long dead and of villages long destroyed, of battles won and a war lost. Through it all, Arnold and I sat in respectful silence. Our confusion was obvious; I had not been there, and even though Arnold had, he had few memories.

"You're shittin' me," Brandon said when Arnold was unable to recall a particular firefight. "Hell, you was right there beside me, no more than twenty meters away. You're tellin' me you don't remember me killin' that damn sniper? Little fucker was shot through the chest, playin' possum, then snappin' off a few rounds once we moved past him. Man, I can still see his eyes, seein' him smilin' up at me even as I lowered the shotgun to his face. He knew he was gonna die, but that didn't stop him from smilin' at me. Yep, them gooks were tough little bastards."

Silence. I played with my coffee cup, mesmerized by Gunny's stories. Jim merely smiled. It was a vacant smile that never reached his eyes. He would shake his head and admit how confusing it was, even after thirty-three years, because he remembered as little about the events of Vietnam now as he did in March 1968, when he lay near death on that hospital bed in Bethesda, Maryland.

Arnold said, "Guess I want to go back and just laugh and smile. I didn't do any of that in my four months in Nam."

More silence. I could feel the anxiety start to take hold of me again. Then Gunny's voice lost its bravado when he admitted that he almost didn't get on the flight that morning. He had been having trouble sleeping; his dead men from Fox had come calling again. Unable to sleep, he found it impossible to eat. Worse yet, he couldn't talk about it with anyone, for fear they might think he was losing his mind.

And here he paused, rubbing his huge hands together, as if trying to ignite kindling, his eyes glassy. Finally he blurted, "Yeah, seein' the faces again and me tryin' to talk to the guys, tellin' 'em I'm so goddamn sorry that they died and . . . well, I don't know. Doesn't seem right that they died and not me."

Jim and I stared at each other. I don't know about him, but my heart was crying out for Gunny.

As if noticing our sadness, Gunny—always the kick-ass gunnery sergeant—regained control of the situation by thrusting his left hand into the air. "By God, I don't want you Marines letting me down," he said, grinning. "Lost this damn thumb over there near the Rockpile. Gotta find it—that's my mission. And I'm countin' on you two helpin' me. Understood?"

Jim and I laughed. It felt good.

We gathered at the Thai Airlines terminal the next morning. Ed Garr, a retired Fox 2/4 captain now working as a tour guide for Military Historical Tours, introduced himself, then introduced those who would be making the trip with us.

Charles Swindell from Raleigh, North Carolina, was short and wiry and had a ready smile. He was a first lieutenant during his tour of Nam, supplying his brethren of the 1st Marine Division. Accompanying Swindell was his older cousin Jack Selby of New-nan, Georgia, an Army vet from the Cold War era who was along to make sure "Charles doesn't do something silly, like inciting them Vietnamese and igniting that damn war all over again." Ann and Jerry Kershner were from Eugene, Oregon. Jerry was a retired lieutenant colonel from the 2/4 command element, a noncombat-ant who had served in Hue shortly after the city was recaptured in 1968, and then helped with the evacuation of Khe Sanh. Bill Hontz was from New Port Richey, Florida. Twice wounded by land mines while driving resupply trucks during the height of the Tet

Offensive, Hontz had a thick neck and a muscular build that would be intimidating if not for his obvious good humor. George and Susan Malone were from Clinton, Maryland. Susan had worked with the Army's intelligence arm, the Studies and Operations Group, in Laos; her husband, a retired lieutenant colonel, was wounded three times while serving as a platoon commander with Alpha Company, 1st Battalion, 9th Marines, in the A Shau Valley in 1969–1970. He is the recipient of the Navy Cross, our nation's second-highest combat decoration. Linking up with us in Bangkok would be Dr. Bryan Crafts and his daughter Laurel, both from Atlanta. Garr told us that Dr. Crafts was a retired Navy anesthesiologist who had worked at the main medical battalion in Phu Bai during Fox's 1968 incursions along the Cua Viet River.

"A few simple things to remember once we land at Danang," Garr said. "At all times be polite and courteous; don't forget to smile. We're visitors, just like we were during the war. It's not our country—it's theirs."

Garr said we were on a set itinerary from which there would be no deviation. We would be spending three days in Danang, visiting Hill 327, China Beach, and Red Beach, and Hills 55 and 65. From there we would head north, stopping at Hai Van Pass and Phu Loc before entering Hue. And then it was farther north to the DMZ, with a short layover at Dong Ha before heading west to the Laos border. Highlights of that part of the tour would be the Lang Vei Special Forces camp, which was overrun during Tet; Khe Sanh, Camp Carroll, the Rockpile, Con Thien, and Gio Linh.

"Everything culminates with a very special ceremony at Mai Xa Chanh, or Mai Xa Thi, as some of you might remember it," Garr said, laying his hand on my shoulder as he explained the significance of the ceremony. He paused while my fellow travelers expressed condolences to me, then reiterated that the Republic of South Vietnam no longer existed.

"Very little of *your* Vietnam remains," Garr said. There are no more firebases, no clear-cut, bulldozed perimeters, no hastily constructed airstrips cut into the jungle. Everything had been reclaimed by elephant grass or returned to rubber and coffee plantations. Ho Chi Minh's goal had been to rid his land of all foreigners. And after almost ninety years of continuous warfare—first against the Chinese, then the Japanese and French, and finally against the United States—he had succeeded.

Garr then told a story about Ed Henry, a fellow MHT guide. On a previous trip, one of the tourists kept telling Henry that he couldn't wait to visit Hill 55 so he could show everyone where he had spent his youth digging fighting holes. Henry tried to soften the blow, telling the vet that that part of Vietnam no longer existed, that all he would see was a huge Communist monument atop the hill. When they got to Hill 55, all that aged Marine could say was, "What the hell did they do to my hill?" In response, Henry told him it was never his hill in the first place.

"Bottom line," Garr said, "is we didn't own that place then, and we sure as hell don't own it now. All the sandbagged bunkers and barbed wire are gone. All that remains are your memories."

We departed for Japan on Sunday, March 18. Twelve hours in the air, an hour's layover at Osaka, then a five-hour flight to Bangkok. Somewhere along the way we lost a day, arriving at Bangkok International shortly after midnight on Tuesday morning. Jim Arnold and I shared sleeping quarters—a large closet with two bunks. He slept while I pumped coffee nonstop. Our flight to Danang departed at nine o'clock that morning. Almost two hours later, Vietnam's lush countryside passed beneath us.

And while I marveled at the sight—both beautiful and formidable, both breathtaking and foreboding—the calm was shattered by war's memories.

"Remember the Cua Viet, Gunny? What was it, something like five thousand NVA artillery rounds an hour being dropped on us from Khe Sanh all the way to the river?" George Malone asked.

Gunny cringed, as did others. Looking into the blanched faces surrounding me, I was greeted by glassy-eyed, vacant stares. Yesterday was closer than anyone imagined. Especially once our plane taxied on the Danang runway and coasted past the terminal, which was adorned with a gigantic Vietnamese flag—blood red with its bold gold star.

Inside the terminal we were greeted by Vietnamese military personnel, complete with dark green uniforms and sidearms. Much to our surprise, some of them smiled.

Although I've seen more than my share of war-ravaged Third World countries, I don't profess to be an expert on Vietnam. What little knowledge I took with me on this journey was the result of having read Graham Greene's *The Quiet American,* Bernard Fall's *Hell in a Very Small Place,* and Michael Herr's *Dispatches.* Nonetheless, when I departed the plane at Danang, I did so as a cherry, the term given to every American soldier who entered the country for the first time during the 1960s and early 1970s.

Vietnam is 180 degrees from what it was at the height of our nation's involvement. Peace reigns, mainly because other than a brief border spat with China and the crushing of the Khmer Rouge, no foreign militants have been stupid enough in the past two decades to consider either occupation or invasion. The populace appears content, mainly because everyone has enough rice to get them through another day. The late Ho Chi Minh's utopia is in full bloom, and his presence remains all-knowing as he cares for his people, even from the grave. Wherever you look, you see Ho— his image adorns the country's currency, his political bent motivates the country's domestic and foreign policy, and almost every billboard erected throughout the countryside has a smiling Ho looking down from it, warning against the spread of AIDS and encouraging the use of condoms. There are other messages, most of which are couched in Lenin's shared mistrust of the proletariat: "It is true that liberty is precious—so precious that it must be rationed."

No one seems to have any complaints. Then again, civil disobedience is not tolerated.

Of course, this is merely an American view of things, which doesn't count for much on either side of the seventeenth parallel. Like those before me, I wasn't here to plant roots. I was merely passing through, taking notes when it seemed prudent, absorbing everything else through the lens of eyes greatly discolored by my own historical slant.

We found no cemeteries containing the remains of either French or South Vietnamese soldiers. Once the victorious North Vietnamese Army and its Viet Cong main force counterparts finally stopped celebrating in the fall of 1975, the remains of their enemies were disinterred and reburied in massive pits throughout the countryside. There were no monuments to their sacrifice, no headstones—nothing to remind anyone of what once was.

Those unfortunate enough to have worn the uniform of the Republic of South Vietnam and somehow managed to survive continued to be punished for their transgressions. They were found throughout the country, pedaling three-wheeled bicycles as they escorted tourists. This was Vietnam's rendition of the taxi driver, and the ex-ARVN soldiers were derisively called "cyclo boys." When the country fell to the Communists in 1975, all ARVN soldiers were rounded up, placed in chains, and then sent to reeducation camps. When Vietnam went to war against the Cambodian Khmer Rouge, the ARVN were repatriated and bore the brunt of the fighting. Approximately 70 percent of them died on the battlefield.

I came by this knowledge through Nguyen Van Son, who was fifty-two and lived in a rented room behind an alley off Hoang Dieu Street in Danang with his wife, four daughters, and his mother and brother. Son was an ARVN paratrooper and was wounded in the 1972 Easter Offensive. By government decree, the only job Son could have is that of a cyclo boy. On a good day he could earn four dollars American pedaling tourists about the city. Son rented his vehicle for twelve dollars a month from the government. He dreamed of owning his own bicycle someday. Also by government decree, Son's wife was not allowed to work, and children of former ARVN were not allowed to be educated.

Wherever a traveler went it was impossible not to stumble upon cemeteries honoring North Vietnam's soldiers. These cemeteries were massive, some stretching over several acres, each with huge granite monuments heralding the people's victory. If an outsider had the time or the patience to tabulate the military dead, surely the number would exceed two million. But that is just a rough guess.

We did not find a McDonald's or an Arby's in Vietnam, certainly not a Hooters. Ditto for gin mills or topless nightclubs. But there were still a lot of whores for foreigners at the top hotels. Rice paddies still dominated the countryside, and water buffaloes still roamed wherever their instincts took them.

The vast battalion medical facility at Phu Bai that still haunts Dr. Bryan Crafts was dismantled two decades ago. All that remained was part of the original runway tower. As a thirty-year-old lieutenant during the 1968 Cua Viet offensive, Crafts remembered the battalion's main hospital ward and its endless rows of young men so horribly injured.

"But most of all I remember one Marine, who was obviously in great pain," Crafts said, fighting back tears. "When I bent over him to administer medication, he refused it. Because his buddies were suffering, he chose to suffer also. What magnificent young men . . ."

Occasionally we saw the disabled, rusting hulk of an American-built armored personnel carrier or an M-48 tank. But other than the placid landscape, still pocked by shell craters that have been partially filled in and gone to grass, you could travel for days without seeing the slightest hint of war. One had to step far from the beaten path to be reminded of what occurred here during the late unpleasantness.

That's what we did on our third day in the country, stumbling across the fire-scarred remnants of a hospital outside An Hoa. While the others relaxed, George Malone slowly made his way through the gutted buildings, his rage obvious as he recalled the carnage that transpired here in 1967, when eight German nurses were executed by a VC assault force.

"To those wonderful women, your nationality or uniform meant nothing. VC or American—if you were wounded, they cared for you," Malone said. "But the VC saw them as a threat, so they butchered them—cutting their throats."

You could spend day after day outdoors and *never* hear the thump, thump, thump of helicopters. The ting of cymbals and the sharp stutter of flutes floated on the air, along with the combined aroma of feces, fish, and mildew, a scent brought to the boiling point by the country's suffocating heat.

For the most part, the countryside had healed; everything was lush and green.

"When I was here in 1967–1968, it was nothing but red dirt and rice—nothing was left standing," Bill Hontz reminisced near his old stomping grounds along "Ambush Alley" that culminated at Hill 55, outside Danang. "I don't even recognize this place now."

Smoothly paved highways did not exist when we visited; every highway had at least one pothole every four square yards. Almost all of the country's population was packed into several thousand villages and a handful of major cities, and you could not find a bed *anywhere* longer than sixty-six inches.

The food was fantastic, but don't attempt to eat the raw octopus. The coffee was very strong yet very good. The populace was graciously friendly and respectful. The young women were beautiful, the children adorable, the elderly seemingly ageless. Motor scooters and bicycles were the norm; automobiles, other than those driven by government officials, were rare. There was only one rule of the road: If you think you can squeeze past, go for it.

Our tour group visited Marble Mountain near Danang, where we encountered several hundred vendors—mostly women and children—who tried their best to separate us from our money. We visited China Beach and spoke with fishermen tending their nets. We visited the Forbidden Purple City Palace of Hue's Citadel; sections of its massive walls still bear mortar and artillery scars from the Tet Offensive. And we visited Khe Sanh, reclaimed by elephant grass shortly after the horrific Communist siege in 1968. If you looked hard enough, you could find a few metal plates from the old runway.

About two miles west, nestled against the Laos border, is where a Special Forces unit was decimated. All that remains of Lang Vei are a couple of gutted bunkers partially hidden by encroaching jungle. It was here that Susan Malone laid flowers and shed her tears for the brave men sacrificed thirty-three years earlier to an overwhelming NVA force supported by tanks.

A few miles to the southwest is the A Shau Valley, where George Malone fought hopeless battles within a triple-canopy jungle. He retained two images of that long-ago chaos: A hand-to-hand fight to the death against one NVA soldier amid the fire and smoke and the ensuing helicopter ride out of the caldron. At the time, the then twenty-two-year-old second lieutenant was badly wounded yet miraculously able to fight another day. Most of the men with whom he had gone into battle weren't as fortunate. Accompanying Malone on that flight were the bodies of a dozen dead Marines.

We visited Hai Van Pass, where vendors assaulted us, hawking crafts fashioned from marble. Gunny Brandon and Charles Swindell relived their youth by hiking to the very top of the mountain. Jim Arnold and I were content to explore French stone-and-concrete machine-gun bunkers that could still be found everywhere in the country.

We never did find Gunny's thumb, the one he lost to a mortar blast in the vicinity of the Rockpile. And Jim Arnold's memories remained as vague as ever, even when he stood upon the very spot at Lam Xuan East where, on March 12, 1968, the enemy rocket round tore through his back. As I snapped a picture of him, Arnold forced a smile.

"One moment it was just the normal noise of battle, lots of AK-47 fire and a few mortar rounds. But then . . ." Arnold took a deep breath, his eyes surveying the killing field that now had regained its original beauty, the placidity it had known before a century of invasion. "Fleming, Watkins, and I were dug in right here," Arnold said, his words clipped and cold as he toed the slight indentation where his fighting hole once resided.

He gazed toward our left to a riverbank, every bit as thick with foliage and foreboding as he remembered it, then slowly turned his head to the right, picturing once again the enemy's seemingly endless green tracers that reached out for them. "One moment we're taking enemy fire, the usual stuff. But then, just as if someone had flipped a switch, it's as if the gates of hell were shoved open."

Arnold turned away.

I stared mindlessly at the rice paddies, forcing myself not to think what tomorrow would bring. And that's when Gunny Brandon moved to my left side, draped his huge arm around my shoulder, and said, "It's gonna be okay, buddy. I'm right here for you. Take your time; don't forget to breathe. It's almost over."

The final leg of our journey was the village of Mai Xa Thi—the hallowed ground upon which my brother had been killed.

24

The Face of the Enemy

Dear Bro: There's a lot going on right now. Lots of movement and all that Gung-Ho crap, but life is getting better. I'm glad the rains have stopped and we can see the sun again. Just wanted to let you know that I'm thinking of you. Don't have much time, so I'll write later. Love you—Your Bro JES

—March 4, 1968

It is Sunday, March 25, 2001, and we were now at the Hieu Giang Hotel, half a block from Dong Ha's bustling marketplace. It was there, standing shoulder-to-shoulder with other shoppers, all of us caught up in the frenzy of bargaining for the best deal, that I was struck with the realization that something odd had swept through me. At first I thought it was simply the change in locale. But that wasn't it, for Dong Ha was no different from any of the other cities and villages I had visited. All were a beautiful, strange mix of overwhelming energy and breathtaking beauty.

But there was something else going on here. Without knowing exactly when or where it happened, I had suddenly lost my hatred for this country and its people.

I suspect the turnaround occurred in bits and pieces, beginning a year earlier, when I finally met my brother's comrades face-to-face and heard their reminiscences. Of course, the final transformation had happened within the past week, maybe upon visiting an ancient temple and reverently bowing before a strange deity, or stepping down the rough-hewn rock ledge that led deep into the bowels of Marble Mountain and into the hospital the VC once used to treat their wounded. Maybe it was the smiling faces of the children or the beauty of their mothers. Or maybe it was the seed planted by my brother Jim, who cautioned me months earlier not to lay a blanket indictment over people and places—instead, to go to the heart of all wickedness and damn governments.

By the time we checked into the Hieu Giang Hotel, we were whipped. It was all Jim Arnold and I could do to hoist ourselves onto our beds. There was no sleep, though, because the shouts and laughter, not to mention the loud instruments from an off-key band, droned on throughout the night. The merriment was another of life's ironies, we would learn, for our visit coincided with the Communists' annual revelry—the celebration of their conquest of the Republic of South Vietnam.

Not that the week-long celebration caused me any grief. Sleep was impossible, noise or not. I was too wired.

"Tell you the truth, brother, I don't know if I can handle any more of this," Arnold said, wetting a towel and draping it over his face. Both of us were in agreement: not only had it taken too damn long reaching our destination, but also we were being tormented by memories.

"For the past few days, all I've been thinking about is Smitty," said Arnold. Seeing Jeff smiling as he crouched behind the mounded Vietnamese grave, seemingly unconcerned about the sniper who was trying to kill them. And then, acting as if he didn't have a care in the world, Jeff reaches into his pocket and hands Arnold the C-rations—a can of fruit cocktail. He opens it, digs his fingers in and scoops out a handful, then hands it back to Jeff; back and forth until it's empty.

Afraid that I would start crying, I could not look Arnold in the eye. So I eased off my bed and, for the hundredth time since this journey began, made sure I hadn't forgotten anything. I dug into my seabag and pulled out the items one by one, arranging them on the bed—the pictures of my mother and father, my brothers and sisters; and the red ribbon that had adorned the wreath that

stood beside my brother's open casket, the ribbon with the stenciled gold "U.S. Marine Corps." We had already discussed the significance of the items—I would place them at the exact spot where
Jeff had died. It was the only way I could think of that would re-
unite our family.

As I thumbed through the pictures again, making sure I had
not left anyone out, my eyes kept darting to the red ribbon. It
seemed to symbolize the darkness within which I had buried myself for more than three decades.

"Don't know why I've held onto this shit for so long," I told
Arnold.

Jim stood, reached into his suitcase, and pulled out a marble
plaque with the Marine Corps emblem etched on it, a memento
he had purchased in Danang. He handed it to me and said it was
his contribution to my brother's memorial. And then he cleared
his throat and turned away.

It was an awkward moment. I hesitated, then reached into my
bag once again and pulled out the can of fruit cocktail. I had
intended to surprise Arnold once we had arrived at Mai Xa Thi; I
would eat a handful of fruit, then pass it to him and Gunny Brandon. Realizing now that it would be unfair to spring that on him at
such a moment, I put my hand on his shoulder and turned him
toward me, then handed him the fruit cocktail.

"Ah, Jesus," Arnold said with a gasp, then hugged me.

I have no idea how long we cried in each other's arms.

I lay in bed that night, oblivious to the fractured noise from the
merrymakers outside in the hallway, my mind racing—torn between yesterday and today, right and wrong, unrepentant grief and
redemption. For most of the previous week I had managed not to
dwell on the gentleman who would be escorting us to Mai Xa Thi,
concentrating instead on the historical significance of the combat
areas we toured—Hill 55, Hue, Lang Vei, and Khe Sanh. But as
our bus neared Dong Ha, Ed Garr brought up the subject again,
reminding us that our guide had been a VC guerrilla leader.

"Anh has lived his entire life in Quang Tri Province," Garr said. "Strange how things turn out. Thirty some-odd years ago he was trying to kill me and I was trying to kill him. And now . . ."

And now, despite Garr's praise of Anh—he was a perfect gentleman, a very nice man, and without doubt a true warrior—I had difficulty thinking of our guide as anything other than the enemy, a monstrosity lurking in the shadows of long ago. That's when the numbness started to move through me, when the darkness began to envelop me once again. I tried to focus on the countryside that floated lazily past my window—the endless stretch of rice paddies, the water buffaloes, the sea of civilians riding bicycles or motorbikes that clogged our passage along the greatly pocked roadway. Noise abutting noise—the dull blast from our bus's horn, the sharp beeping of response from hundreds of bicycle horns as the wave of humanity slowly parted for us, then re-formed in our wake.

Garr's praise of Anh was lightly received, dismissed. But after pointing out that because of the isolation of the area north of us, we would be boarding a sampan early the next morning to travel up the Cua Viet River to Mai Xa Thi, Garr received my full attention when he said that he had already spoken with Anh about the significance of this leg of the journey.

"Anh knows all about your brother," Garr said. "In fact, he was there that day—on the other side, of course."

No surprise. Everything considered, I had assumed as much. But I had never bothered to connect the dots completely until now. Before I could ask the obvious, Garr said, "Actually, Mr. Anh was in command of the unit that ambushed Fox that day."

As soon as I dropped onto my bed at the Hieu Giang Hotel, my mind, a scary animal even at the best of times, started to roar with rage and my fists tightened into calcified stumps of wrath as I awaited the inevitable.

Honest to God, I didn't know if I could go through with this, standing on or near the exact spot where my brother was killed—standing shoulder-to-shoulder with the man responsible for my brother's death. I feared it as much as I had ever feared anything. I closed my eyes and listened to the music of the demented—the thudding of my headache, the thumping of my heart, the fingernails-on-blackboard vehemence in the voice carried on the chill ill wind that said, "You have an obligation to your brother."

An obligation to honor Jeff's memory, his sacrifice to our country?

Or an obligation to kill the man responsible for my brother's death?

While the battle raged inside me—conscience versus vanity or pride or whatever the hell you wish to call it—I prayed as never before. Calling upon God throughout the night. Still calling upon Him, pleading for strength, wisdom, and compassion as a new day's sun burned away the early-morning mist. And never being certain as to which side would triumph until that tenuous, fractured moment of reckoning as I stood on the banks of the Cua Viet and came face-to-face with the enemy—the focus of my nightmares.

Much to my surprise, Duong Tu Anh looked nothing as I had imagined he would. No squinty-eyed leer or gap-toothed sneer. No arrogance or boisterousness. He was simply an old man, quaint and unpretentious.

Gunny Brandon stood at my side as the introductions were made, his thick arm draped around my shoulder—protecting me, I'm sure, from doing something stupid. I remember my knees suddenly growing weak. I also remember my breath catching in my throat, being light-headed and numb all over as the roaring bombarded my ears. I bowed slightly, then hesitantly extended my right hand, which Mr. Anh grasped warmly with both of his.

I have no idea what I said, if anything. Nor do I have a recollection of Anh's words, if he said any. We merely gripped hands, respectfully bowed to one another, and then stepped up into the sampan. Anh took a seat in the bow, me in the stern. And then the oarsmen pushed us away from the bank, guiding us up the river toward Mai Xa Thi.

Seated beside me was Dr. Bryan Crafts. He placed his hand upon my shoulder and assured me that I was among friends, among brothers, all of whom were here to support me.

"In the past year—having met your brother's friends and filled in many of the missing pieces of his life—you have traveled 340 degrees," Crafts said, his eyes sad. "Now it is time for you to walk the rest of the circle."

It began to rain, yet I hardly noticed. My mind raced between yesterday and today. I lost track of distance and time, shaken from my reverie only when the boat brushed against shore.

We had arrived.

Duong Tu Anh was, at age sixty-three, a kindly gentleman whose manners were faultless. He was short, wiry, soft-spoken, and unassuming. He smiled readily, which he told me later that evening had much to do with the beauty of his wife and his three lovely children, the oldest of whom was twenty-five. Until recently, Anh had been the provincial chief of Quang Tri, which is as close to sitting at the right hand of God as any Communist could hope for.

But long before he attained this lofty governmental rank, Anh was the commander of K-400, the main force Viet Cong guerrilla company whose job was to harass and keep American forces from penetrating farther south into the Cua Viet River region. It was Anh and his troops who triggered the ambush at Lam Xuan East on March 12, 1968, destroying most of Fox Company's 1st Platoon, which resulted in the deaths of Thomas Fleming and Ken Watkins and wounded Steve Klink and Jim Arnold.

Anh also was responsible for laying the defensive groundwork that resulted in the near-annihilation of the remainder of the 2nd Battalion, 4th Marines at the Battle of Dai Do six weeks later.

Long before the last American departed Vietnam in April 1975, Anh's actions on the battlefield were considered legendary. Tenacious and unyielding, he led his troops with honor and heroism. And along the way he suffered. He was shot through the left wrist at Dai Do and sustained three wounds at Lam Xuan East, the worst of which was one in the lower part of his left leg, which never healed properly. But Anh's most grievous injuries occurred on March 7, 1968, at Mai Xa Thi, when he was wounded in the head and groin.

"Battle, it is a terrible thing," Anh told me through an interpreter as we began to retrace the lengthy walk of the past, moving south along the banks of the Cua Viet, exiting what once had been the Fox Company base camp and traipsing across grassland that had been rice paddies thirty-three years earlier. This was the route Fox had taken on March 7, moving out in single file, in search of an enemy that was always elusive.

Ours was an eerie journey, one taken for the most part in silence, each participant filled with awe and wonder, each stepping lightly toward the past, solemnly intruding on memories long suppressed. Gunny Brandon could not stop the muscle memory—his head was on a constant swivel, ever vigilant for the first sign of trouble. As we neared a bend in the river, he grabbed my arm and pulled me close. And then, in a voice barely above a whisper, he said, "It was like fighting ghosts, trying to catch smoke with your hands."

Brandon took a few steps, pulling me along, then stopped once again to get his bearings. We were close, he assured me. It was just a matter of time. Once he lined up that pagoda with the Vietnamese grave . . . he would know it when he saw it.

But Gunny never did, for when we finally arrived at the spot where Fox Company had been ambushed, two pagodas stood in what once had been a rice paddy. And where once there had been one mounded Vietnamese grave, now there were three. Gunny looked at me in disbelief, then circled the area, hoping to catch a glimpse of yesterday. When Anh approached and asked, again through an interpreter, what it was that we searched for, I told him about the sniper who had opened fire on my brother and Jim Arnold, and how they had sought cover behind one of these graves.

Without hesitation, Anh gently took me by the arm and led me to the middle grave. "It was *here* your brave Marine brother died," he said, then bowed and stepped aside. I stood transfixed for what seemed like an eternity.

Anh shook me out of the deadness, again gently taking me by the arm and handing me the flowers and incense sticks. Where these came from, I have no idea. But I do know that the Buddhist ceremony was Anh's idea, his way of honoring a fellow warrior.

We laid the flowers at the very spot where Jeff had been killed. Once I had arranged the pictures of my family, Arnold's Marine Corps marble plaque, and the aged ribbon from my brother's burial wreath on the hallowed ground, Anh, Arnold, and Gunny took turns lighting the incense sticks. George Malone read a passage from his Bible; then I knelt, for if I hadn't, I would have collapsed. I opened the can of fruit cocktail, ate a handful, then passed the can to Arnold, who ate and in turn passed the can to Gunny.

And then, much to my surprise, I cried like never before, dumping three decades of suppressed grief and hatred at my brother's feet.

I don't know how long I wept. I remember Gunny, Arnold, and the others from our tour group consoling me. And I remember Anh's embrace. But most of all I remember his eyes, full of compassion and sorrow.

We made the sampan ride back to Dong Ha in silence.

Mr. Anh and I talked over dinner that evening. He told me about his youth, how Mai Xa Thi had always been a poor village, explaining in great detail how he and his neighbors made their living from the rice and the river. But when the Marines and their helicopters arrived, he said they had no choice but to fight for what little they had.

"Fate dictated that our village was essential for that war," he said, pointing out that it was his job to stop the Marines from entering Dai Do, to the south. So Anh and his soldiers entered the tunnels and waited one week, all the while watching the Marines' movements from the concealment of the tree line. It was during the hours of darkness that his men brought in the mortars and rockets, then moved back underground, waiting for the right moment when "we could stop the war by fighting."

Anh's eyes never left mine as he relived all this, his hands spread flat upon the table. Silence as we peered deep into each other's heart; then he lifted his hands and laid them over mine. Then he said, "And then, on that day, the Marines came to us, and your brother was killed. My sorrow is with you."

He paused and bowed his head, then asked if I had questions, which I did. Hundreds of them, but only *one* of real importance—

did he know who killed my brother? It was obvious to me that Anh knew more about Jeff's death than he was willing to divulge. My gut told me so. But I could not bring myself to pursue the matter any further.

As soon as Anh said, "My sorrow is with you," what Dr. K. Mundy Smith-Hamm, the psychiatrist at Brawner's, had told me nineteen years earlier finally made sense: "As painful as [Jeff's] death continues to be for you, you are never ever going to get better until you release him."

Until this moment, I thought I had released Jeff. Instead, I had merely boxed up my brother's memory and set it aside, unwittingly prolonging the inevitable.

But now, with Anh's hands on mine, with our eyes locked upon each other's, and our hearts as one, I knew the time had come for me to bury my brother once and for all, at long last, to allow the dead to rest in peace.

Just like that, Anh became human, just another pawn on life's chessboard, which we explored in great detail for more than an hour. Finally I told Anh about my family, how my brother's death had destroyed us, pitting brother and sister against brother; that my mother blamed my father for Jeff's death; how my parents had divorced and gone their separate ways. That our family self-destructed, all because of the death of one young Marine.

And then I reached across the table, took Anh's hands in mine, and said, "I'm not proud of this, Mr. Anh, but if I had met you a year earlier—before I had finally found my brother's friends, before my heart had started healing—I would have killed you."

The old warrior did not flinch. Instead, he nodded knowingly, his eyes locked onto mine, and said, "I know this; I understand. But now our war is over. It is good to have peace, and I hope your children will have no war."

Anh paused and smiled, then added, "It is good to no longer see the anger in your eyes. It was there this morning on the boat. But no more. Peace, it is good for both of us."

* * *

I slept like a baby that evening. I dreamed of Jeff, not war. My brother and I were playing basketball. He would dribble toward the basket, then stop and give me a shoulder fake, then spin through the air and flip the ball toward the basket, just out of my reach. Then it was my turn to dribble past him and score, keeping pace, the score always tied, neither of us gaining on the other. Brothers forever. And we couldn't stop laughing.

And after our one-on-one shoot-out, we took a breather and talked about Mom and Dad, about our younger brothers and sisters, about my wife, June, and our four daughters. I don't remember exactly how our conversation went. But I can still feel the warm glow that moved through me that night in Dong Ha. I remember the peace, the tranquillity, the lightness of my heart.

It was the heat in my hand that awakened me in the middle of the night. My eyes snapped open, and I remained very still, immobile until I gained my bearings. Once I had, I realized that my right arm was outstretched. And honest to God, I felt another's hand in mine. The warmth, the tenderness of the grip, was like nothing I had ever felt before.

I stared into the darkness, seeing no one, yet feeling flesh pressed into mine.

I know of no other way to explain what happened next, other than to say I *felt* Jeff's words: "You're gonna be all right, bro. It's over now. You can relax."

Epilogue

In the agonizing months that I went in search of Jeff's Vietnam buddies and their memories of him, I came to love them like family. At first I respected them for what they had gone through and appreciated their love and kindness toward my brother. That respect and appreciation has not diminished. But to it has been added genuine affection for each of them, as unique as each one of them is, and for what they stand for.

I also am flattered that these warriors accepted me into their company and bound me to them in ways great and small. What began as shared grief, tears, and knowledge of wasted years and of unfathomable anguish became something else equally unfathomable.

Like some alchemic equation, the negatives fused, at least for me, into a startling and unexpected process in which I began to heal from the inside out. I think I saw something similar happening with those who long ago also shared a bond with my brother and like me have suffered since that bond was severed.

I would not go so far as to say that any of us are good as new, but I know for me, and I think for most of them, scar tissue has begun to bridge what were wounds.

I hope and pray that my immediate family has an easier time letting go of Jeff than I did. But I have seen progress, if not partial healing, among us. Although we are separated by hundreds of miles, we are now on speaking terms. I have shared my memories of Jeff and those of his war buddies with everyone, and they in turn continue to share a family's love with me.

My dad is now eighty-four, but you wouldn't know it, especially if you played a round of golf with him at his home course in Phoenix. He shoots his age.

My brother Joe finally put his uniform away, retiring from the Army as a sergeant major. He is now an ROTC instructor at a high school in El Paso, Texas.

My sister Jude has moved to Whitewater, Wisconsin, and once again is attending college, hoping to obtain a teaching degree. I know she will make it.

Much to my surprise, my brother Jim finally tired of scouring the ocean for Spanish treasure off the coast of Key West, Florida. He has returned to Wisconsin, having been bitten once again by the political-campaigning bug.

But the greatest miracle of all has happened to my sister Jane. She has confronted her demons and conquered them. Equally as important, she has truly found the love of her life, her husband, Tom.

Although I began this journey alone, new brothers accompany me now. Professionally, they have little in common: a lawyer, three civil servants, a common laborer, a town manager, an engineer, a motorcycle rowdy, and a minister. Collectively, they are bound by esprit de corps. They are not crazed misfits enslaved by post-traumatic stress. Although most have physical limitations because of their wounds—quite understandable considering that combined they have nineteen Purple Hearts—they came home, got jobs, married, raised children and a little bit of hell. But for the most part, they turned their grief inward and conducted themselves as ordinary citizens. That a war-weary nation disdained their patriotism and heroics still does not sit easy with them. But what the hell, they'll tell you—if nothing else, they have each other. Brothers in blood, brothers forever.

The last of these brothers is Jim Wainwright, who was Jeff's platoon commander. Wainwright and I finally met at a Marine reunion in November 2002 in West Point, Virginia. Ron Dean, Jeff's squad leader, hosted the gathering, and there was plenty of laughter once our tears had subsided. Funny that hard-assed Marines—well, at least we think we're hard-assed—should cry so much.

We also ate well and drank well, and did our damnedest to outdo each other as storytellers. We even tried our hand at karaoke, emulating Merle Haggard, Waylon Jennings, and Marty Robbins.

Long after the laughter had faded, Wainwright and I retired to the front porch.

We talked long into the night, about war and peace, about dreams and ideals, about why it is that some young men die and others survive. And near the end of our conversation, Wainwright said that it would do me a lot of good to visit Vietnam. There was a gentleman over there, a man against whom Wainwright had fought, whom he said I should meet.

"The man's name is Anh," Wainwright said, "and he led the guerrilla unit we faced along the Cua Viet."

I held my breath and tongue.

"I know this might sound hard to believe, but it *truly* is a small world we live in," Wainwright said. "I was wounded through the elbow the day your brother was killed. I don't remember how Jeff died, though; there was too much confusion. But Anh was there that day, fighting us. And Anh was there the day I was wounded again, at Dai Do, when a rocket hit the armored personnel carrier I was riding atop."

How miraculous that three decades later, upon Wainwright's return to Vietnam, he should strike up an acquaintance with Duong Tu Anh, his battlefield counterpart. It was amid their sharing and comparing of wartime memories that Anh recounted that he fired only four rockets during the entire Cua Viet campaign, one of which he said hit an armored personnel carrier, killing almost everyone aboard.

"Can you believe that? It was Anh who fired the rocket that wounded me," Wainwright said, his voice barely above a whisper. "Of all the people I should meet over there, it's the man who almost killed me."

Wainwright lapsed into silence, then said that the second rocket Anh fired hit another armored personnel carrier but failed to detonate. His third rocket sailed high and wide of its target, exploding harmlessly far away from Wainwright's troops.

As for the fourth rocket, Wainwright said that Anh was a little unclear about that.

"All he said was that he looked through his binoculars and saw two Marines hiding behind a grave, smoking cigarettes. Anh said he fired the rocket; he thought he killed both Marines."

Of course, Mr. Anh was wrong. He killed only my brother.

It has taken a lifetime, but I forgive him.

Index